TRUTH IS A LONELY WARRIOR

UNMASKING THE FORCES BEHIND GLOBAL DESTRUCTION

JAMES PERLOFF

REFUGE BOOKS

BURLINGTON, MASSACHUSETTS

Also by James Perloff:

The Shadows of Power:
The Council on Foreign Relations and the American Decline (1988)

Tornado in a Junkyard:
The Relentless Myth of Darwinism (1999)

The Case against Darwin:
Why the Evidence Should Be Examined (2002)

Freedom Shall Return (2003) (music CD)

Thirteen Pieces of the Jigsaw:
Solving Political, Cultural and Spiritual Riddles,
Past and Present (2019)

———————

Published by Refuge Books
25 South Bedford Street
Burlington MA 01803

ISBN 13: 978-0-9668160-2-0
ISBN 10: 0-9668160-2-1

Printed in the United States of America

"My people perish for lack of knowledge." –Hosea 4:6

CONTENTS

INTRODUCTION

The original title of this book was to be *How Satan Rules in the World*. However, I was advised that this would hamper the book's sales. Our secular world discounts the existence of Satan, just as it does God, claiming that these were beings dreamed up by primitive cultures. If by "Satan" one means a cartoon character with horns and a pitchfork, I'd agree. However, at least the reality of *evil* is acknowledged by most people, except for a handful of extreme relativists (those who might say nothing—not even machine-gunning a group of children—could be called evil, since morality is "a matter of opinion").

The Bible views Satan as a real being, God's chief enemy, who has played a major hand in generating evil throughout history, usually through deception. *Truth Is a Lonely Warrior* contends that Satan influences global events, and that among his instruments is a powerful organization of men on Earth. This organization has fomented many wars, revolutions and other cataclysms of the past several centuries. Their ultimate goal: establish a world government run by Satan's puppet—a figure the Bible calls "the beast" or "Antichrist." However silly that might sound right now, I ask that you read on, as we view history in a way that will contradict, in many ways, the accounts presented in mainstream media.

☺ Hold on, dude! Red flag! "Not presented in the mainstream media"? That basically translates to: *you're a whack job*!

This book will make the case that this organization is so powerful that it controls most of the major media, and therefore can keep both its agenda and its very existence unknown.

☺ So we add "paranoid conspiracy theorist" to your resumé. Um—in fact, let's make that *ultra*-paranoid.

By the way, this little fellow ☺ is Marvin, my critic. Marvin serves to occasionally present common objections—from both liberal and conservative viewpoints—to what this book says.

☹ Yeah, right! Like readers of this book are r-e-eally gonna get a fair hearing from me—when *you*, Perloff, are actually putting words in my mouth like a ventriloquist's dummy! Let's face it, I'm nothing but a straw man—you're gonna set me up to lose all the arguments, right?

That's still a better deal than lots of books give people, Marvin, so clam it for a while, huh? Now I realize Marvin may seem like a frivolous distraction to some of you, so I'll limit his interruptions.

This book will examine history in a way some of you have never heard it told before. For now, all I ask is that you read with an open mind.

Note: *Truth Is a Lonely Warrior* refers to a number of web pages (which in the Kindle version can be instantly accessed with a click). Due to the Internet's transient nature, it is predictable that some of these web pages will eventually disappear after this book's publication. In such cases, please use Web search engines to locate the subject matter discussed.

Chapter 1
SIX WARS

Pearl Harbor

We begin with one of the most tragic events in American history. On December 7, 1941, the Japanese navy attacked the United States fleet at Pearl Harbor in Hawaii, sinking or heavily damaging 18 naval vessels (including eight battleships), destroying 188 planes, and leaving over 2,000 Americans dead. This, of course, was the event that propelled America into World War II.

After the shocking news, a question plagued Americans: "How could this disaster have happened to our country? Why were we caught off guard?"

President Franklin D. Roosevelt appointed a commission to answer this question. Called the Roberts Commission, it was headed by Owen Roberts, a Supreme Court justice friendly with Roosevelt. Also appointed: Major General Frank McCoy, a close friend of Army Chief of Staff George Marshall; Brigadier General Joseph McNarney, a member of Marshall's staff chosen on his suggestion; and retired Rear Admiral Joseph Reeves, whom Roosevelt had given a job in Lend-Lease. Admiral William Standley was the only member who seemed to lack close ties to the Washington Establishment.

The Commission conducted two days of hearings in Washington and 19 in Hawaii. Its report declared that Washington officials had discharged their duties in an exemplary fashion. The fault for Pearl Harbor, it concluded, lay with our commanders in Hawaii: Admiral Husband Kimmel, commander of the Pacific Fleet, and General Walter C. Short, the Army commander in Hawaii. It alleged these men had failed to take adequate defensive measures and surveillance of the waters surrounding Pearl Harbor. Kimmel and Short were relieved of their duties. The words "dereliction of duty" were emblazoned on headlines across the country. The two were inundated with hate mail and received death threats. It was claimed their neglect had caused the deaths of thousands of Americans. Some members of Congress said the pair should be shot.

Kimmel and Short, however, protested the findings of the Roberts Commission, which they viewed as a kangaroo court. Roberts had run an unusual hearing—initially, evidence was heard without being recorded, and statements not made under oath. Kimmel and Short were denied the right to ask questions, cross-examine witnesses, or have fellow officers present to serve as legal counsel. They also found that the Commission's report omitted significant testimony.

Members of Congress demanded that they be court-martialed—which was exactly what the two officers wanted: to resolve the issue of Pearl Harbor in a bona fide courtroom, using established rules of evidence, instead of Owen Roberts's personal methods. Courts-martial, however, were feared by the Roosevelt administration, which had secrets concerning Pearl Harbor it wished to conceal. Therefore, it was announced, courts-martial would be held, but delayed "until such time as the public interest and safety would permit." Roosevelt knew that, if three years elapsed, the statute of limitations would expire, and Kimmel and Short could no longer be required to face court-martial.

However, the two officers waived the statute of limitations, and in June 1944 a Congressional resolution mandated the trials. That August, the Navy Court of Inquiry and Army Pearl Harbor Board convened.

At these proceedings, the attorneys for Kimmel and Short presented undeniable proof that Washington had *complete foreknowledge of the Pearl Harbor attack, but had withheld this information from the commanders in Hawaii.* As the evidence was presented at the Navy Court of Inquiry, two of the admirals, including chairman Oran Murfin, flung their pencils on the floor in outrage. The court exonerated Admiral Kimmel of all charges and laid the blame squarely on Washington. The Army Pearl Harbor Board also concluded that Washington had full foreknowledge of the attack. Its report closed with these words: "Up to the morning of December 7, 1941, everything that the Japanese were planning to do was known to the United States."[1]

The American people had reacted with wrath when Kimmel and Short were condemned by the Roberts Commission. How do you suppose they responded to this reversal? The answer: they didn't respond, because the Roosevelt administration ordered that the trial verdicts be made confidential. The public remained in the dark.

However, after World War II, a number of books strove to reveal the truth. These included *Pearl Harbor* (1947) by *Chicago Tribune* reporter George Morgenstern, *The Final Secret of Pearl Harbor* (1954) by Rear Admiral Robert Theobald, and *Admiral Kimmel's Story* (1955) by Admiral Kimmel. The "Establishment" press gave these books scant attention, but they were out there for anyone seeking the truth.

A real breakthrough came in 1982 with publication of *Infamy: Pearl Harbor and Its Aftermath* by John Toland, the Pulitzer Prize winner known as the dean of World War II historians. By the time of Toland's book, witnesses and information had emerged that had not been available to earlier investigators.

In 1986, I summarized the finding of Toland and other authors in a cover story for *The New American* magazine. In 1989, the BBC produced a documentary, *Sacrifice at Pearl Harbor*, viewable on YouTube, repeating much of what we had stated in *The New American*; it later aired on the History Channel.

☹ Hold on, Mr. Perloff! You've been yammering about Washington having this supposed "foreknowledge" of the attack. But you haven't even given us one shred of evidence yet! Isn't this just a scurrilous, irresponsible accusation?

How *did* Washington know Pearl Harbor was coming?

First, through decoded messages. In 1941, relations between Japan and the United States were deteriorating. The Japanese used a code called "Purple" to communicate to their embassies and major consulates throughout the world. Its complexity required that it be enciphered and deciphered by machine. The Japanese considered the code unbreakable, but in 1940 talented U.S. Army cryptanalysts cracked it and devised a facsimile of the Japanese machine. As the result, U.S. intelligence was reading Japanese diplomatic messages, often on a same-day basis.

Copies of the deciphered texts were promptly delivered in locked pouches to President Roosevelt, as well as to Secretary of State Cordell Hull, Secretary of War Henry Stimson, Army Chief of Staff General George Marshall, and the Chief of Naval Operations, Admiral Harold Stark.

These messages revealed:

• that the Japanese were planning to rupture relations with the United States and had ordered their Berlin embassy to inform the Germans (their allies) that "the breaking out of war may come quicker than anyone dreams."[2]

• that Tokyo had ordered its Consul General in Hawaii to divide Pearl Harbor into five areas and, on a frequent basis, report the exact locations of American warships there. Nothing is unusual about spies watching ship *movements*—but reporting precise whereabouts of ships in dock has only one implication.

• that, one week before the attack, the Japanese had ordered all of their North American diplomatic offices to destroy their secret documents (once war breaks out, the offices of a hostile power lose their diplomatic immunity and are seized).

In the 1970 movie *Tora, Tora, Tora*, a Hollywood depiction of the events surrounding Pearl Harbor, Japan's ambassadors are shown presenting their declaration of war to Secretary of State Cordell Hull, after the attack on Hawaii, and Hull reacts with surprise and outrage.

In reality, however, Hull was not shocked at all. On the previous day (December 6), he had already read the translated intercept of Japan's declaration of war—13 parts of the 14-part message—as had President Roosevelt.

During 1941, the Roosevelt administration also received several personal warnings regarding Pearl Harbor:

• On January 27th, our ambassador to Japan, Joseph Grew, reported to Washington: "The Peruvian Minister has informed a member of my staff that he has heard from many sources, including a Japanese source, that in the event of trouble breaking out between the United States and Japan, the Japanese intended to make a surprise attack against Pearl Harbor with all their strength. . . ."[3]

• Brigadier General Elliot Thorpe was the U.S. military observer in Java, then under Dutch control. In early December 1941, the Dutch army decoded a dispatch from Tokyo to its Bangkok embassy, forecasting an attack on Hawaii. The Dutch passed the information to Thorpe, who considered it so vital that he sent Washington a total of four warnings. Finally, the War Department ordered him to send no further warnings. You can see Brigadier General Thorpe interviewed in the BBC documentary *Sacrifice at Pearl Harbor*.

• The Dutch Military attaché in Washington, Colonel F. G. L. Weijerman, personally warned U.S. Army Chief of Staff George Marshall about Pearl Harbor just days before the attack.[4]

• Dusko Popov was a Yugoslavian double agent whose true allegiance was to the Allies. Through information furnished by the Germans, Popov deduced the Japanese were planning to bomb Pearl Harbor. He notified the FBI; subsequently FBI Director J. Edgar Hoover stated that he warned Roosevelt, who told him not to pass the information further, but to leave it in his (the President's) hands. Popov is interviewed in *Sacrifice at Pearl Harbor*.

• Senator Guy Gillette of Iowa received information from Kilsoo Haan of the Sino-Korean People's League that the Japanese intended to assault Hawaii "before Christmas." Gillette briefed the President, who said the matter would be looked into.[5]

• U.S. Congressman Martin Dies of Texas came into possession of a map revealing the Japanese plan to attack Pearl Harbor. He later wrote:

As soon as I received the document I telephoned Secretary of State Cordell Hull and told him what I had. Secretary Hull directed me not to let anyone know about the map and stated that he would call me as soon as he talked to President Roosevelt. In about an hour he telephoned to say that he had talked to Roosevelt and they agreed that it would be very serious if any information concerning this map reached the news services … I told him it was a grave responsibility to withhold such vital information from the public. The Secretary assured me that he and Roosevelt considered it *essential to national defense.*[6]

In 2001, Disney produced a movie starring Ben Affleck, *Pearl Harbor*, a standard rendering that depicted Washington as completely surprised by the attack. That year, *The New American* asked me to write a new cover story on Pearl Harbor, not only in response to the film, but because new information had surfaced. In his book *Day of Deceit: The Truth about FDR and Pearl Harbor*, Robert Stinnett proved, from documents obtained through the Freedom of Information Act, that Washington was not only deciphering Japanese diplomatic messages, but *naval dispatches* also.

It had long been presumed that as the Japanese fleet approached Pearl Harbor, it maintained complete radio silence. This was not the case. The fleet observed discretion, but not complete silence. U.S. Naval Intelligence intercepted and translated numerous dispatches, which President Roosevelt had access to. The most significant was sent by Admiral Yamamoto to the Japanese First Air Fleet on November 26, 1941:

The task force, keeping its movement strictly secret and maintaining close guard against submarines and aircraft, shall advance into Hawaiian waters, and upon the very opening of hostilities shall attack the main force of the United States fleet and deal it a mortal blow. The first air raid is planned for the dawn of x-day. Exact date to be given by later order.[7]

We have only looked very briefly at Pearl Harbor. If you would like more details, please see my articles online, available at www.thenewamerican.com ("Hawaii was Surprised; FDR Was Not," "Scapegoating Kimmel and Short," and "Motives behind the Betrayal"). I should comment that when these 2001 articles were transferred to the Internet years after publication, alterations made some paragraphs incoherent. Nevertheless, the articles provide substantial additional evidence of Washington's foreknowledge of the attack. However, I'd like to add here a bit of testimony that did not surface until after I wrote them. The June 2, 2001 *Washington Times* quoted Helen E. Hamman, daughter of Don C. Smith, who directed the Red Cross's War Service before World War II:

> Shortly before the attack in 1941, President Roosevelt called him [my father] to the White House for a meeting concerning a top-secret matter. At this meeting, the president advised my father that his intelligence staff had informed him of a pending attack on Pearl Harbor, by the Japanese. He anticipated many casualties and much loss; he instructed my father to send workers and supplies to a holding area. When he protested to the president, President Roosevelt told him that the American people would never agree to enter the war in Europe unless they were attacked within their own borders. . . . He followed the orders of his president and spent many years contemplating this action, which he considered ethically and morally wrong. I do not know the Kimmel family, therefore would gain nothing by fabricating this situation, however, I do feel the time has come for this conspiracy to be exposed and Admiral Kimmel vindicated of all charges. In this manner perhaps both he and my father may rest in peace.

Many people, when they first learn the foregoing facts about Pearl Harbor, think: "Hey, I never knew there was any controversy about Pearl Harbor. I never read about it in school, or in the *New York Times*." This book will examine many other suppressed stories of American history.

The *Lusitania*

Pearl Harbor embroiled America in World War II. What brought us into World War I? Though historians cite various factors, the *Lusitania* affair probably inflamed public opinion the most. In 1915, Britain was at war with Germany. The United States later joined the conflict on Britain's side, but at this point was still neutral. The *Lusitania*, a British passenger ship en route from America to England, was sunk by a German submarine. 128 Americans were among the passengers lost. Americans were told the Germans torpedoed the ship out of a wanton desire to kill innocent women and children.

However, many facts were denied the public. The Germans sank the *Lusitania* because she was transporting millions of rounds of ammunition, shrapnel shells, gun cotton, and other munitions. Germany and Britain were at war, and the navies of both were attempting to cut each other's arms supplies.

The *Lusitania* sank in just eighteen minutes after being struck by one torpedo. Survivors stated there had been two explosions—a smaller one followed by a huge one. The first was the torpedo hitting, the second very possibly the munitions detonating. This version of events—a single torpedo, followed by a massive explosion—was confirmed by the log book of the submarine, the *U-20*.

Even more significant is evidence the *Lusitania* was deliberately sent to her doom. Prior to the incident, Winston Churchill, then head of the British Admiralty, had ordered a study done to determine the political impact if the Germans sank a British passenger ship with Americans on board. And just before the sinking, Edward Grey, the British foreign minister, asked Edward Mandell House, top advisor to President Woodrow Wilson: "What will America do if the Germans sink an ocean liner with American passengers on board?" House's reply: "I believe that a flame of indignation would sweep the United States and that by itself would be sufficient to carry us into the war."[8]

The British had cracked Germany's naval codes, and knew the approximate locations of her U-boats at that time, including the *U-20*. Commander Joseph Kenworthy, then in British Naval Intelligence, wrote: "The *Lusitania* was sent at considerably reduced speed into an area where a U-boat was known to be waiting and with her escorts withdrawn."[9]

At the U.S. hearing investigating the *Lusitania* incident, a critical piece of evidence was missing. President Woodrow Wilson ordered that the ship's original manifest, listing her munitions, be hidden in the archives of the U.S. Treasury.

☹ Oh, come on! Aren't these just sensationalistic claims? Do any serious historians buy into this?

In his book *The Lusitania*, British historian Colin Simpson recounted the foregoing facts; many of them aired in the documentary *In Search of the Lusitania*, seen on the History Channel and viewable today on YouTube in two parts. Patrick Beesly is considered the leading authority on the history of British Naval Intelligence, in which he was long an officer. In his book *Room 40*, Beesly writes: "I am reluctantly driven to the conclusion that there *was* a conspiracy deliberately to put the *Lusitania* at risk in the hopes that even an abortive attack on her would bring the United States into the war. Such a conspiracy could not have been put into effect without Winston Churchill's express permission and approval."[10]

Remembering the *Maine*

In the mid-1890s, "yellow journal" newspapers, such as William Randolph Hearst's *New York Journal*, were pushing for the United States to drive the Spanish out of Cuba, which had been a colony of Spain since 1511. Cuba had become the world's wealthiest colony and largest sugar producer by the nineteenth century, and its sugar plantations were coveted by the Rockefellers' National City Bank. The American public was suddenly regaled with phony atrocity stories, such as the Spanish roasting Catholic priests and feeding Cubans to sharks.

William Randolph Hearst paid bribes to have the private correspondence of Spanish ambassador Enrique Dupey de Lôme spied upon. In a private letter to a friend, the ambassador criticized U.S. President William McKinley. In violation of diplomatic immunity, the letter was stolen and reprinted in Hearst's *Journal* under the headline "THE WORST INSULT TO THE UNITED STATES IN ITS HISTORY," driving anti-Spanish feelings to fever pitch.

Just two days later—on February 15, 1898—an enormous explosion tore apart the American battleship *Maine* in Cuba's Havana Harbor. Most of the crew died—266 men. Although a Naval Court of Inquiry could not determine who was behind the incident, U.S. newspapers swiftly blamed the Spanish government. The Spanish-American War ensued, with Americans rallied by the cry "Remember the *Maine!*"

However, to this day, historians continue to ponder: What really sank the *Maine*?

This much is certain: The Spanish had no motive to provoke America, and desperately tried to avoid war. Spain still had mostly wooden warships, many in disrepair, which could not match the firepower of America's increasingly steel navy. The Spanish government's internal memoranda indicate they knew that a war against the mighty United States would be unwinnable. Spain acceded to every U.S. demand except complete withdrawal from Cuba, and offered to submit the matter of the *Maine* to arbitration.

Of the potential suspects for who sunk the *Maine*, Spain was least likely. According to Ferdinand Lundberg in his classic *America's Sixty Families*, President McKinley was beholden to John D. Rockefeller and Standard Oil. While governor of Ohio, McKinley went bankrupt, and was secretly bailed out by a syndicate headed by Rockefeller front man Mark Hanna, who had known John D. since they were high school classmates. Hanna became McKinley's political manager. Many considered him the real White House boss; critics called the President "McHanna."

On January 24, 1898, the inflammatory decision to send the *Maine* to Cuba was made at a White House meeting—of which no minutes were kept. Although the Spanish were advised that a warship would eventually visit, they were not expecting the *Maine* when it sailed into Havana January 25. This was unknown to the ship's commander, Captain Charles Sigsbee, who wrote: "It became known to me afterward that the *Maine* had not been expected, even by the United States Consul General."

With potential war looming, by what "oversight" did Washington fail to notify both Spanish and American officials in Havana of the battleship's arrival? However, if anyone hoped shooting would erupt in the harbor, leading to war, they were disappointed. The Spanish, courteously if coolly, welcomed the *Maine* and permitted her to dock.

It is notable that the war was financed with a $200 million loan from the Rockefellers' National City Bank. How was the loan to be repaid? Since no income tax then existed, a telephone tax was levied on the American people. That tax remained in place for 108 years.

Mark Twain wrote:

> How our hearts burned with indignation against the atrocious Spaniards.... But when the smoke was over, the dead buried and the cost of the war came back to the people in an increase in the price of commodities and rent—that is, when we sobered up from our patriotic spree—it suddenly dawned on us that the cause of the Spanish-American War was the price of sugar.

And who acquired Spain's lucrative Cuban sugar industry—then known as "white gold"? Lundberg notes that "the Cuban sugar industry gravitated into National City's hands."

For a detailed review of the Spanish-American War, see this author's 2012 online article "Trial Run for Interventionism" at www.thenewamerican.com.

The Korean War

We started with Pearl Harbor and moved back in time. Now let's move forward. Next on our war survey: Korea. On June 25,

1950, Kim Il-sung, North Korea's communist dictator, sent his troops to invade South Korea. American forces, fighting under UN authority, came to South Korea's defense, in a bloody three-year war that ended in stalemate.

But most people cannot answer this question: How did Kim Il-sung and the communists come to power in North Korea? The answer: We—the United States—put them there, in a round-about way.

During World War II, the U.S. fought the Germans in Europe and the Japanese in Asia. The Soviet Union, then under Joseph Stalin's brutal rule, was our "ally" during this war. The Soviets, however, only fought Germany; they maintained a nonaggression pact with Japan.

But at the "Big Three" conferences at Teheran and Yalta, President Roosevelt asked Stalin if he would break his treaty with Japan and enter the Pacific war. Stalin agreed—on condition that the United States supply him with all the weapons, vehicles and materiel his Far Eastern army would need for the expedition. Roosevelt agreed, and some 600 shiploads of supplies were sent across the Pacific to Russia to equip Stalin's army to fight Japan.[11]

This was an absurd foreign policy decision. Stalin was a well-known aggressor. The 1939 invasion of Poland, which officially began World War II, had actually been a *joint* venture by the Germans and Soviets. In 1940, Stalin had invaded Finland, Latvia, Estonia and Lithuania, and annexed part of Romania. No one could seriously believe he would bring benevolence to Asia.

Stalin did not send his army into the Far East until five days before the war ended; Japan, already struck by the atomic bomb, was ready to surrender. Soviet forces moved into China, where, after very limited fighting, they accepted the surrender of huge Japanese weapons depots. They then turned these weapons, plus their own American lend-lease supplies, over to communist rebel Mao Tse-tung. Thus armed, the Chinese communists ultimately overthrew the Nationalist government.

But what about Korea? At the time, it was a Japanese protec-torate. In April 1944, *Foreign Affairs*—America's most influential journal of foreign policy—published an article entitled "Korea in the Postwar World." It proposed dividing Korea into a trusteeship, its fate similar to that of East and West Germany and Berlin. We would control Korea's southern half, while our "noble" Soviet allies would take custody of the North. Naturally, Stalin agreed with this idea, and the Soviets received power over North Korea.

Considering that the Soviets did nothing to win the Pacific war, North Korea was an enormous trophy to give the dictator Stalin, well known to have murdered millions of his own people. Stalin swiftly established a communist government under Kim Il-sung in North Korea, and equipped him with the tanks, MiGs and other weapons needed for the 1950 invasion—which could have been *completely avoided had we not made overtures to Stalin to bring him into the Far East.*

☹ Aw, look, Jim. The people who make our foreign policy are just good Joes, like you and me. And sometimes, like you and me, they make mistakes. Jim, are *you* perfect? You're not? Gosh, what a surprise! Well, neither are the guys who make our foreign policy! Granted, maybe they were a bit naive in thinking that Stalin would make a good steward for North Korea—but, look, hindsight is 20-20. It's easy for *you* to sit there and criticize that decision decades after the fact! There's no reason to get all paranoid about it, with your feathers all ruffled, going around making a lot of irresponsible accusations! Just chill, Jim! The fact is, there's a very simple explanation for what happened in Korea: ACCIDENTS HAPPEN.

This little "accident" resulted in a war that killed more than 50,000 American soldiers, as well as over one million Koreans. In addition, North Koreans have suffered for over 60 years under one of history's most oppressive dictatorships.

So before we dismiss this as "accident," let's quote James Forrestal, Secretary of Defense under President Truman. Seeing that certain diplomats made decisions that invariably favored the Soviet Union and harmed the United States, he said: "Consistency has never been a mark of stupidity. If the diplomats who have mishandled our relations with Russia were merely stupid, they would occasionally make a mistake in our favor."

On May 22, 1949, Secretary Forrestal fell to his death from a window on the 16th floor of Bethesda Naval Hospital. Of course, some people might say:

☺ Dude! I'm sure there's a simple explanation for that. ACCIDENTS HAPPEN. Doubtless Forrestal was walking down the corridor, slipped on a banana peel, and took a header out the window. Hey, things like that happen every day!

Secretary Forrestal's brother Henry believed he was murdered. Anyone doing a little research will find that many questions were left unanswered by the official story of Forrestal's alleged suicide, which occurred at a time when he had become critically in conflict with American foreign policy.

Vietnam

In 1964 Congress passed the Tonkin Gulf Resolution, authorizing President Lyndon B. Johnson to intervene in the Vietnam War, to which he committed hundreds of thousands of troops. The justification given for the resolution was two alleged attacks on U.S. destroyers by Vietnamese torpedo boats in the Tonkin Gulf, on August 2 and 4, 1964.

President Johnson described the first attack as an "unprovoked assault" against a "routine patrol." Actually, the destroyer was supporting a South Vietnamese military operation against the North.

The second attack never occurred at all. Admiral James Stockdale, recipient of the Congressional Medal of Honor, was a pilot stationed in the Tonkin Gulf at the time. Later shot down, he spent seven years in a communist POW camp. After returning home, he summarized his experiences in his book *In Love and War*.

Stockdale was called to the scene of the alleged August 4 attack, but saw no Vietnamese boats during one and a half hours of overflight. Let's pick up his narrative from his return to the aircraft carrier *Ticonderoga*:

> Wheeling into the ready room I had hurriedly left three hours before, I came face to face with about ten assorted ship's company, air group, and staff intelligence officers—all with sheepish grins on their faces. The mood of the group was mirthful; obviously they had some big joke to tell me. "What in the hell has been going on out there?" they laughingly asked.
>
> "Damned if I know," I said. "It's really a flap. The guy on the *Maddox* [destroyer] Air Control radio was giving blow-by-blow accounts just like he did on Sunday. Turning left, turning right, torpedoes to the right of us, torpedoes to the left of us—boom, boom, boom! I got right down there and shot at whatever they were shooting at. I came around toward the destroyers once, right on the deck, chasing some imaginary PT boat they said was running up behind them, and fired every type of weapon I had—including a *sidewinder!*" ...
>
> I was rather giddy by this time, and delivered this "debriefing" with elaborate gestures as a kind of catch-on hilarity enveloped the room.
>
> "Did you see any boats?"
>
> "Not a one. No boats, no boat wakes, no ricochets off boats, no boat gunfire, no torpedo wakes—nothing but black sea and American firepower. But for goodness' sake, I must be going crazy. How could all of that commotion have built up there without *something* being behind it?"[12]

Stockdale then describes being woken the next morning:

> After what seemed like a very short night, I felt myself being shaken. . . .
>
> "Who are you?" I asked.
>
> "I'm the junior officer of the deck, sir. The captain sent me down to wake you. We just got a message from

Washington telling us to prepare to launch strikes against the beach, sir. . . ."

"What's the idea of the strikes?"

"Reprisal, sir."

"Reprisal for what?"

"For last night's attack on the destroyers, sir."

I flipped on my bed lamp and the young officer left.

I felt like I had been doused with ice water. How do I get in touch with the President? He's going off half-cocked. . . . We were about to launch a war under false pretenses. . . .

The fact that a war was being conceived out here in the humid muck of the Tonkin Gulf didn't bother me so much; it seemed obvious that a tinderbox situation prevailed here and that there would be war in due course anyway. But for the long pull it seemed to me important that the grounds for entering war be legitimate. I felt it was a bad portent that we seemed to be under the control of a mindless Washington bureaucracy, vain enough to pick their own legitimacies regardless of the evidence.[13]

What shall we say? That the Washington decision-makers were, once again, just "good Joes who goofed," who misunderstood the reports from Tonkin Gulf? That yet another "accident" cost over 50,000 GIs their lives? It was eventually revealed that the Tonkin Gulf Resolution was written *before* the alleged incident—i.e., the document was simply awaiting an excuse to activate it.

Iraq

The Iraq War is also controversial—and a sensitive subject, because it is so recent. For now, we make only one observation: the justifications currently given for the war—bringing "freedom and democracy" to the Iraqi people—were not the original reasons presented.

On February 5, 2003, before the conflict began, U.S. Secretary of State Colin Powell told the UN he had absolute proof that

Saddam Hussein possessed weapons of mass destruction (WMDs) that were an immediate threat to world security. He declared: "My colleagues, every statement I make today is backed up by sources, solid sources. These are not assertions. What we are giving you are facts and conclusions based on solid intelligence . . . ."[14]

President Bush declared in his radio address of March 8, 2003: "Saddam Hussein and his weapons are a direct threat to this country, to our people, and to all free people. . . . I will not leave the American people at the mercy of the Iraqi dictator and his weapons."[15]

British Prime Minister Tony Blair told the House of Commons: "Saddam Hussein's regime is despicable, he is developing weapons of mass destruction, and we cannot leave him doing so unchecked."[16]

But after the invasion, David Kay, the chief U.S. weapons inspector, acknowledged that months of searching had turned up no weapons of mass destruction in Iraq, and in his opinion they hadn't existed there since the 1991 Gulf War. Furthermore, Colin Powell, who had made such definite assertions before the UN, has admitted that his claims were based on faulty intelligence.

Scotland's *Sunday Herald* exposed the prewar doctoring of WMD evidence:

> Britain ran a covert "dirty tricks" operation designed specifically to produce misleading intelligence that Saddam had weapons of mass destruction to give the UK a justifiable excuse to wage war on Iraq.
>
> Operation Rockingham, established by the Defence Intelligence Staff within the Ministry of Defence in 1991, was set up to "cherry-pick" intelligence proving an active Iraqi WMD programme and to ignore and quash intelligence which indicated that Saddam's stockpiles had been destroyed or wound down.
>
> The existence of Operation Rockingham has been confirmed by Scott Ritter, the former UN chief weapons inspector, and a US military intelligence officer. He knew members of the Operation Rockingham team and

described the unit as "dangerous," but insisted they were not "rogue agents" acting without government backing. "This policy was coming from the very highest levels," he added. "Rockingham was spinning reports and emphasising reports that showed non-compliance (by Iraq with UN inspections) and quashing those which showed compliance. It was cherry-picking intelligence."

Ritter and other intelligence sources say Operation Rockingham and MI6 were supplying skewed information to the Joint Intelligence Committee (JIC) which, Tony Blair has told the Commons, was behind the intelligence dossiers that the government published to convince the parliament and the people of the necessity of war against Iraq. Sources in both the British and US intelligence community are now equating the JIC with the Office of Special Plans (OSP) in the US Pentagon. The OSP was set up by Defence Secretary Donald Rumsfeld to gather intelligence which would prove the case for war. In a staggering attack on the OSP, former CIA officer Larry Johnson told the *Sunday Herald* the OSP was "dangerous for US national security and a threat to world peace," adding that it "lied and manipulated intelligence to further its agenda of removing Saddam."[17]

What Is Patriotism?

☹ Hey, Jimbo! All these criticisms of U.S. wars—you sound like a damn hippie antiwar protestor. "Peace, baby!" So what's the difference between you and Jane Fonda and Michael Moore and the Hollywood left? Don't you support our troops?

I consider patriotism one of mankind's noblest virtues. My values and motives are completely different from those of "the left," as is over 95 percent of my information. Teddy Roosevelt said of patriotism:

Patriotism means to stand by the country. It does not mean to stand by the President or any other public office save exactly to the degree in which he himself stands by the country.[18]

He further stated:

To announce that there must be no criticism of the President, or that we are to stand by the president, right or wrong, is not only unpatriotic and servile, but is morally treasonable to the American public.[19]

On these particular points, I agree with Teddy Roosevelt. Who is it more patriotic to support? The brave victims of Pearl Harbor, or the lying politicians who denied them the information needed to defend themselves? Is it more patriotic to stand behind Admiral Stockdale, who told the truth about Tonkin Gulf, or the bureaucrats who distorted it? I hope it will be clear to my readers that this book is motivated by a desire for truth and justice, and not by unpatriotic feelings.

Chapter 2
THE POWERS THAT BE

Consider now:

- Spanish-American War (1898)

- World War I (1917)

- World War II (1941)

- Korean War (1950)

- Vietnam War (1964)

- Iraq War (2003)

One could soundly argue that, in each war, American involvement was based on a deception, a false pretext, or—putting it most charitably—a mistaken pretext.

And these wars have *another* common denominator: *The same group was behind our participation in each.*

☺ News flash, Jim! Don't you think the guys behind the Spanish-American War would be kind of, like, *dead* now? So how could *they* be behind the Iraq War? D-u-u-u-h!

We're discussing a group that has survived through generations. This is true of many organizations. For example, Marx and Engels issued *The Communist Manifesto* in 1848. Yet more than a century later, long after they and other founders of communism were dead, the communists seized power in China. There are millions of Republicans in America today, but the party's first members, from Abraham Lincoln's day, are now dead. The Christian church has existed for two millennia. The Mafia is said to date at least as far back as the 19th century. Many more examples exist. That's the type of organization we're discussing—one that adds new members as older ones die off.

Different terms have been used to describe this organization. We'll start with a familiar one.

The "Establishment"

When I was hippie (about 1970), I commonly heard other hippies say something like: "You know, Man, it's really *the Establishment* that's running this country!" Hippies liked to characterize themselves as "anti-Establishment."

By "Establishment," they meant that, in America, a rich, powerful elite really calls the shots. I agree with that. Where I disagree with the hippies is their *characterization* of the Establishment. In their view, it was: (A) conservative; (B) patriotic; (C) anti-communist; and (D) mostly Christian.

Syndicated columnist Edith Kermit Roosevelt, granddaughter of President Theodore Roosevelt, penned an accurate, though restrained, definition of "Establishment":

> The word "Establishment" is a general term for the power elite in *international finance*, business, the professions and government, largely from the northeast, who wield most of the power *regardless of who is in the White House*. Most people are unaware of the existence of this "legitimate Mafia." Yet the power of the Establishment makes itself felt from the professor who seeks a foundation grant, to the candidate for a cabinet post or State Department job. It affects the nation's policies in almost every area.[20] (emphasis added)

I italicized two phrases Roosevelt used: "international finance"—because, as this book will show, these people are rooted in banking and Wall Street—and "regardless of who is in the White House"—because it doesn't matter whether the President is Democrat or Republican; the Establishment still rules.

☺ Aw, that's ridiculous! Mr. Perloff, you obviously don't know squat about American government. If you did, you'd know that we have "government of the people, by the people, and for the people." You see, Jim, we *elect* our leaders. The President and members of Congress are merely *public servants*. We're their *boss*. So obviously, whatever happens in our foreign policy represents the *will of the people*. Nothing "sinister" is going on. And you know what, Jim? If we don't like the job our leaders are doing, all we have to do is vote the rascals out come the next election! So there's no "power behind the throne" in America—except for us, the sovereign voters.

I certainly agree that power is supposed to belong to the American people *in principle*. I disagree that they hold very much power *in fact*.

Aside from the questionable integrity of computerized vote-counting (see, just as one example, the testimony of computer programmer Clinton Eugene Curtis before the Ohio state legislature on YouTube), the Establishment has two major means of getting around our electoral system. First, through their influence within the two major parties, as well as the media, they can pretty much predetermine the Democratic and Republican nominees for President. Elections are not a major focus of this book, but I don't wish to leave this point unsupported, so let's take an example.

In 1976, Jimmy Carter was elected President.

Trivia question: According to a Gallup poll, taken just seven months before Carter was nominated at the Democratic National Convention, what percent of Democratic voters favored him for President?

Answer: less than 4 percent.[21]

Carter was governor of Georgia; few people outside the state even knew who he was.

What happened? As Lawrence Shoup noted in his 1980 book *The Carter Presidency and Beyond*:

> What Carter had that his opponents did not was the acceptance and support of elite sectors of the mass communications

media. It was their favorable coverage of Carter and his campaign that gave him an edge, propelling him rocket-like to the
top of the opinion polls. This helped Carter win key primary
election victories, enabling him to rise from an obscure public
figure to President-elect in the short space of 9 months.[22]

The media blitz included adulatory pieces in the *New York
Times*, and a *Wall Street Journal* editorial declaring that Carter was
the best Democratic candidate. Before the nominating convention, his picture appeared on the cover of *Time* three times, and
Newsweek twice. *Time*'s cover artists were even instructed to make
him look as much as possible like John F. Kennedy.[23] The major
TV networks inundated the public with his image.

How did Carter acquire this media following? It began with a
dinner with David Rockefeller—kingmaker of the Establishment—
at the latter's Tarrytown, New York estate. Also present was
Zbigniew Brzezinski, who helped Rockefeller found the interna-
tionalist Trilateral Commission, and whom Carter would later
appoint National Security Adviser. Former Arizona Senator Barry
Goldwater said of this meeting:

> David Rockefeller and Zbigniew Brzezinski found Jimmy
> Carter to be their ideal candidate. They helped him win the
> nomination and the presidency. To accomplish this purpose,
> they mobilized the money power of the Wall Street bankers,
> the intellectual influence of the academic community—which
> is subservient to the wealth of the great tax-free foundations—
> and the media controllers represented in the membership of
> the CFR and the Trilateral.[24]

Not surprisingly, Carter got the nomination at the Democratic
Convention. But did he win it because (A) all across America,
sovereign voters spontaneously decided he was the best candidate;
or because (B) he was picked in a high place, and then packaged
and sold through the media? I respectfully suggest it was the latter, and that furthermore this has been true for most major-party
Presidential nominees of the last few decades.

However, the Establishment has a second, even more powerful means of subverting the people's will: bridges of influence
to the elected President. The most important is the Council on
Foreign Relations (CFR), headquartered in New York City with
a branch in Washington, DC. It is the subject of my book *The
Shadows of Power*.

We'll discuss how the Council on Foreign Relations impacts
American foreign policy, but first, what is the Council's *goal*?

One World

The goal of the Council on Foreign Relations is *world
government*.

Admiral Chester Ward, former Judge Advocate General of the
U.S. Navy, was a CFR member for sixteen years before resigning in
disgust. In 1975, he stated that the Council's objective is "submer-
gence of U.S. sovereignty into an all-powerful one-world government." He also said: "This lust to surrender the sovereignty and
independence of the United States is pervasive throughout most
of the membership." "In the entire CFR lexicon, there is no term
of revulsion carrying a meaning so deep as 'America First.'"[25]

In a 1996 editorial, the *Boston Herald* called the Council's
members "foreign-policy fuzzy thinkers who worship world
government."[26]

Congress's Special Committee to Investigate Tax-Exempt
Foundations (the Reece Committee) stated that the CFR's "productions are not objective but are directed overwhelmingly at
promoting the globalist concept."[27]

But we need not rely on critics to establish that the Council
advocates world government. The CFR publishes the influential journal *Foreign Affairs*. The following are typical of its
pronouncements:

In 1993, F. A. Kenichi Ohmae stated in *Foreign Affairs*: "The
nation state has become an unnatural, even dysfunctional unit for
organizing human activity and managing economic endeavor."[28]

Richard N. Gardner, in his 1974 article "The Hard Road to World Order," wrote: "An end run around national sovereignty, eroding it piece by piece, will accomplish much more than the old-fashioned frontal assault."[29]

In its first year of publication, 1922, *Foreign Affairs* declared: "Obviously there is going to be no peace or prosperity for mankind so long as it remains divided into fifty or sixty independent states... The real problem today is that of world government."[30] Note well the words "peace" and "prosperity"—globalists have consistently paired them to promote world government during the last century.

The Shadows of Power documents many more examples of CFR advocacy of world government. And just what *is* world government? One regime ruling the planet. Obviously, we don't have that today—the Brazilian government runs Brazil, the Japanese government Japan, etc. In world government, national boundary lines would be obliterated, with a single government taking authority over the Earth.

☺ How totally far-fetched. Jim, it would be a zillion years before anything like that would ever happen! So why worry about it?

It is being established progressively right now. It is modeled in Europe, where once-mighty nations that oversaw empires, such as Britain and Spain, have become little more than provinces of the European Union (EU). There has long been a plan to dismantle their sovereignty. In the July 1968 *Spectacle du Monde*—well before Americans ever heard the phrase "European Union"—Raymond Bourgine wrote:

> The Europe of Jean Monnet is the famous "Supranational Europe" to which member States will progressively surrender their attributes of national sovereignty. In the end their economies will be integrated by Administrators in Brussels while awaiting a European Assembly, elected by popular vote, which will turn itself into a legislative one and give birth to a

new European political power. The national states will then
wither away.[31]

Bourgine's prophecy is being fulfilled. Parliaments of EU
countries are becoming subservient to the European Parliament.
Laws are increasingly uniform throughout the Union. National
currencies are consolidating into the "Euro." The European Court
of Justice can issue arrest warrants against citizens of any member country. Militaries are combining as a "European Pentagon"
is discussed. The EU has its own ambassadors, and a European
Constitution is in development. Furthermore, the Union is not
finished—it's a work in progress. Advocates of world government
plan a universal version of the EU model for the planet.

How do globalists justify world government? By promising
"peace and prosperity." Their argument has traditionally run along
this line: *Look, nothing's worse than war, right? And the only reason
we have war is because the world is divided into nations, who keep
fighting each other. If we just got rid of nations, and replaced them
with a world government, war would end, and mankind would live
as one happy family.*

This pretext is flawed, however. Rudolph Rummel, professor
emeritus of political science at the University of Hawaii, published
a study demonstrating that, in the 20th century, *six times more
people were killed by their own governments than were killed in
wars.*[32] In other words, wars are *not* the deadliest thing—governments are.

This raises a question: If we had a world government, who
would run it? Globalists are fond of pointing out that international
alliances have defeated dictators such as Saddam Hussein. But what
if a man like Hussein *took over* a world government?

Today, if a tyrant enslaves a nation, its people may hopefully
escape to another country. But if a dictator ruled a *world* government, where could one escape?

America's founding fathers recognized the dangers of concentrating power in one place. They therefore split government power
into branches—the President's authority was balanced by Congress;

and even within the legislature, the House and Senate could offset each other. The President and Congress were further balanced by the Supreme Court. And—at least in the Founding Fathers' original vision—the power of the entire federal government was to be held in check by the states themselves.

Granted, there has been corruption within each federal branch; nonetheless, decentralization of power has spared us the oppression of totalitarian dictatorship that other nations have known. James Madison, fourth President of the United States and known as "Father of the Constitution," said: "The accumulation of all power—legislative, executive, and judiciary—in the same hands ... may justly be pronounced the very definition of tyranny."[33]

Countries *themselves* act as a check and balance on each other. If one nation becomes despotic or belligerent, another can rise up to stop it. Thus global government, concentrating all world power in a single regime, could create the most unrestrained tyranny in history.

This has spiritual implications. The Bible predicts that, in the final days before the return of Jesus Christ—commonly referred to as "the End Times"—there will be a satanic world dictator known as the "Antichrist" or "beast."* The book of Revelation says "he was given authority over every tribe, people, language and nation. . . . He also forced everyone, small and great, rich and poor, free and slave, to receive a mark on his right hand or on his forehead, so that no one could buy or sell unless he had the mark . . . ."[34]

[*I realize some Christians believe the prophecies about the Antichrist were fulfilled in the past, especially the 1st century AD. I believe ancient figures like Nero may have *foreshadowed* the Antichrist, but I concur with the widely held view that the Antichrist's ultimate reign is a future event.]

To rule the world, the Antichrist (or anyone) would clearly need a world government. Suppose France's President, François Hollande, came to the United States and said: "I am the Antichrist! All you Americans, bow down and obey me!" We'd laugh ourselves silly. We'd say, "Buzz off, Hollande! Go back to Paris and eat a baguette! You've got no authority here!" And that would be correct.

A national ruler has only national authority. To *govern the world* requires a *world government*.

When the Antichrist comes, he won't create his regime with a wave of a wand, saying: "Hocus-pocus, allahkazam! There's my world government!" We contend that this government is being organized *now*, step by step, with few people even realizing it.

What about this Council on Foreign Relations? How did it begin? Its roots trace to the 1919 Paris Peace Conference, where the Allied powers, victorious in World War I, were settling the postwar world. U.S. President Woodrow Wilson traveled there with his top advisor, Edward Mandell House, who lived in the White House, wielding such influence that *Harper's Weekly* called him "Assistant President House."

House was also known as a front man for the banking community. His official biographer, Charles Seymour, referred to him as the "unseen guardian angel" of the Federal Reserve Act.[35]

In the next few pages, we'll examine the people and events that led to the founding of the Council on Foreign Relations. In doing so, this book may seem to have "switched gears" from political affairs to banking. However, the American foreign policy establishment is inextricably linked to the banking establishment. One cannot fully understand one without understanding the other. As we proceed, the connection should become clear.

Chapter 3
THE DEVIL AS BANKER

I see in the near future a crisis approaching that unnerves me and causes me to tremble for the safety of my country. Corporations have been enthroned, an era of corruption will follow, and the money power of the country will endeavor to prolong its reign by working upon the prejudices of the people, until the wealth is aggregated in a few hands, and the republic destroyed. –Abraham Lincoln, November 21, 1864.[36]

On general principles, it shouldn't surprise us that a *sinister scheme for world control* has ties to banking.

Sinister? The Bible says "the love of money is the root of all evil." And: "Is it not the rich who are exploiting you?"

Control? We say "money makes the world go round." Humanly speaking, probably nothing is more influential than money.

To find who is behind something, we say "follow the money." So let's do that—follow the money and see who is behind the Council on Foreign Relations and the campaign for world government.

Inflation

Americans know they have inflation. In 1962, a postage stamp cost four cents; today it's 46. A candy bar cost a nickel in 1962; now around 75 cents to a dollar. A 1962 movie ticket was 50 cents; today $8.00. Annual tuition at Harvard then was $1,520; you could buy a new imported Renault automobile for $1,395; and the average cost of a new house was $12,500. Since 1913 the dollar's purchasing power has declined over 95 percent—i.e., it won't buy what a nickel did a hundred years ago.

What causes rising prices? The "Establishment" media propound various explanations. A typical one runs like this: "Inflation

31

is the American worker's fault. Joe goes to his employer and says, 'Boss, my wife's expecting. How about a raise of fifty dollars a week?' The boss says, 'Joe, the only way I can afford that is by raising our prices fifty dollars a week—I'll have to pass the cost on to our customers.' Then firms doing business with Joe's company say, 'Yo! You've raised your prices fifty dollars a week! That means we'll have to raise *our* prices fifty dollars a week.' And so, there's a ripple effect—across America, prices rise, all because greedy Joe, and other selfish workers like him, asked for a raise."

We are told inflation is "inevitable, like death and taxes." Indeed, based on the recent Consumer Price Index (CPI)—the broad index used to measure inflation—that seems true. America has experienced general price increases every year since 1955 (with one exception)—i.e., for nearly sixty years, America has only had inflation, not *de*flation.

But as we can easily prove, inflation is *not* inevitable. Figure 1 depicts American price levels from 1665 to the present.

Note there was no net inflation for the first 250 years. Little inflationary blips are on the graph, as during the American Revolution, War of 1812 and Civil War, when the United States printed large quantities of money to pay for those conflicts. Of course, increasing the supply of money diminishes its value, causing prices to rise. But notice that, after the wars, money always returned to its normal value. A dollar in 1900 was worth the same as in 1770: you could expect to pay the same for bread or shoes in 1900 as you did in George Washington's day.

But look at the graph's right side. During World War I, our currency inflated, but instead of resuming its normal value afterwards, inflated out of sight. American money, stable for 250 years, began to rapidly and permanently lose its value. This did not happen by chance; every effect has a cause. Around the time of World War I, something significant must have happened to induce this transformation.

US Price Levels 1665 to estimated 2014, with 2003 = 100

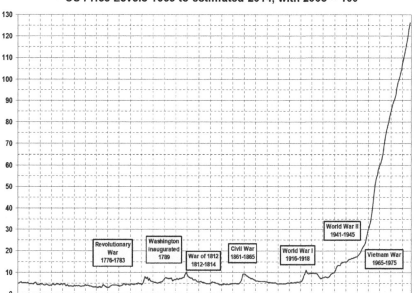

Figure 1. Source: Robert Sahr, Oregon State University

The change came from a single factor: creation of the Federal Reserve Bank in 1913. Though most Americans have heard of it, few know much about it.

Ben Bernanke is current chairman of the Federal Reserve Board; Alan Greenspan held that position from 1987 to 2006. The Fed chairman has been called America's economic czar, because he and the board set U.S. interest rates. This in turn impacts the stock market's direction. If interest rates rise, CDs and other interest-bearing securities appear more profitable, causing money to flow out of the riskier stock market. But if interest rates fall, investors tend to return to stocks. Mutual fund managers try to stay ahead of curve; when the Fed chairman holds a news conference, their fingers are poised over the "buy" and "sell" buttons, hoping the chairman will reveal some hint about the direction of interest rates.

The Fed was established when Congress passed the Federal Reserve Act in 1913. But the original legislation was introduced by Senator Nelson Aldrich, a front man for the banking community.

You may not have heard of Aldrich, but you have probably heard of billionaire Nelson Rockefeller, who was Gerald Ford's Vice President, long New York's governor, and one of America's richest men. His full name: Nelson Aldrich Rockefeller—named for his grandfather, Nelson Aldrich. Aldrich's daughter married John D. Rockefeller, Jr., and his son Winthrop served as chairman of the Rockefellers' Chase National Bank. When Nelson Aldrich spoke on Capitol Hill, insiders knew he was acting for the Rockefellers and their allies in high finance.

Jekyll

The legislation he introduced in the Senate, which became the basis of the modern Federal Reserve System, was not written by him. It was crafted by several of America's richest bankers, at a secret nine-day meeting in 1910, at a private club on Jekyll Island off the Georgia coast. At that time, Jekyll Island was an exclusive retreat of the wealthy elite—the Rockefellers, Morgans, Vanderbilts and Astors.

☹ Oh, come on! Only conspiracy theory screwballs believe that sort of rubbish!

The Federal Reserve's origination at the Jekyll Island meeting is well-established. Today Jekyll Island is open to the public. You can visit the Jekyll Island Club Hotel, and sit in its "Federal Reserve Room" where the Fed was birthed.

The first reporter to break the Jekyll Island story was B. C. Forbes, founder of *Forbes* magazine.

We have already mentioned National City Bank (forerunner of today's Citibank), and the $200 million loan with which it financed the Spanish-American War of 1898. That loan was negotiated by Frank Vanderlip, assistant secretary of the U.S. Treasury. When he left office, National City Bank rewarded Vanderlip by making him its president. In that capacity, he attended the Jekyll Island meeting and discussed it in a memoir 25 years later:

> There was an occasion near the close of 1910 when I was as secretive, indeed as furtive, as any conspirator . . . . I do not feel it is any exaggeration to speak of our secret expedition to Jekyll Island as the occasion of the actual conception of the Federal Reserve System. . . . We were told to leave our last names behind us. We were told further that we should avoid dining together on the night of our departure. We were instructed to come one at a time and as unobtrusively as possible to the terminal of the New Jersey littoral of the Hudson, where Senator Aldrich's private car would be in readiness, attached to the rear end of the train for the South. Once aboard the private car, we began to observe the taboo that had been fixed on last names. . . . Discovery, we knew, simply must not happen. If it were to be discovered that our particular group had got together and written a banking bill, that bill would have no chance whatever of passage by Congress.[37]

The participants designed America's central bank, crafting the name "Federal Reserve System" to deceive Americans. While "Federal" implied public control, it is in fact owned by private shareholders. "Reserve" suggested it would hold reserves to protect banks, but it does not.* "System" implied its power would be diffuse (through regional Federal Reserve banks), whereas actual power would be centralized in the Board and the New York Fed.

[*The Fed keeps Treasury bonds as "reserves," but since bonds are debts, they cannot be reckoned as genuine assets.]

Attending this meeting were agents from the world's three greatest banking houses: those of John D. Rockefeller, J. P. Morgan, and the Rothschilds. Together, they represented an estimated 25 percent of the world's entire wealth. Acting for the Rockefellers were Senator Aldrich and Frank Vanderlip. Representing the Morgan interests were: Benjamin Strong, head of J. P. Morgan's Bankers Trust Company; Henry Davison, senior partner in J. P. Morgan & Co.; and Charles Norton, head of Morgan's First National Bank of

New York. But the most important figure, who actually ran the meeting, was the Rothschilds' agent, Paul Warburg.

Few people recognize Paul Warburg's name today, but if you've seen the *Little Orphan Annie* comic strip, or the musical based on it, *Annie*, you have seen him caricatured. Annie had a benefactor, the world's richest man, Daddy Warbucks. He was a takeoff on Paul Warburg—the cartoonist simply changed the name to War*bucks*.

Paul Warburg belonged to a prominent German banking family associated with the Rothschilds. The latter, the world's most powerful banking dynasty, had grown rich by establishing central banks that loaned money to European countries. Its patriarch, Amschel Mayer Rothschild, said: "Permit me to issue and control the money of a nation, and I care not who makes its laws."

In 1901, Paul Warburg came to America intending to establish a similar central bank in the United States. Shortly after immigrating, he became a partner in Kuhn, Loeb and Co., the Rothschilds' powerful banking satellite in New York City.

The Rothschilds had long been allies of America's two foremost banking families, the Rockefellers and Morgans. They had provided the seed money for John D. Rockefeller's Standard Oil Company, and had helped bail out J. P. Morgan when his firm was financially distressed.

The axis of Warburg/Rothschild, Morgan and Rockefeller, and their Wall Street confederates, became known as "the Money Trust." In 1922 New York City Mayor John F. Hylan declared of this destructive coalition:

> The real menace of our republic is the invisible government which, like a giant octopus, sprawls its slimy length over our city, state and nation. At the head is a small group of banking houses generally referred to as "international bankers." This little coterie of powerful international bankers virtually run our government for their own selfish ends.[38]

The Money Trust worked in unison to force a central bank on America. In 1907, J. P. Morgan, who controlled numerous newspapers, began a false rumor concerning the insolvency of a rival bank—the Trust Company of America. This led to a *run** on the bank that nearly destroyed it.

[*The term "run" may be unfamiliar to some younger readers. Banks loan out money they have on deposit—this is their main means of profit. However, if a bank loaned out too much, and many depositors panicked and simultaneously demanded their money, the bank could collapse. A run is depicted in the famous film *It's a Wonderful Life*. Runs are rarely seen today due to the advent of FDIC insurance.]

The frenzy spread to other banks, and became what historians call the Panic of 1907. Subsequently, Morgan's and Rockefeller's newspapers clamored for a central bank to prevent further crises; Senator Aldrich echoed the call in Congress; and Paul Warburg traveled the country lecturing on why the change was needed.

All this materialized in the Federal Reserve, which ultimately resulted from the legislation, penned on Jekyll Island, that Senator Aldrich introduced. Because of the Senator's well-known ties to Wall Street, Congress rejected the Aldrich Bill. But the bankers gained passage of a very similar act, the Glass-Owen Bill, which created the Fed officially. It was passed on December 23, 1913—when Congress was eager to adjourn for Christmas.

Motive No. 1: Stocks and Bondage

Why did the bankers want the Fed? Well, who do you suppose President Wilson named vice chairman of the Federal Reserve Board (a position from which national interest rates would be set)? *Paul Warburg.* Who was appointed to run the New York Fed, the system's nucleus? *Benjamin Strong.* The very men who had secretly planned the bank now controlled it. The foxes were in charge of the henhouse. At the time, neither Congress nor the public had any inkling of the Jekyll Island meeting.

Paul Warburg's annual salary at Kuhn, Loeb and Co. had been $500,000—the equivalent of well over $10 million in today's dollars. He relinquished that for a Federal Reserve Board position that paid only $12,000. Why?

☺ I'll bet this guy Warburg, after immigrating to the U.S., got all choked up with patriotism, and altruistically decided to sacrifice his salary at Kuhn, Loeb so he could stabilize the American economy!

Try this instead: Paul Warburg told himself, "Why should I settle for a measly $500,000 at Kuhn, Loeb when I can make countless millions, for myself and my associates, by controlling American interest rates? I snap my fingers once—stock market's goin' up. I snap them twice, it's goin' *down!*"

☹ What?!? You think the Federal Reserve is a *conspiracy*? Only cross-eyed loony-tune nut-cases believe something like that! You probably also think that Elvis is alive on a UFO! "Gnaa! Look out! The government's out to get us!" Yeah, *right!*

I'll quote *another* conspiracy nut—Charles Lindbergh, Sr. Most people are familiar with Charles Lindbergh, *Jr.*—"Lucky Lindy"—who made the first solo nonstop transatlantic flight. Fewer people know that his father, Charles, Sr., was a distinguished member of the U.S. House of Representatives. Congressman Lindbergh helped lead the fight—yes, fight—against the Federal Reserve Act. Many congressmen and Senators joined, but I'll quote Lindbergh because his name is most familiar. In December 1913 he declared on the floor of the House:

> This act establishes the most gigantic trust on Earth. When the President signs this act the invisible government by the money power, proven to exist by the money trust investigation, will be legalized.

By "the money power," Lindbergh referred to the Rothschild-Rockefeller-Morgan alliance. Continuing the quote:

> The money power overawes the legislative and executive forces of the nation. I have seen these forces exerted during the different stages of this bill. From now on depressions will be scientifically created. The new law will create inflation whenever the trust wants inflation. If the trust can get a

period of inflation, they figure they can unload stocks on the people at high prices during the excitement and then bring on a panic and buy them back at low prices. The people may not know it immediately, but the day of reckoning is only a few years removed.[39]

Lindbergh's words were prophetic. Did inflation follow the Fed's establishment? Yes, as Figure 1 graphically proves. Were stocks unloaded on the people at high prices, then bought back at low prices after a panic? Yes. The "day of reckoning" Lindbergh predicted came with "Black Thursday" and the Great Crash of 1929.

The October 1929 stock market collapse wiped out millions of small investors—but not the Money Trust. Warburg, Rockefeller, Morgan, Bernard Baruch and other top insiders had exited the market. Friendly biographers attribute this to their fiscal "wisdom." But fiscal *foreknowledge*, especially of the Federal Reserve policy they were controlling, is more like it. Congressman Louis McFadden, chairman of the House Committee on Banking and Currency from 1920 to 1931, said of the crash:

It was not accidental. It was a carefully contrived occurrence. The international bankers sought to bring about a condition of despair here so that they might emerge as rulers of us all.[40]

McFadden stated further:

When the Federal Reserve Act was passed, the people of the United States did not perceive that a world system was being set up here…. a superstate controlled by international bankers and international industrialists acting together to enslave the world for their own pleasure.[41]

Senator Robert L. Owen, who co-sponsored the Federal Reserve Act (the Glass-Owen Bill), testified before the House Committee on Banking and Currency in 1938:

The powerful money interests got control of the Federal Reserve Board through Mr. Paul Warburg, Mr. Albert Strauss, and Mr. Adolph C. Miller.... In 1920 that Reserve Board deliberately caused the Panic of 1921. The same people, unrestrained in the stock market, expanding credit to a great excess between 1926 and 1929, raised the price of stocks to a fantastic point where they could not possibly earn dividends, and when the people realized this, they tried to get out, resulting in the Crash of October 24, 1929.[42]

Several strategies were used to precipitate the 1929 crash. One was interest rates. The Federal Reserve increased the discount rate from 3.5 percent in January of that year to 6 percent in late August.

Another tactic was calling loans used to purchase stock. In the relatively unregulated investing environment of 1929, one could heavily buy stocks "on margin" (with 90 percent borrowed money). But many of these were "24 hour call loans"—meaning the loan could be called at any time, requiring immediate repayment. For most investors, the only way to repay was to sell the stock. Simultaneously calling huge numbers of these loans would, of course, cave in the stock market. In *The United States' Unresolved Monetary and Political Problems*, William Bryan reported:

When everything was ready, the New York financiers started calling 24 hour broker call loans. This meant that the stock brokers and the customers had to dump their stock on the market in order to pay the loans. This naturally collapsed the stock market and brought a banking collapse all over the country because the banks not owned by the oligarchy were heavily involved in broker call claims at this time, and bank runs soon exhausted their coin and currency and they had to close. The Federal Reserve System would not come to their aid, although they were instructed under the law to maintain an elastic currency.[43]

Curtis Dall, son-in-law of President Franklin D. Roosevelt, was the syndicate manager for Lehman Brothers. He was on the floor of the New York Stock Exchange on the day of the crash. He said of it: "Actually, it was the calculated 'shearing' of the public by the World Money powers, triggered by the planned sudden shortage of call money in the New York money market."[44]

The Money Trust also helped stimulate the collapse by heavily short-selling the market, which pressured stocks downward. (In short-selling, you sell a stock you don't own yet, pledging to purchase it later. This investment strategy will be profitable if one knows in advance that stock prices are going down.) William J. Gill highlights an example:

> Albert H. Wiggin, chairman of the Chase National Bank, was unmasked as one of the premier villains when it was discovered he had sold short some 42,500 shares of Chase stock beginning a full month before Black Thursday, thus making a personal contribution to the crash. Using a "front" company, he had financed the deal with a $6.5 million loan from his own bank. Wiggin picked up more than $4 million in profits on this one transaction at a time when investors not plugged into Chase's inside information were losing their shirts. Yet Wiggin was kept on as Chase chairman for an additional three years and the bank's board, in gratitude for the splendid example he had set, voted him a lifetime salary of $100,000 per year upon his retirement.[45]

The combination of higher interest rates, called loans and short-selling caused a plunge that snowballed into a complete panic. Afterwards, the Money Trust moved back into the market—exactly as Congressman Lindbergh had predicted. They bought up stocks that once sold for $10 per share at $1 per share, widening their ownership of corporate America.

Motive No. 2: Something from Nothing

But controlling the stock market was not the only purpose behind the Federal Reserve. Another was *creating money from nothing.* An outstanding book that explains this—and the Fed itself—is G. Edward Griffin's *The Creature from Jekyll Island.*

As you've probably noticed, the U.S. government is very expensive. Its deficit for 2009, 2010, 2011 and 2012 was over $1 trillion for each year. This means that every day, on average, the government spent over $3 billion more than it took in.

How does the government *get* money? Chiefly from taxes and sale of government bonds. (The latter is a poor funding method, since money from bonds must be *repaid later with interest.*) But these revenues never satisfy the federal budget's demands.

Still, despite insufficient income, the government always meets its obligations. It continues to pay federal employees, defense contractors, Social Security and Medicare recipients, etc. How does the government manage this?

It happens through a little-known mechanism. We'll loosely borrow from an illustration given by Griffin. Let's say that, this week, the federal government is short one billion dollars needed to pay its employees. It sends a Treasury official to the Federal Reserve building, where a Fed officer literally writes out a check for $1 billion to the Treasury, in exchange for government bonds that could not otherwise have been sold. This check, however, is not based on any assets the Fed actually holds. It is "fiat money"—created from nothing. Now, if you or I wrote a check, with no assets to back it up, we'd go to jail. But for the Federal Reserve, it's perfectly legal. The technical term the Fed uses for this is "monetizing the debt."

☺ Well, Jim, that helps our government! Why would private bankers care about that?

Warburg and his accomplices already had this figured out. Fiat money gave the government the potential to spend without limit. The banking cartel was intimately linked to corporations that did business with the U.S. government. This meant these corporations (in modern culture, your Halliburton, Bechtel, Enron, Raytheon, etc.) could earn virtually unlimited revenues from government contracts. Wars could be financed without raising taxes. And where do you suppose much of the money came from for the recent Wall Street bailout?

And the mechanism benefitted the bankers in other ways. In our example above, what do you suppose the federal employees will do with that billion dollars in salary? Deposit it in their banks. How does a bank make profits? By loaning out deposited money. The more money in, the more they can loan out. Thus, *out of nothing*, the Fed has created a billion loanable dollars for the banks. Furthermore, this billion automatically becomes *nine* billion. Why? Because under Federal Reserve rules, a bank need only keep 10 percent of deposits in reserve. For every dollar deposited, nine may be loaned. Thus the Fed's creation of $1 billion from nothing actually manufactures $9 billion in loanable money for the banks.

In Europe, the Rothschilds had perfected this system of fabricating bank deposits through central banks. Warburg essentially copied the model to design the Federal Reserve. For the banks, the system meant endless profits, but for the rest of us, endless inflation. Why? Because every time the Fed creates dollars from nothing, it increases the amount of money in America, *thereby decreasing money's value.*

You may have heard of the German inflation of the early 1920s. Defeated in World War I, Germany was compelled to pay the Allies massive reparations. To meet this obligation, it printed huge quantities of money. This decreased the value of German currency so badly that by November 1923, a loaf of bread cost 80 billion marks. People carted paper money around in wheelbarrows; some used it as fuel for stoves.Whenever the Fed "monetizes" the debt, it does the same thing as Germany, only on a smaller scale. In today's high-tech world, of course, printing money is no longer necessary; the Fed can simply create money electronically—but the inflationary result is the same. That is why, following 250 years of stable prices, we've had pernicious inflation since the Fed's birth in 1913. Every effect has a cause.

☹ You're forgetting one thing, Jim! The bankers wouldn't want inflation either, would they? Because they have to face those rising prices too!

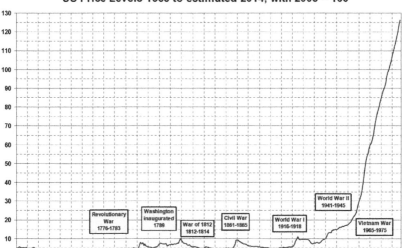

US Price Levels 1665 to estimated 2014, with 2003 = 100

Who cares about five or ten percent inflation when you're making billions from nothing? Here's an analogy. Suppose you built a printing press capable of producing counterfeit $20 bills, and it made you fabulously wealthy. And let's say you actually created so much of this counterfeit cash that it caused slight inflation. You'd gladly accept this, knowing it was a small price to pay for your personal wealth. The bankers feel the same way. But inflation *is* painful to the rest of us, who survive on relatively fixed incomes.

Incidentally, Washington politicians love this system. By letting the Fed finance their expenditures with money made from nothing, politicians know they can *spend without raising taxes*. Tax increases are a "kiss of death" at reelection time (as President George Bush, Sr., learned in 1992 after voters rejected him for breaking his pledge of "Read my lips, no new taxes."). When the Fed produces more currency, making prices rise, who do we blame? Not the Fed. Not politicians. Instead, we blame the local retail store. "Why are you guys jacking up your prices again?" Or we blame the candy company for making a smaller chocolate bar, or the cereal company for putting less corn flakes in the box. But these businesses are simply trying to cope with the same dilemma as us: inflation. *The culprit is the Federal Reserve,* and the problem is not that *prices are going up,* but that *money's value is going down.*

Did you notice that George Bush, Jr., waged war against Iraq without increasing taxes? He even introduced new tax credits and rebates! How did he manage this? Instead of raising taxes like his father, he simply had the Fed finance the war with fiat currency. This caused massive U.S. inflation: the cost of housing, food, energy, college tuition—everything soared.

By the way, inflation *is* a tax—a hidden one the public generally doesn't perceive as such. And it is more unfair than conventional taxes, which are scaled by income. Inflation affects all equally, making no exceptions for the needy.

(Note: Subsequent to this book's publication, an economic crash *could* cause a period of *de*flation. During an economic debacle, prices tend to drop because many people are out of work and can't afford to buy things. As the graph illustrates, this occurred during the Great Depression of the 1930s.)

Motive No. 3: Soaking the American People

After developing this scheme, the bankers still faced a problem. The billions deposited in their banks, which had been created from nothing, *still belonged to depositors.* To make it profitable, the bankers had to loan it to someone.

To whom do you suppose they wanted to loan the money? Someone like you or me? Forget it! Individuals don't borrow that much, and if our businesses failed, we might not repay the loans.

The bankers wanted to loan the money to *one man in particular:* Uncle Sam! Yes, right back to the government through which they had manufactured it. Why? Because Uncle Sam would borrow astronomically *more* than businesses or individuals, would *not* go belly up, and would always *guarantee repayment.* Government debt (borrowing) is generated through sale of bonds. The Federal Reserve was empowered to buy and sell U.S. government bonds. The Establishment's own banks and investment firms could now buy these bonds, redeeming them at interest rates set by their friends in the U.S. Treasury Department.

We thus see yet another motive for the Fed: *interest on government loans.*

But the Jekyll Island bankers still had a problem. How would America pay back all the interest on those loans? In 1913, the U.S. government had few revenue sources—its largest was tariffs collected on foreign imports.

The bankers' solution? *Income tax.* Though now an accepted way of life, income tax was not always around. The original U.S. Constitution excluded it; in 1895 the Supreme Court ruled it would be unconstitutional.

Therefore the only way the Money Trust could establish income tax was by legalizing it through a Constitutional Amendment. Which Senator introduced that Amendment in Congress? You get one guess.

Nelson Aldrich—the same Senator who introduced the original Federal Reserve legislation.

Why did Americans accept income tax? Because it was originally only one percent of a person's income, for salaries under $20,000 (the equivalent of about $500,000 in today's dollars). Senator Aldrich and other supporters of the tax issued assurances it would never go up. So patriotic Americans said: "If Uncle Sam needs one percent of my salary, and I can always keep the rest, it's OK by me!"

But you know what happened. Congress later dolefully informed Americans it needed to raise taxes a smidge. A few smidges later and, depending on bracket, we're losing 15, 25, 28 or 33 percent of our income to federal tax.

It's said that if you want to boil a frog, you can't just toss him in boiling water. Instead, you put him in lukewarm water, and gradually turn up the heat. That way, the frog never realizes he's been boiled. This, in effect, is what the bankers did to Americans, knowing that once we became accustomed to taxes, the amounts could incrementally be turned up to "boil." *It was a long-range plan.*

☹ Hold on, Mr. Perloff. These rich bankers would *never* have wanted an income tax. After all, it "soaks the rich"—the wealthier you are, the more taxes you pay.

It's true that income tax is graduated. If an American today earns $100,000 or $200,000 per year, he or she usually owes lots of tax. But not the *super-rich*. The Warburg-Rockefeller-Morgan axis had no intention of paying substantial income tax.

In 1970, at age 18, I worked making minimum wage: $1.80 per hour. Yet I paid more income tax that year than billionaire Nelson Rockefeller, who didn't pay one cent. (We know this because when Rockefeller sought to become Gerald Ford's Vice President, he had to disclose his tax returns.)

Likewise, the Senate's Pecora Hearings of 1933 discovered that none of the 17 partners of J. P. Morgan & Co. had paid any income tax in 1931 and 1932.

How did the Money Trust escape taxes? The means were numerous, but a major one was placing their assets in tax-free foundations. The Carnegie and Rockefeller foundations were already operational by the time income tax passed. The cartel's foundations, while fronting as "charitable" organizations, use their grants to advance its agenda. For example, they help finance the CFR and pour countless millions of dollars into universities to motivate them to teach "politically correct" doctrines.

Summing up the Money Scheme

Let's review the scenario. In 1913, the bankers created the Federal Reserve, which not only gave them control over interest rates and thus the stock market, but empowered them to create billions of dollars from nothing, which they would then loan to America. Also in 1913, the bankers installed income tax, enabling them to exact repayment on these interest-bearing loans to the government.

Only one thing was still missing: *a significant reason for America to borrow.* In 1914, just six months after the Federal Reserve Act passed, Archduke Ferdinand was assassinated, triggering the start of World War I. America participated; as a result, our national debt grew from a manageable $1 billion to $25 billion. Ever since, America has been immersed in skyrocketing debt—now said, officially, to exceed $15 trillion.

☹ Actually, Mr. Perloff, there's an easy explanation for all that stuff— the Fed, the taxes, the war. Those things were just *coincidences*. Hey, stuff happens, dude!

Some readers of this book are familiar with my creation-evolution books, *Tornado in a Junkyard* and *The Case against Darwin*. I am often asked what connection exists between those books and the topic of this one.

When discussing creation-evolution, I present evidence that the world and living things reveal evidence of *design*—i.e., they were not produced by chance, as materialists claim.

In *Truth Is a Lonely Warrior*, we examine the flip side: *evil* also results from design. Satan wanting to deny God's existence was the root motive behind Darwin's theory of evolution. But Satan, at least for now, doesn't want us knowing *he* exists either. Hence Establishment historians dismiss the march of history as accidental, just as Darwin did with the development of life itself.

Alexandre de Marchenches, who for 11 years headed France's intelligence service, the Service of External Documentation and Counter-espionage, wrote: "The most astute move of the devil was to make people believe that he does not exist."[46] Do I believe in accidents? Absolutely. But not very often in politics.

☹ Accidents or not, Mr. Perloff, the Federal Reserve and income tax are part of America—they're two of the cornerstones of our free enterprise system! Your criticizing them makes you sound like a communist!

Marvin, read *The Communist Manifesto*. In it, Karl Marx laid down tens steps he proclaimed necessary to establish a communist state.

Step 2 was: "A heavy progressive or graduated income tax."

Step 5 was: "Centralization of credit in the hands of the State, by means of a national bank with state capital and an exclusive monopoly."

Thus, in 1913, the United States enacted two of Marx's conditions for a communist totalitarian state. Income tax and central banks have nothing to do with free enterprise or the American way of life.

The original Constitution excluded an income tax, which the Founding Fathers opposed. Concerning money, the Constitution declares (Article 1, Sec. 8): "Congress shall have the power to coin money and regulate the value thereof." The Federal Reserve Act transferred this authority from our elected representatives to private bankers.

In America today, many young couples work hard. Commonly, both spouses hold jobs. A young man might say: "Wow! When my great-grandfather came to this country, he worked only one job, but he owned a house, had seven kids, and his wife never worked outside the home. But me and Mindy, we're working two jobs, we have only one kid, and can barely pay the rent. What are we doing wrong? We must be spending too much!" And the couple begins arguing over money.

But it's hardly their fault. When great-grandpa came to America, income tax didn't exist. Today's average workers lose about 50 percent of their pay to taxes: federal income tax, state income tax, social security tax, real estate tax, sales tax, excise tax, utilities tax, etc. (The American colonists went to war with Britain when the only tax was a 3-cent customs duty on a pound of tea.) If half a family's wages go to taxes, won't it need *two* jobs to maintain the same standard of living? Furthermore, great-grandpa had a stable dollar—it didn't plummet in value every year like now.

But you'll be glad to know the bankers are sorry about the trouble they've caused (sniff, sniff, boo-hoo) and want to help us! They realize people can't make ends meet (boo-hoo), and they've found a solution! That's why they send us *multiple credit card offers in the mail every day*. Can't afford this month's groceries? No problem! Just swipe some plastic! Er, of course, the banks *will* charge double-digit interest on that.

Catch the circle? The banking cartel created inflation and income tax, robbing us of our income; therefore we don't have enough to live on, forcing us to borrow from … them!

Postscript: Today, corruption at the Fed has reached a new zenith. In 2011, a limited audit of the Fed by the Government Accountability Office (GAO) revealed that, from 2007 to 2010, the Fed had handed out $16 trillion in financial assistance to multinational banks and corporations. Top recipients included Citigroup ($2.5 trillion) and Morgan Stanley ($2.04 trillion). Those aren't typos; that's *trillions*, not billions.

Technically, these were loans, but the loans were given at *zero percent interest*, and very little has been repaid. In short, these were basically gifts that Ben Bernanke bestowed on his elitist friends, without informing Congress or the people. U.S. Senator Bernie Sanders of Vermont stated: "As a result of this audit, we now know that the Federal Reserve provided more than $16 trillion in total financial assistance to some of the largest financial institutions and corporations in the United States and throughout the world. This is a clear case of socialism for the rich and rugged, you're-on-your-own individualism for everyone else."[47] The GAO's audit of the Fed may be read online.[48]

Chapter 4
HOW THE CARTEL HAS RUN AMERICA

Wilson, House and the League

Let's now connect the banking to the politics. When the plotters met at Jekyll Island, Republican William Howard Taft was President. Taft opposed the Aldrich plan for a central bank, and the cartel sought to replace him with someone more compliant.

We earlier quoted Franklin D. Roosevelt's son-in-law, Curtis Dall, who knew many of Washington's inside stories. In his book *FDR: My Exploited Father-in-Law*, he described how Woodrow Wilson pledged to banker Bernard Baruch to do four things if elected President: (1) lend an ear to advice on who should occupy his cabinet; (2) support creation of a central bank; (3) support income tax; and (4) lend an ear to advice should war break out in Europe.[49]

The Money Trust knew that Wilson, a stiff-looking Princeton professor, could never defeat the popular incumbent Taft. So they backed former Republican President Teddy Roosevelt on the short-lived "Bull Moose" ticket. This effectively split Republican votes between Taft and Roosevelt. Wilson, the Democratic Party candidate, won the election with only 42 percent of the popular vote.

Watch Wilson's career:

1910–President of Princeton, little-known to Americans, he has no political experience. But with the Establishment's power supporting him, Wilson's fortunes take off.

1911–He is elected governor of New Jersey (they needed to give him *some* political credential before running him for President).

1912–Having only one year of political experience, but with the Establishment press exalting him, Wilson is elected President.

1913–His first year in office sees passage of both income tax and the Federal Reserve.

1914–World War I begins.

1915–The *Lusitania* is sunk; Wilson later orders the ship's manifest hidden.

1916–He is reelected on the campaign slogan "He Kept Us Out of War."

1917–Safely reelected, he secures a Congressional declaration of war.

1918–The Germans surrender after U.S. entry into the war shifts the power balance against them.

1919–Wilson heads to the Paris Peace Conference.

Trivia time. Who did Wilson appoint to head the American delegation to the peace conference? Paul Warburg—who he'd also named vice chairman of the Federal Reserve! How could Warburg—a recent immigrant—be the only person qualified for these critical positions?

More trivia. Who did Wilson bring to Paris as his chief economic advisor? Bernard Baruch, to whom he made those campaign pledges.

And as always, the President was under the watchful eye of Edward Mandell House, the bankers' front man. Wilson did not invite any leading Democratic Party members to travel with him to Paris—not a single Senator or congressman accompanied him; only the bankers and their entourage.

At this conference, of course, Wilson presented his famous "Fourteen Points," the most important calling for establishment of the League of Nations. Many people think he invented the League, but it originated with House and the bankers.

Ray Stannard Baker, Wilson's official biographer, said that "practically nothing—not a single idea in the Covenant of the League—was original with the President."[50] Charles Seymour, House's official biographer, said Wilson "approved the House draft almost in its entirety, and his own rewriting of it was practically confined to phraseology."[51]

What were the bankers seeking in the League? It was a plan for a *world government*.

☹ Hold on, Mr. Perloff! Earlier you said the Establishment wanted an *all-powerful* world government. The League of Nations was in fact rather feeble.

Correct. In 1919, nations wouldn't have accepted a powerful world government. The plan was to start with a weak association, and gradually strengthen it. If you want to boil a frog …

The Paris Conference produced the Versailles Treaty, which officially established the League of Nations. Ironically, though the American President had proposed the League, the United States did not join. The U.S. Constitution stipulated that no President could single-handedly make a treaty; the Senate had to ratify it.

The Senate rejected the Versailles Treaty. Americans had helped win the war, but saw no reason to join an organization that might infringe on their sovereignty. When news of the Senate vote reached Paris, the bankers reacted swiftly. They held a series of meetings, culminating with a dinner at the Majestic Hotel, at which they resolved to form a new organization in the United States. Its purpose would be to change the climate of American opinion so that the nation would accept world government. In 1921, that organization was incorporated in New York City as the Council on Foreign Relations (CFR).

Examination of the Council's original roster reveals that most members were bankers or lawyers affiliated with J. P. Morgan and Co. For example, J. P. Morgan's personal attorney, John W. Davis, was the CFR's founding president; Morgan attorney Paul Cravath was the founding vice president; Morgan partner Russell Leffingwell was the first chairman.

Conscious that this peculiar uniformity would look unsuitable for a foreign affairs association, the Council diversified its roster by adding college professors. However, these came from universities receiving large grants and endowments from the Morgan interests. The professors, carefully screened, could be counted on to attend

Council meetings, then return to their university classrooms and preach the glories of world government.

By the late 1920s, the Rockefellers had brought their people into the Council. David Rockefeller was the CFR's chairman for many years, and was still honorary chairman as of this book's publication.

The Council's Influence over Policy

How does the Council influence American foreign policy? One method is its publications, including many books and especially its periodical *Foreign Affairs*, which *Time* magazine has called "the most influential journal in print."[52] Most people haven't heard of *Foreign Affairs*, but it's a virtual instruction manual for U.S. foreign-policy makers.

The CFR also has numerous interlocks with the media and universities. According to the Council's 2011 annual report, more than 1,000 members were in media or education.

But the CFR's most important means of controlling foreign policy is *supplying cabinet-level and sub-cabinet level personnel to the government*.

As of February 2013, 21 Secretaries of Defense/War, 19 Treasury Secretaries, 18 Secretaries of State, and 16 CIA directors have been Council members. Bill Clinton selected 12 cabinet members from the Council's roster. Under President George Bush, Jr., members included Vice President Dick Cheney, Secretaries of State Colin Powell and Condoleeza Rice, Assistant Secretary of Defense Paul Wolfowitz, Deputy National Security Advisor Stephen Hadley, and innumerable others. Obama's CFR picks have included Treasury Secretary Timothy Geithner, Defense Secretary Robert Gates, Depart of Homeland Security Secretary Janet Napolitano, Deputy Secretary of State James Steinberg, and many others.*

[*See my book *The Shadows of Power* for recaps of CFR presence in Presidential administrations through that of Reagan; see my article "Council on Foreign Relations: Influencing American

Government" at www.thenewamerican.com for a more comprehensive listing of CFR members in the Obama government.]

Obama Secretary of State Hillary Clinton, speaking at the Council's Washington branch, frankly stated:

> I have been often to, I guess, the mother ship in New York City, but it's good to have an outpost of the Council right here down the street from the State Department. We get a lot of advice from the Council, so this will mean I won't have as far to go to be told what we should be doing and how we should think about the future.[53]

What policies has the Council created? Let's take three examples from immediately after World War II.

The UN

The League of Nations had effectively collapsed with that war's onset. Its successor, of course, was the United Nations—a bolder step toward world government.

My public school teacher recited a typical explanation of the UN's origins: "You see, children, after World War II, all the countries were really sick of war! So they got together and formed a new organization that would prevent war!"

That's not what happened. The United Nations began with a group of CFR members in the U.S. State Department. Working under Secretary of State Cordell Hull, they called themselves the "Informal Agenda Group"—selecting this innocuous name to arouse no suspicion. The group drew up the original plan for the UN. They then consulted three attorneys, all CFR members, who declared the scheme constitutional. Subsequently they met with President Roosevelt, who approved the plan and publicly announced it the same day.[54] After that, FDR made establishing the UN his central priority for postwar planning (just as the League had been to Wilson). And when the UN held its founding conference in San Francisco in 1945, most of the American delegates—47 of them—were CFR members.

Marshalling Our Assets

How about the Marshall Plan, America's postwar program of aid to Europe? Allegedly it was the brainchild of General George Marshall, who proposed it in a Harvard commencement speech.

In reality, however, the plan was not conceived at all by Marshall, but by a CFR study group with David Rockefeller as secretary.[55] They originally intended President Truman to announce the proposal and call it the "Truman Plan." However, after deliberating they decided against this, realizing that Truman, as a Democrat, might fail to win support from Congressional Republicans (the latter might have viewed it as a "Democratic Party spending scheme").[56] Marshall, a CFR cohort, was chosen to reveal the plan because, as a military figure, he would be misperceived as politically neutral and win more bipartisan support. The strategy worked.

Americans were told the funds were for Europe's needy. They were not told, however, that the goods sent to Europe, which their tax dollars purchased, came mostly from multinational corporations linked to the CFR, which had hatched the scheme.

But the Marshall Plan had an even more sinister aspect. Unknown to most Americans, Europeans were required to pay for Marshall Plan goods with printing press money called "counterpart funds." CFR member John J. McCloy, appointed High Commissioner to Germany, was put in charge of this cash. He was then approached by Jean Monnet, renowned as founder of the Common Market, predecessor of today's European Union; *Time* called him "the Father of Europe." Foreign policy specialist Hilaire du Berrier commented on Monnet's ties to the world government intrigue:

> Sometime in 1913 Monnet was taken into the conspiratorial Canadian and British group planning a United Europe as a step towards a single government for the world. The Americans, Canadians and Britishers were not alone in this plot. During World War II the French initiates smuggled a truckload of papers from Paris to Lyon for safe-keeping. Lyon

was near the Swiss border and had become an escape hatch for all sorts of conspirators. After the Germans occupied the city, French police searched for anything that might get them in trouble if the Germans found it first, and among the documents in a Lyon cellar they stumbled onto an elaborately bound volume containing detailed plans for a revolutionary one-world empire. According to this master plan the first step for the establishment of a federalist world was the forming of a regime "in which all power would be concentrated in the hands of a High Power and representatives duly mandated by banking groups, especially designated from each country." They were all there: Monnet's interlocking supporters in "the City," [London] the Rothschilds and Lazards in France, the Rockefellers in America and Societe Generale in Belgium. Study of the secret files revealed that the French wing had been active since 1922, when Monnet and Colonel House and their associates were drawing up plans for a world state as they proposed to shape it.[57]

In 1947, Monnet sent agents to McCloy, who put millions of dollars in counterpart funds at their disposal. This money jump-started the movement for European unity. According to du Berrier, McCloy's handouts financed Common Market propaganda, a European union youth movement, establishment of schools and universities that would promote European consolidation, the Council of Europe's first meeting in 1949, and election campaigns of favored political candidates.[58]

Journalist Richard Rovere called McCloy "Chairman of the Establishment."[59] A true Insider's Insider, when he returned to the U.S. he became chairman of both the Council on Foreign Relations and the Rockefellers' Chase Manhattan Bank.

Global Banks

McCloy was also second president of the World Bank, which, along with its dark sister, the International Monetary Fund (IMF), needs investigation.

☹ Oh, I know about them! They're nice, charitable branches of the UN that help poor countries with their debt problems! They got started at the Bretton Woods Conference.

Although the 1944 Bretton Woods Conference *officially* created the World Bank and IMF, all the initial planning and groundwork were done by the Economic and Finance Group of the CFR's War and Peace Studies Project.

As with the Marshall Plan, the motive wasn't charity. After World War II, the New York banks wanted to continue loaning money to governments. However, they worried that some war-torn nations might have difficulty repaying. What if an interest payment was missed? How tragic! A fall guy was needed to guarantee the loans. Can you guess who the sucker was?

Yes, taxpayers—especially American ones.

Here's how the scheme would work. Chase Bank lends Poland $50 million. The Poles start repaying the loan, but eventually can't make an interest payment. So the IMF or World Bank bails them out with taxpayer money. Chase wins; Poland wins—only the taxpayer loses.

The World Bank and IMF gave *carte blanche* to the New York banks. They could now make virtually any loan to foreign governments, no matter how foolish. If the transaction went sour, their profits were still guaranteed. Why, they asked, should they pay for their own mistakes? Let the chumps and the suckers—secretaries, clerks, guys who pump gas for a living—let *them* dig into their pockets and ante up.

U.S. Senator Jesse Helms, once chairman of the Senate Foreign Relations Committee, said in 1987: "The New York banks have found important profit centers in lending to countries plunged into debt. This has been an essentially riskless game for the banks because the IMF and World Bank have stood ready to bail the banks out with our taxpayer's money."[60]

Noted British author A. K. Chesterton declared: "The World Bank and International Monetary Fund were not incubated by hard-pressed governments, but by a Supra-national Money Power which could afford to look ahead to the shaping of a postwar world that would serve its interest."[61]

Furthermore, these institutions provide loans for infrastructural projects—dams, roads, building construction, etc.—typically executed by Establishment multinational corporations: Halliburton, Bechtel, etc.

But profit was not the only motive. Through their grant-making power, the World Bank and IMF can make or break politicians. For example, a few years ago, when Russian President Boris Yeltsin was in political trouble, the World Bank loaned Russia six billion dollars. Yeltsin got reelected (amazing what $6 billion will do for your popularity).

Furthermore, the World Bank often attaches conditions to loans. It may demand a voice in government policy. For example, it might dictate that a country privatize part of its industry (to multinational corporations) before money comes through. Thus the World Bank and IMF are instruments of both profit *and* control.

Incidentally, these loans do little to improve the lot of people in Third World nations—except for their corrupt leaders. As Hilaire du Berrier noted:

> It is misleading to call these handouts "loans." There is nothing to show for them save a high level of inflation, lots of automobiles, luxury items and Swiss bank accounts for the families in power.[62]

The CFR has shaped U.S. foreign policy in many other ways (see my book *The Shadows of Power*). We will soon discuss what's happening today, but first let's examine one of American history's most critical episodes.

CHAPTER 5

VIETNAM

Few events have impacted America more than the Vietnam War. It spawned a vast protest movement, to which the subsequent "counterculture" generally traces its roots.

☹ I'll explain it to the folks, Jim. The war was a *quagmire*. It was the military's fault. They told Washington that beating the communists would be a piece of cake. But they underestimated the patriotic fervor of the Vietnamese, who loved communist leader Ho Chi Minh. So we sent 100,000 troops—that didn't do any good; 200,000 didn't either. Finally we sent 500,000 troops—no use! You see, the war was *unwinnable*. But those gosh-darn right-wing, patriotic hawks were too proud to pull out. So the war dragged on for 14 years, until finally we gave up, and South Vietnam fell to the communists. That's all there was to it—a big mess, a quagmire, that nothing could fix.

Thank you, Marvin. You have just encapsulated the Establishment media's explanation—invented for public consumption—of the Vietnam disaster. On a Google search I once found over one million websites pairing the words "Vietnam" and "quagmire."

But now let's view Vietnam through the Establishment's hidden maneuverings and motives.

Until 1954, Vietnam had been a French colony. As du Berrier noted:

> According to Mr. Charles Bohlen's minutes of the Cairo-Teheran papers, it was by secret agreement between President Roosevelt and Joseph Stalin on December 1, 1943, that France's premature elimination from Southeast Asia and the sowing of wars to come were effected. Franklin D. Roosevelt, we are told by Mr. Bohlen,

"was 100% in agreement [at Teheran] with Marshal Stalin that France should not get back Indochina."[63]

After World War II, U.S. foreign policy dictated that France quit Vietnam. Few recall that the United States initially *supported* Ho Chi Minh, first by intervening to have the British release him from a Hong Kong jail. Then, in 1945, the OSS—forerunner of the CIA—trained Ho's army and provided him with guns and 20,000 cartridges to fight the French. In the meantime the U.S. press extolled him. In 1946, *Newsweek's* Harold Isaacs compared him to George Washington.

In 1954, with its troops hemmed in by Ho's forces at the critical battle of Dien Bien Phu, France begged the United States to intervene. A one-hour aircraft carrier strike would have averted disaster, but the U.S. government refused.

Following the French pullout, and division of Vietnam into North and South, U.S. foreign policy's next objective was removing emperor Bao Dai, the one man capable of uniting the country. Through a rigged plebiscite, Ngo Dinh Diem—hand-picked by the CFR—was installed as South Vietnam's president, and the emperor ousted. The South Vietnamese hated the corrupt and oppressive Diem, who drove many Vietnamese into the communists' arms.

In the meantime, CIA Colonel Edward Lansdale (CFR) oversaw the disarming and destruction of three powerful anti-communist groups in Vietnam: the Cao Dai sect, Hoa Hao sect, and Le Van Vien's private army.

Thus, even before U.S. troops went to Vietnam, our CFR-dictated foreign policy had ravaged the country, sponsored Ho Chi Minh, and destroyed his opponents at every level—French, imperial, and local.[64]

What about the catastrophic war itself, which lasted from 1961 until 1975? Let's give it context. In World War II, the United States fought on two fronts—Europe and the Pacific. The German and Japanese forces were extremely tough and well-equipped. Yet we crushed both those military empires, with our allies' help, in just three and a half years. On the other hand, we spent 14 years fighting little North Vietnam and failed. Something's wrong with the picture!

In the March 1968 *Science & Mechanics*, Lloyd Mallan interviewed nearly a dozen retired high-ranking U.S. military officers. Each, queried separately, said the Vietnam War could be won quickly—in weeks or months. They were nearly unanimous in their recommendations: (1) declare war on North Vietnam; (2) take the war directly against the North by invasion plus decisively bombing strategic targets; and (3) blockade Haiphong Harbor, where North Vietnam received some 90 percent of its war supplies.

The communists were sending those supplies south via the Ho Chi Minh Trail. President Johnson periodically permitted bombing of the trail, but historically, bombing had not been very effective at halting supply lines. The Reds, forewarned of approaching bombers detected by radar, would simply pull off the trail, wait until the bombs fell, then resume their trek. Officers interviewed by Mallan observed we should have *blocked* the trail with troops.

U.S. Secretary of Defense Robert McNamara was forbidding the Air Force to strike over 90 percent of the strategic targets it wanted to hit. (A CFR member, he left the Defense Department to become president of the World Bank.)

Then there were the Rules of Engagement, not declassified until 1985, when they consumed 26 pages of the *Congressional Record*'s fine print. According to the Rules of Engagement, American soldiers weren't allowed to shoot at the enemy first, but had to wait until fired upon. If a pilot saw a MiG (fighter plane) on the ground, he couldn't attack—he had to wait until it was airborne and showing hostile intent. If a surface-to-air missile launch site was under construction, he couldn't bomb it—he had to wait until it was fully operational.

Imagine if we had fought World War II that way. A pilot spots several Luftwaffe planes on a German airfield, but his squadron commander says, "Sorry, boys, leave them alone. We have to wait until they're in the air and shooting at us." If we had approached World War II like we did Vietnam, the Axis would have defeated us.

Clearly, we didn't lose in Vietnam because its people loved communism or Ho Chi Minh, but because our soldiers were chained. Washington politicians, not the military, authored those restrictions. Without them, the war would have ended in months, and would now be a little-remembered episode in U.S. history.

Who was responsible for this tragedy? At the time, I was a hippie, anti-war protester; we were always told that the people behind the war were right-wing, anti-communist jingoes—Archie Bunker types!

Let's check that. The first U.S. combat troops went to Vietnam in late 1961. President Kennedy authorized sending about 10,000 on the advice of the State Department's Walt Rostow, who had just returned from a fact-finding mission to Vietnam.

☺ Well, Jim, obviously this Rostow must have been a big anti-communist—otherwise he never would have made that recommendation!

To the contrary: his father had been a Marxist revolutionary in Russia. Two of his aunts belonged to the U.S. Communist Party. His brother, Eugene Debs Rostow, was named after Socialist Party leader Eugene Debs. The Eisenhower State Department rejected Walt Rostow for employment three times as a security risk. The Kennedy administration could only get him in by firing Otto Otepka, the State Department's head of security. An entire book was written on that subject: *The Ordeal of Otto Otepka*, by William J. Gill. Rostow's background resonated with communism, *not* anti-communism.

☺ OK, so maybe he wasn't a big anti-communist—but I'll bet he was a flag-waving ultra-nationalist!

Let's quote Rostow's book *The United States in the World Arena*, published the year before his advice to Kennedy on Vietnam:

> It is a legitimate American national objective to see removed from all nations—including the United States—the right to use substantial military force to pursue their own interests. Since this right is the root of national sovereignty, it is there-

fore an American interest to see an end to nationhood as it has been historically defined.[65]

The preceding was a classic globalist pronouncement, typical of the CFR—to which Rostow belonged.

As we noted earlier, Congress authorized President Johnson to intervene in Vietnam through the 1964 Tonkin Gulf Resolution. It was written *before* the two alleged North Vietnamese attacks on the U.S. Navy; Admiral Stockdale testified that the second never even occurred.

Who prematurely authored the Tonkin Gulf Resolution? William P. Bundy, Assistant Secretary of State for Far Eastern Affairs.

☺ Well, if Bundy wrote that resolution, he must have been an anti-communist.

In the 1950s, Bundy headed the defense fund for the notorious Soviet spy Alger Hiss.* No anti-communist would have even considered doing that.

[*Although Hiss claimed innocence, his guilt has been proven conclusively by the release of the Venona files—FBI decodings of Soviet intercepts from the 1940s.]

☺ But surely he was a Yankee Doodle boy! I bet he went skipping down the street, waving the flag as he sang about Mom, baseball and apple pie.

After Bundy left the State Department, David Rockefeller appointed him editor of *Foreign Affairs*, the journal of the Council on Foreign Relations, America's leading opponent of national sovereignty.

In 1964, President Johnson successfully ran for reelection against Republican Barry Goldwater, whom the press branded a "war-monger." But after the election, Johnson himself suddenly began escalating the war, committing hundreds of thousands of troops. *Why?* Few people know that he made the decision at the urging of a secret clique called "the Wise Men," fourteen senior advisors, twelve of whom were CFR members.

☹ I don't buy it! Only conspiracy nuts believe such tripe.

These meetings are described in the book *The Wise Men*, by Walter Isaacson and Evan Thomas, themselves CFR members. The book does not condemn the Wise Men, but overflows with praise for them.

Actually, Johnson had not wanted to escalate, but the Wise Men insisted. Their leader, who *led the charge in demanding escalation*, was former Secretary of State Dean Acheson.

☺ Acheson must have been a big reactionary anti-communist to give Johnson that advice.

To the contrary, even before the United States recognized the USSR in 1933, the murderous dictator Joseph Stalin selected the young attorney Dean Acheson to represent Soviet interests in America. While Truman's Secretary of State, Acheson surrounded himself with communists, known spies and security risks—such as John Stewart Service, John Carter Vincent and Lauchlin Currie. He promoted Service even after the FBI caught him passing government secrets to communist agents. In the late 1940s, Poland's new communist regime hired Acheson's law firm to win U.S. recognition. His law partner was Donald Hiss—brother of Soviet spy Alger Hiss and a secret member of the Communist Party.

In short, the men who maneuvered us into Vietnam were not anti-communist, but *soft on communism* or even *pro-communist*. Although not "card-carrying" Party members, it defies credibility that they would seek to defeat communism through war. Nor were they flag-waving patriots—they were quite the opposite: CFR globalists who opposed nationalism in favor of world government.

Incidentally, Bundy, who drafted the Tonkin Gulf Resolution, *was Acheson's son-in-law.* This was a small, tight group. Furthermore, nearly all key American policy planners during the Vietnam War were CFR members. When we realize that the same clique *that got us into the war* authored the Rules of Engagement and other restrictions *preventing victory*, it is clear that Vietnam was not a "quagmire" or the result of "blunder," but happened as planned.

One of their goals—successfully implemented—was to provoke a huge American political slide to the left. College students, many of whom previously thought little about politics, were transformed into Marxists and revolutionaries. Wars have traditionally been exploited to sow revolution. Lenin, for example, used World War I to ignite the Russian Revolution.

In *The Strawberry Statement: Notes of a College Revolutionary*, student radical James Kunen described the 1968 annual meeting of Students for a Democratic Society (SDS), which spearheaded the war protest movement:

> Also at the convention, men from Business International Round Tables—the meetings sponsored by Business International—tried to buy up a few radicals. These men are the world's leading industrialists and they convene to decide how our lives are going to go. They are the left wing of the ruling class. They offered to finance our demonstrations in Chicago. We were also offered Esso (Rockefeller) money. They want us to make a lot of radical commotion so they can look more in the center as they move to the left.[66]

Jerry Kirk, one-time member of SDS and the Communist Party, testified before the House and Senate Internal Security Panels:

> Young people have no conception of the conspiracy strategy of pressure from above and pressure from below. . . . They have no idea that they are playing into the hands of the Establishment they claim to hate. The radicals think they are fighting the forces of the super rich, like Rockefeller and Ford, and they don't realize that it is precisely such forces which are behind their own revolution, financing it, and using it for their own purposes.[67]

Thus the Establishment played a double game, arranging the war on one hand, financing the resulting rebellion on the other.

Part of the plan was to touch off a furor of *anti-patriotism*, epitomized by the burning of American flags on college campuses. Destroying patriotism, of course, is prerequisite to absorbing nations into a world government. To put it in Marxist Hegelian lingo, war was the thesis, revolution the antithesis, world government the synthesis.

CHAPTER 6
THE PLAN TODAY

Today, the Establishment still offers us "peace and prosperity." They proclaim prosperity will come through international trade accords, and peace through "the war on terror." We'll examine trade first.

Exporting Our Economy

Over the last few years, you may have noticed America becoming embroiled in various trade agreements and organizations with acronyms—GATT (General Agreement on Trade and Tariffs); WTO (World Trade Organization); NAFTA (North American Free Trade Agreement); SPP (Security and Prosperity Partnership—a strengthened NAFTA); and the proposed FTAA (Free Trade Area of the Americas—a projected extension of NAFTA to the entire Western Hemisphere).

You may have also noticed that American jobs are disappearing—going overseas.

In 1994, we signed the GATT Treaty, making us a member of the World Trade Organization. Congress bitterly debated the treaty, whose proponents assured us it would not undermine our trade balance: exports *and* imports would increase; everyone would win!

However, the following year, America's trade deficit shot from $75 billion to a record $103 billion. Since then, the deficit has steadily increased, reaching a staggering $721 billion by 2007. The biggest item we export is jobs.

This occurred because GATT and other recent trade treaties eradicated America's *tariff structure*. A tariff, of course, is a charge a government puts on foreign goods. It raises the cost of imports for consumers, but also provides revenue for the American government.

Years ago, a woman shopping at Wal-Mart would see two comparable plastic products—one manufactured in China, one in America. The Chinese product, made by virtual slave labor, cost $4.50, its price increased by a tariff. The American product cost $5—a bit more expensive, but it looked nicer, so the woman would buy it.

But now comes the GATT Treaty. The tariff on the Chinese import vanishes. It now sells for $1.25, reflecting the labor's true cost. Meanwhile, the American product is still $5. The woman sighs, "Well, the American one *looks* nicer—but I can't pass up a bargain." She buys the Chinese item, as do other consumers. Result: the American manufacturer must either close his business, or move his factory to China (or Mexico, or wherever labor is cheap).

That, in a nutshell, is what happened to American industry. Textiles, steel, electronics—cheap imports have destroyed virtually all manufacturing sectors. Unfortunately, many conservatives accepted the trade treaties *under the illusion that removing tariffs constitutes "free enterprise."* For a refutation of this widely accepted myth, see Appendix I.

When we ratified the GATT Treaty in 1994, Europe received 30 votes in the World Trade Organization; Africa 35. America? *One vote.* Our voting power equals that of the island nation Antigua, population 64,000. Thus we are at the mercy of other countries, many hostile to America, who set trading rules we are compelled to obey. By whim of a majority vote, we can be forced to accept cheap imports, while certain other nations bar our products.

But who *pays* for the WTO's administrative costs? Naturally, U.S. taxpayers foot the lion's share. This is what America's Founding Fathers called "taxation without representation." Thus the WTO not only rapes our economy, *we actually have to pay them to do that.*

Who dreamed up international alliances like WTO and NAFTA? Was it the American people? Pete's getting a haircut at Joe's barber shop and says, "You know, Joe, I was thinking—we ought to form a trading union with Mexico and Canada." "Gee, Pete," says Joe, "That's a swell idea! Let's write our congressman about it!" Does anyone really believe that's how American foreign policy is made?

Before Congress voted on the GATT Treaty, the Senate Commerce Committee, chaired by South Carolina's Ernest Hollings, held hearings on the treaty's merits. The Establishment then brought out one of their big guns. Felix Rohatyn, CFR member and Lazard Freres investment analyst, advocated the treaty before the committee, warning that if wasn't ratified, the markets would react adversely. That very same day, Alan Greenspan and the Fed unexpectedly raised short-term interests rates 0.75 percent, sparking a steep five-day drop in the stock market. Congress and the country grew nervous. Finally Bob Dole, Minority Leader of the Senate's Republicans, hurried to the White House and, standing next to President Clinton, vowed that the GATT Treaty would receive bipartisan support in Congress. The market immediately rebounded, and the treaty passed. This was not the only time the Establishment has manipulated the markets to suit its purposes.

Shortly before the vote, Senator Hollings declared on the Senate floor:

> They [multinational corporations and banks] have got the Trilateral Commission, and the foreign affairs association [CFR] up there in New York. If you ever run for President, they'll invite you. And when you come at their invitation, what they'll do is, they want you to swear, on the altar of free trade, almighty faith forever and ever. "Are you a free trader?" "Yeah, I'm for free trade." That's all they want. You can get out, you can get their contributions, you can get their support—I've been there, I know what we're talking about! But that is what our "friend" David Rockefeller and his Trilateral Commission and all that got that steam together—it's money, not jobs, money! ... Well, *they're* getting rich and we're losing jobs! ... They are debilitating and destroying us![68]

I would go beyond Senator Hollings's remarks; these trade treaties signify more than job destruction. Henry Kissinger said NAFTA "will represent the most creative step toward a new world order taken by any group of countries since the end of the Cold War."[69]

In the *Wall Street Journal* in 1993, David Rockefeller said of NAFTA: "Everything is in place—after 500 years—to build a true 'new world' in the Western Hemisphere."

Andrew Reding of the World Policy Institute said: "NAFTA . . . will signal the formation, however tentatively, of a new political unit—North America. . . . *With economic integration will come political integration. . . .* By whatever name, this is an incipient form of international government. . . . Following the lead of the Europeans, North Americans should begin considering formation of a continental parliament."[70] (emphasis added)

Although international trade treaties propose *economic* consolidation, they're really about *political* consolidation. The European Union began with the Common Market, foisted on Europeans as a purely economic arrangement. The Common Market's official name was European Economic Community. Eventually, however, the word "Economic" was simply dropped, a European Parliament was formed, then the European Union.

The EU is progressively destroying the sovereignty of Europe's nations. As we have elsewhere noted, their parliaments now do little more than ratify EU decisions; and their laws, currencies, and militaries are gradually being consolidated.

The Terror Angle

How does the war on terror fit into this? The Department of Homeland Security has given the U.S. government unprecedented power to intrude on citizens' private lives. The Department's ostensible purpose: combat terrorism. We all oppose terrorism, but many of us wonder how that word might eventually be defined. After 9-11, Anna Quindlen wrote a *Newsweek* column entitled "The Terrorists Here at Home." She was referring to the pro-life movement, characterizing it as ultraviolent. Interplaying images of pro-lifers and 9-11 attackers, Quindlen wrote: "There's no real ideological difference between these people and the people who flew planes into the World Trade Center. One of the leaders of Operation Rescue once sent his followers a letter that concluded 'Return to the training so that God may use you.' Sound familiar?"[71]

Comparing 9-11 to the pro-life movement was quite a stretch. Thousands died in a single day at the World Trade Center. By contrast, since Roe v. Wade in 1973, a total of seven people had been killed working at abortion clinics. Yet Quindlen attempted to broad-brush the entire movement as "terrorists" based on the acts of a handful of extremists.

Quindlen's comparison is ominous, because if pro-lifers were reclassified as terrorists, they could be detained without trial, with their websites shut down and assets frozen. The same restrictions could plague anyone else the latest administration deemed "terrorists."

The concept of Homeland Security did *not* originate after the attack on the Twin Towers, but with a 1998 proposal by the United States Commission on National Security, which had twelve members, nine of whom belonged to the CFR. They recommended a "National Homeland Security Agency"—the very phrase President Bush used nine days after 9-11.

Consolidating the Continent

What connects the *trade agreements* and *war on terror*? Both are being used to justify a North American Union.

In 2004, the CFR's Robert Pastor wrote in *Foreign Affairs*: "Security fears would serve as a catalyst for deeper integration. That would require new structures to assure mutual security.... The Department of Homeland Security should expand its mission to include continental security—a shift best achieved by incorporating Mexican and Canadian perspectives and personnel into its design and operation."[72]

Pastor is thus suggesting that *security concerns* warrant combining NAFTA's *economic* partners—America, Canada and Mexico—into a continent-wide Homeland Security Department.

But it doesn't stop there. On March 23, 2005, in Waco, Texas, President Bush met with Mexican President Vincente Fox and Canadian Prime Minister Paul Martin to discuss broadly integrating their three countries. The union is initially being called the "Security and Prosperity Partnership" or SPP. (In Establishment vocabulary, "security" has replaced "peace" in the phrase "peace and prosperity" because the public now perceives terrorism as more threatening than war.) Total convergence is ultimately planned: if fulfilled, our borders with Mexico and Canada would be eliminated, all citizens issued a North American ID card, and the dollar replaced by a continental currency (the "Amero")—in short, we would copy the European Union. No one in the major media commented on the Waco meeting except CNN's Lou Dobbs, who said of it: "President Bush signed a formal agreement that will end the United States as we know it, and he took the step without approval from either the U.S. Congress or the people of the United States."[73] Dobbs, of course, is no longer with CNN.

Can you guess where the SPP was dreamed up? As *The New American* reported in 2006:

> The Council on Foreign Relations (CFR) serves as the intellectual incubator for most of the foreign policy direction followed by the executive branch of the federal government. Before the trilateral meeting between the heads of state in Waco on March 23 of last year, the CFR had already undertaken an initiative with its counterparts in Mexico and Canada (Consejo Mexicano de Asuntos Internacionales and the Canadian Council of Chief Executives) to study the possibility of integrating the three nations. Laying the foundation for the Waco meeting, the CFR produced a document entitled *Creating a North American Community: Chairmen's Statement of the Independent Task Force on the Future of North America.* The document called for "the creation by 2010 of a commu-

nity to enhance security, prosperity, and opportunity for all North Americans."[74]

The only reason the North American Union has not progressed according to the Establishment's timetable is that it has been so bitterly opposed by American patriots, including some members of Congress.

Regional alliances such as the EU and SPP are not ends in themselves, but *stepping stones* to world government. Leading Establishment figure Zbigniew Brzezinski declared at Mikhail Gorbachev's October 1995 State of the World Forum: "We cannot leap into world government in one quick step. . . . The precondition for genuine globalization is progressive regionalization."

Even Soviet dictator Joseph Stalin recognized this principle as integral to communist plans for domination, saying: "Populations will more readily abandon their national loyalties to a vague regional loyalty than they will for a world authority. Later, the regionals can be brought all the way into a single world dictatorship."[75]

We are headed for world government, which is world tyranny.

CHAPTER 7
THE MEDIA, AND THE NATURE OF TRUTH AND LIES

We now interrupt our history review to ask: Is this book true?

☺ Mr. Perloff, a simple litmus test can discredit everything you've said in this book. There can be no real secrets in America, because the Founding Fathers gave us freedom of the press. It's right there in the First Amendment of the Constitution.

Yes, but freedom of the press shouldn't be confused with *accuracy* of the press.

The Media

Thomas Jefferson, who advocated freedom as much as anyone, deprecated the press. In 1807 he said:

> Nothing can be believed which is seen in a newspaper. Truth itself becomes suspicious by being put into that polluted vehicle. The real extent of this state of misinformation is known only to those who are in situations to confront facts within their knowledge with the lies of the day. I really look with commiseration over the great body of my fellow citizens, who, reading newspapers, live and die in the belief, that they have known something of what has been passing in the world . . . . I will add, that the man who never looks into a newspaper is better informed than he who reads them; inasmuch as he who knows nothing is nearer to truth than he whose mind is filled with falsehoods and errors.[76]

☹ OK, granted you can't believe *everything* you read. Nevertheless, the general accuracy of the press is guaranteed by the *diversity* of information resources. For daily news, you can read *The New York Times*. If you don't like that, there's the *Washington Post, Boston Globe, LA Times*—take your pick. If you want it in a weekly format, there's *Time, Newsweek* or *US News & World Report*. And if you don't like to read—and I suspect you don't, Jim—then there's television news: NBC, CBS, ABC, CNN, Fox, PBS . . .

And that's just a sampling! Now, these sources act as *checks* on each other. For example, when I get up in the morning, I read news online with AOL. If I have any doubts about a story, I can easily cross-check its accuracy by turning on CNN. Later in the week, I'll receive my *Time* magazine, which provides yet another cross-check. When a story has been *independently confirmed* by different sources like that, you can pretty much rest assured it's true.

Furthermore, news reporters are always looking for a *big scoop*. Mr. Perloff, if your stories were true, they'd certainly qualify as "scoops." Are you seriously trying to tell me that *all* the reporters in *all* these media outlets somehow missed them? That's absurd! Why should we believe a goofball like you, when we can turn to a trusted information source like the *New York Times*? Tell you what, Perloff: this guff you're dishing out? I'll believe it when the *Times* reports it. Until then, don't waste my time!

During the Cold War, one commentator ironically noted that the Soviet people were actually less brainwashed than Westerners. In the USSR, people would receive *Pravda* and immediately toss it in the trash, saying "Ah! Party propaganda!" But in America, people would get the *New York Times* and believe every word, under the illusion that "we have a free press, so we can't possibly be brainwashed."

Although America has a free press *in principle*, I disagree that it has one in fact. To achieve its objectives, the Establishment always knew it needed to control the media—the primary molder of public opinion. In Chapter 12 of *The Shadows of Power*, I documented the CFR's powerful media interlocks. For this book's purposes, we'll take the *New York Times*.

In the 19th century August Belmont (real family name: Schoenburg) served as a Rothschild financial agent in the United

States. He reportedly offered Abraham Lincoln a Rothschild loan to finance the War Between the States—at 27.5 per cent interest. According to the story, possibly apocryphal, Lincoln had Belmont literally thrown out of the White House.

But not everyone was so discriminating. Later, with J. P. Morgan, Belmont helped finance Adolph Ochs, who purchased the *New York Times*—then a tiny newspaper with a circulation of 9,000. International banking's might behind him, Ochs transformed the *Times* into the world's most powerful newspaper. The *Times* was built on money, not journalistic integrity. Ownership passed from Ochs to his son-in-law Arthur Hays Sulzberger (1935-61), then Orvil Dryfoos (1961-63), and Arthur Ochs Sulzberger (1963-1992), the latter three all CFR members.

The *New York Times*' editorial policy has consistently paralleled the Establishment's agenda. When members of Congress opposed Paul Warburg's nomination to the Federal Reserve Board, the *Times*' editorial page lobbied on his behalf.

When communist Fidel Castro was trying to seize Cuba in 1959, a series of articles by *New York Times* reporter Herbert L. Matthews—CFR member—persuaded Americans that Castro was simply the George Washington of Cuba.

During the Vietnam War, the *Times* demoralized the public by publishing an alleged exposé of the war's origins—the Pentagon Papers, a leaked Defense Department study. Leslie Gelb, who oversaw the study, went on to be a *Times* correspondent and editor. So, one might ask, will Gelb do an exposé of the CFR too? Not likely. He was the Council's President for ten years (1993-2003) and remains its President Emeritus. Many *Times* executives, editors and reporters have been CFR members. Some current ones include director Robert E. Denham, editorial page editor Andrew Rosenthal, assistant managing editor Susan Chira, business columnist Andrew Sorkin, foreign affairs columnist Thomas L. Friedman, and op-ed columnist Nicholas Kristof.

The *Times* will never expose the CFR *because they both belong to the same hierarchy.* A similar picture can be sketched of the other major news organs. The media's "diversity" is illusory. Marvin

(☹) thought he could confirm an AOL news story's accuracy by checking it against CNN and *Time*. The problem: AOL, CNN and *Time* are owned by a single corporation—Time Warner, Inc., which also owns Warner Brothers Studios, HBO, New Line Cinema, *Sports Illustrated, People, Fortune, Money*, and scores of other media organs.

The New York Times Company owns the *Boston Globe*; The Washington Post Co. owns *Newsweek*; Disney owns ABC; CBS owns Simon & Schuster. Most of America's major media—TV and radio networks, movie studios, newspapers, magazines and publishing houses—are owned by about a dozen large corporations; and these, in turn, have directors that interlock through membership in the CFR. Thus the Establishment can guarantee the public receives a uniform viewpoint.

At the height of the Vietnam War, Congressman John Rarick declared:

> There are many attempts to shift all the blame to the military in the eyes of the people. But no one identifies the Council on Foreign Relations, a group of some 1400 Americans which includes almost every top level decision and policy maker in the Vietnam War. CBS tells the people it wants them to know what is going on and who is to blame. Why doesn't CBS tell the American people about the CFR and let the people decide whom to blame for the Vietnam fiasco? … *Who will tell the people the truth if those who control "the right to know machinery" also control the government?*[77] (emphasis added)

On June 5, 1991, speaking before the Bilderbergers (a CFR affiliate we will later discuss), Council Chairman David Rockefeller described the media-policymaker marriage:

> We are grateful to the *Washington Post*, the *New York Times*, *Time* magazine, and other great publications whose directors have attended our meetings and respected their promises of discretion for almost forty years. It would have been impossible for us to develop our plan for the world if we had been

subject to the bright lights of publicity during these years. But the world is now more sophisticated and prepared to march towards a world government which will never again know war but only peace and prosperity.[78]

What did Rockefeller promise? Peace and Prosperity!

The Big Lie

Through its ownership of the media, the Establishment creates an illusion of "reality." They achieve this through a psychological mechanism called "the big lie."

Suppose you had unrelenting abdominal pain. You describe it to a friend who's an operating room nurse. She asks, "Have you ever had your appendix out?" You say, "No." She says, "It sounds like appendicitis. You better see your doctor right away." You go online and Google "Appendicitis." Yes, you seem to have the classic signs and symptoms.

Next you visit your physician. You wince as he pushes on your abdomen and tells you, "Looks like appendicitis for sure. It'll have to come out." You say, "Listen, Doc, I trust your judgment, but I have a *really* busy week ahead. Any chance this might just be some inflammation that'll go away by itself? I'd hate to have surgery if I didn't need it. Would you mind if I got a second opinion?"

The doctor says, "OK, I understand your concern. Let's have Dr. Barrett see you over at the hospital—he's the best surgeon in town."

Dr. Barrett tells you: "Well, no question in my mind that you need your appendix out. But, we'll do a CT scan to be absolutely sure."

After the test, Dr. Barrett shows you the scan's image. "See that? Your appendix is completely swollen. If you don't have it out, it may burst—that'll cause *much worse* problems and a long hospital stay."

At this point, you say, "OK, I'm convinced!" And you'd be reasonable to do so. When a clear-cut consensus of trusted opinion agrees on something, we normally accept it as true.

However, it is also possible to make a *lie* look true through *artificial* consensus. This we call a "big lie," defined by *Webster's New World Dictionary* as "a gross falsification or misrepresentation of the facts, with constant repetition and embellishment to lend credibility."

The big lie can be demonstrated in many ways. When I was a boy in the early 1960s, *Candid Camera* was a popular television program. It would film unsuspecting persons in embarrassing and/or amusing situations.

For one episode, official-looking street signs that said "BACKWARD ZONE" were placed on a city sidewalk. Actors, posing as ordinary folks, would stroll up to the signs and start walking backwards. The camera would then follow real pedestrians who, seeing the actors walking backwards through the "zone," would do the same, no questions asked.

The hilarious results made a point: people will often accept an absurdity if a majority of others appear to believe in it.

Conformity research at universities has affirmed this. In the famous Asch experiments, an individual would be invited to partake in a vision test. He or she entered a classroom with several other participants, who were secretly confederates of the person running the experiment. The subjects were asked which of a set of lines was longest. The confederates all deliberately named the wrong line. The unwitting person frequently went along, agreeing the wrong line was longest. When queried later about why they'd said this, it was often from fearing what others might think of them—but sometimes the person truly doubted his own judgment, believing that the others, being unanimous, must be right.

A wounded German soldier, hospitalized during World War II, recounted this story:

One day a boy soldier who happened to be a farmer's son was assigned to our room and, for lack of other things to talk about, told us of his house pet, a white rabbit with red eyes. We all knew that white rabbits have or can have red eyes but that didn't stop one fellow from loudly disputing the fact that any animal, rabbits included, can have red eyes. When the rabbit's owner insisted that he was right, we all chimed in on the side of the detractor, and for days on end we assembled "scientific proof," including getting some wounded fellows from other rooms involved, that the farm boy was in this matter suffering from delusions. It took a week or two but after that the poor fellow sincerely admitted that he had been wrong.[79]

These examples underscore that people will deny reality when enough others insist a falsehood is true.

In 2008, a spectacular joke was played on Philadelphia Phillies pitcher Kyle Kendrick. Widely publicized, it is viewable on YouTube. Kendrick was told he'd been traded to Japan. Everyone was in on the prank, including Kendrick's teammates, the manager (who sadly informed him of the deal, presenting him with the "contract" which he dutifully signed), Kendrick's own agent, and even media reporters, who held mikes before Kendrick, asking how he felt about going to Japan.

In a less humorous context, cults employ the same device, bringing prospective members to remote areas and inundating them with ideas that, with adequate repetition, become "true."

The Establishment media parallels the above illustrations. Coordinating multiple news outlets fabricates a spurious consensus about events. As in the Asch test, people are convinced because "that many sources couldn't be wrong." And of course, government spokesmen—also under CFR control—affirm what the media say. Thus are generated "big lies" for public consumption.

☺ Whoa, fella! How do you know *you're* not the victim of "big lies"? You never thought of that, did you? You've obviously been inundated with a bunch of stupid theories. Boy! Some people believe *everything*! And you have the gall to criticize the *New York Times*! Just what are *your* resources? Some stupid website called "conspiracy.com"?

My Resources

This book's resources are myriad, and are identified within the text and endnotes, but let's review some significant ones.

• Distinguished Jewish author Myron Fagan was a leading Broadway playwright in the early 20th century and dramatic editor of the *New York Globe*. Politically well-connected, he was public relations director for Charles Evan Hughes, the 1916 Republican Presidential candidate opposing Woodrow Wilson. Later Herbert Hoover asked him to serve in the same capacity. After World War II, Fagan became a leader in the fight against communism. He discovered the CFR's secret role in controlling politics, and was among the first to expose it. Go to YouTube and type in "Myron Fagan" to find his taped speeches on the subject.

• Count Arthur Cherep-Spiridovich was a major general in the Russian army and president of the Slavonic Society of Russia. Shortly before his "suicide" in 1926, he published a book in the United States entitled *The Secret World Government*, which described the same forces as this book. Despite occasional vanity discernible in his writing, Cherep-Spiridovich contributed unique insights into the powers manipulating European politics and the Czar's overthrow.

• Admiral Sir Barry Domville headed British Naval Intelligence from 1927 to 1930. He discovered that England's foreign policy was run from behind the scenes by a wealthy elite—the CFR's English counterpart. He wrote:

> From that time onwards I had a strong suspicion that there was some mysterious Power at work behind the scenes controlling the actions of the figures visibly taking part in the Government of the country.... We always vaguely referred to this hidden control amongst ourselves as the Treasury.[80]

As Domville attempted to learn more about this group and expose it, he was stripped of rank and imprisoned. This occurred without due process—no trial or charges; he was simply incarcerated under an old British defense regulation called 18B, by which the government could detain anyone suspected of "acts prejudicial to public safety." Domville told his story in his book *From Admiral to Cabin Boy*.

• William Guy Carr served with the Canadian Intelligence Service during World War II; he also worked as a police investigator and newspaperman. He developed far-reaching intelligence contacts and discovered the same conspiracy as Fagan, Cherep-Spiridovich and Domville. Carr wrote three books about it—one, *Pawns in the Game*, I consider perhaps the best single volume on the subject.

• Despite a very French name, Hilaire du Berrier was an American, originally from North Dakota. Working for the OSS in China during WWII, he was captured and tortured by the Japanese. After the war, he left the OSS (which changed its name to CIA) but maintained numerous international contacts, and ran his own intelligence newsletter out of Monaco from 1958 until his death in 2001. Du Berrier wrote extensively on the Council on Foreign Relations, the European Union movement, and the forces behind them.

• Pierre de Villemarest was a hero of the French resistance during WWII. Well-connected with the French intelligence community, he was long editor of the conservative news weekly *Valeurs Actuelles*. He, too, wrote books exposing the CFR and EU.

• Ted Gunderson was a 29-year veteran of the FBI; before retiring in 1979, he last served as Special Agent-in-Charge for Los Angeles, with over 700 FBI personnel under him. He specifically corroborated works of William Guy Carr written 50 years earlier, and warned of the coming satanic world order. After his death in 2011, his website, www.tedgunderson.net, went down but much information is available at http://educate-yourself.org/tg/ and numerous interviews of him may be seen on YouTube.

• Dr. John Coleman was an officer in MI6, Britain's equivalent of the CIA. In MI6, Coleman learned of the international cartel controlling our world. His outstanding books and monographs, available at www.coleman300.net, are among the most informative resources available.

The works of these eight men don't agree on every minor detail, but all concur that the Council on Foreign Relations sets U.S. foreign policy, and that the CFR is only one element of a larger international scheme to impose world government.* I find it significant that they all reached this conclusion, even though they came from different backgrounds, and to a large extent, different nations and time frames. Very possibly you've never heard of any of these men—because they're outside the box; never mentioned by CNN or the *New York Times*. To understand the box, you must step outside it. CNN and the *Times* are *part of* the box.

[*Cherep-Spiridovich did not specifically mention the CFR in his discussion of world government, but his premature death by "suicide," shortly after the Council's founding, virtually precluded that.]

Can we trust these men, unrecognized by the "respectable" Establishment media? I ask Christian readers to remember that Jesus and His apostles were not "respectable" by the world's standards.

Suppose I lived in a pillared marble mansion, and before people could see me, they first had to go through a fussy butler, and then a snooty secretary with a British accent. Some might leave my mansion saying: "Well, he's certainly done well for himself! We should pay attention to what he said." Regrettably, that's how the world often judges. But while money buys superficial respectability, it has very little bearing on truth.

This book contains over 250 endnotes. Feel free to check sources and see if I misquoted anyone or took them out of context.

However, a comment on documentation: The fact that I, or any author, quotes a source, does not mean that source itself is accurate. I could have 1,000 endnotes to 1,000 *bad* sources, and give you 1,000 pieces of misinformation.

How, then, can you determine if I'm right?

The Nature of Truth

In physical science, facts are relatively easy to establish. Water boils at 100 degrees centigrade—repeated experiments have established that; anyone can test it.

Historical truths are different, however. They are unrepeatable, one-time events. Eyewitnesses may testify about what took place, but they may contradict each other, making erroneous statements, honestly or deliberately. Determining what happened in the past can be very difficult—just look at the controversy and innumerable theories still swirling over John F. Kennedy's assassination.

Your role, as this book's reader, might compare to a jury member. My role is akin to a district attorney. I am arguing that crimes have been committed against humanity, and am producing witnesses and evidence to support that contention.

The defense attorney in this case is the Establishment media. They say everything can be explained as coincidences/accidents, and that the accused are innocent victims of paranoid conspiracy theories. (If anyone feels I have not adequately presented the Establishment's side, it is easily found in their well-distributed media.)

Let's address the distinction between paranoia and evil. Paranoia does exist. A person sometimes has delusions that others are trying to hurt him when they're not. But can we also agree there is *real evil*?

To illustrate the two perspectives: Suppose you're an office worker, carrying a stack of reports down a corridor. Another employee, Joe, comes in the opposite direction. He bumps into you and the reports fall. If you said, "Joe, you *deliberately* did that!" it would be pretty paranoid. But let's say you picked up the reports and Joe bumped you again, knocking them to the floor. If you're a patient, forgiving person, perhaps you'd make no accusation, but you might at least feel annoyed and say something like, "Well, Joe, I guess we've got the dropsies today, huh?" However, suppose you picked up the reports, and Joe bumped you a third time, sending them flying. At this point, you'd probably say, "All right, Joe! *What's going on?*" You'd know he had acted deliberately. Your conclusion would not be paranoid. And it only took three times to establish pretty firmly that Joe acted by design, not blunder. The same criteria apply in politics.

Thomas Jefferson said: "Single acts of tyranny may be ascribed to the accidental opinion of a day; but a series of oppressions, begun at a distinguished period, and pursued unalterably through every change of ministers, too plainly prove a deliberate systematical plan of reducing us to slavery."[81]

James Forrestal, quoted in Chapter 1, expressed the same viewpoint in saying: "Consistency has never been a mark of stupidity. If the diplomats who have mishandled our relations with Russia were merely stupid, they would occasionally make a mistake in our favor."

Congressman Walter Judd, speaking in the context of China's fall to communism, made a similar observation: "On the law of averages, a mere moron once in a while would make a decision that would be favorable to the United States. When policies are advocated by any group which consistently work out to the Communists' advantage, that couldn't be happenstance."[82]

Forrestal and Judd saw the same group of officials—the Acheson-Hiss clique in the State Department—were involved in decision after decision that supported the Soviet Union and harmed America: giving North Korea to the Russians; ceding parts of Northern China to Russia without China's permission; granting the Soviets three votes in the UN while we got one; agreeing that all Russians displaced during World War II would be forcibly repatriated to the USSR; etc. Like "bumping Joe" at the office, these guys weren't blundering, they were *perpetrating.*

So when we observe that Paul Warburg and Benjamin Strong secretly planned the Federal Reserve, without the knowledge or consent of the people or Congress, and that these very same men were then appointed to *run* the Fed, it's not "paranoia" to connect the dots and say this happened by design, not coincidence.

District attorneys regularly make such correlations to prove criminal cases. Killers rarely commit murder right in front of witnesses, or while being videotaped—so prosecutors have to accumulate *indirect* evidence of guilt. For example, they might show that the accused owned the murder weapon, or that his fingerprints were on it, or that the victim's blood was on his clothing, that he was observed leaving the crime scene, that he had a motive, etc. Are district attorneys *paranoid* to do this? No; it's essential to solving crimes. A preponderance of evidence can prove criminal intent, and that is what this book seeks to establish.

As I note in my works on creation vs. evolution, there is a principle called "design proves a designer." We know the Mount Rushmore Monument did not arise by chance because it's too well designed. Likewise, policemen, prosecutors and judges understand that artfully planned crimes cannot be dismissed as the result of a series of accidents.

In most trials, neither side can *absolutely* prove they are right. Neither can I. Criminal conspiracies are inherently secretive, and exposing them takes considerable detective work. So ask yourself: Which side does truth seem to be on? Whose explanation makes more sense, and is most consistent? If you distrust the ideas I present, thanks for at least considering them. Perhaps the pattern of future events will eventually confirm them to you.

Chapter 8
THE DESTRUCTION
OF NATIONS

Let's return to world government. This book's outset described the questionable circumstances that led America into six wars, but didn't explain the motives behind them.

Although not the only rationale, establishment of world government was a major factor in these wars, especially World War I (used to create the League of Nations), World War II (United Nations), and the Korean War (used to validate the UN as a peacekeeper).

The Council on Foreign Relations has always opposed national sovereignty, because *destroying nations* is prerequisite to forming a world government. This was another reason for the wars: while the CFR's publications supplied an *intellectual* attack on nations, wars, along with revolutions, provided *physical* attacks.

I believe that the Bible is true. Chapters 8 and 9 of the book of Genesis recount how a flood devastated the Earth; only those on Noah's Ark survived. Chapter 10 details how their descendants became the world's tribes and nations. Chapter 11 describes how, when the people started building the Tower of Babel, God scattered them into different lands with different languages. This was for their own protection, to restrain evil. National sovereignty really began with the scattering after Babel. We may reasonably understand world government as Satan's attempt to reverse the dispersion God ordained.

Immigration

In this context, we briefly address immigration. For many centuries, there were mainly Japanese in Japan, Russians in Russia,

Italians in Italy, Irishmen in Ireland, and so forth. After Babel, national identity became established not only by language, but by unique racial and ethnic characteristics.

Recent years have seen huge pushes to relax U.S. immigration laws. President George W. Bush was criticized by his own party for being notoriously weak on restricting immigration; in 2007 he even joined forces with liberal Democratic Senator Ted Kennedy to create a bill that would have naturalized all illegal immigrants.

Immigration is integral to the globalist plan. The European Union, for example, encourages free movement within members states. *Why?* Notice that nations are becoming harder to characterize. Britain had only 10,700 Indians and Pakistanis in 1955; by 2001 that figure had risen to over 1.8 million. France today has over five million Muslims, most of them immigrants from its former North African colonies; they constitute a state within a state—as witnessed by the rash of violence and fires in 2005 that French police couldn't contain.

The Establishment encourages such situations because *if you confuse national identity, you weaken national sovereignty.* When Africans Muslims come to France, they usually don't consider themselves Frenchmen—and ethnically they aren't. A country not unified by a distinct identity is far easier to strip of sovereignty because the subjects themselves feel little allegiance to country, flag, and each other. "Multiculturalism" is politically correct today, but its purpose is to *fragmentize nations.*

Colonialism

Another method of destroying nations, now almost fully accomplished: severing them from their colonies. Britain, France, Germany, Spain, Portugal, Italy, Belgium and the Netherlands, among others, once governed colonies that furnished them with abundant natural resources. The U.S. State Department and CIA were two of the Establishment's chief agents in ending these relationships.

We already commented (Chapter 5) on how the U.S. pushed the French out of Indochina after World War II. No sooner was this achieved than the State Department began demanding France evacuate its colony Algeria. Likewise, the U.S. gave the Dutch an ultimatum to leave Indonesia. Anti-colonialism became a universal agenda.

The American media fed the process by portraying colonizing nations as "oppressors," while communist-inspired insurgents (as in Algeria) were "seeking democracy." I would agree that colonialism included oppression; however, hospitals, schools, churches, roads and telephone lines were also built. The bloodbaths and corruption ravaging Africa in recent years are hard to argue as improvement on colonial rule. "Democracy," translated, meant dictatorship. In Zaire (formerly the Belgian Congo) CIA-backed Mobuto stashed some $5 billion in foreign bank accounts and acquired sumptuous European chateaus for himself. When he finally fell from power in 1997, garbage had not been collected in seven years and brush was overgrowing the roads built by the Belgians; government employees were rarely paid—and when they were, received about enough to buy a loaf of bread.

In 1976, Henry Kissinger imposed sanctions against Rhodesia (now Zimbabwe), forcing the white government to abdicate in favor of black majority rule. The result of American-inflicted "democracy" was tyranny under terrorist Robert Mugabe. Once a prosperous food-exporting nation, Zimbabwe is now in economic chaos. Food production plummeted after Mugabe seized farms and distributed them to his cronies; inflation in 2008 reached a staggering 100,000 percent. Yet when Mugabe got married, he held a three-day binge for 25,000 guests and built his young bride a 30-room house.[83]

The Establishment dismantled colonialism to reduce nations like Spain and the Netherlands from global empires to weak countries which the European Union could rule. As for the new African "democracies," they became members of the UN, where their votes could be relied on to support the New World Order agenda. African dictators, converting foreign aid into personal fortunes, would do as told to keep wealth coming. And when their countries collapsed, in would come the World Bank and IMF with bailouts—contingent on "privatizing" industries, i.e., handing them over to Establishment multinational corporations. Thus the vast mineral wealth and resources, originally developed by colonizers and entrepreneurs, would fall into the hands of the global cartel.

Forms of Government

Besides immigration and anti-colonialism, the Establishment has wielded an even more profound means of destroying national sovereignty: changing the forms of government which nations use.

The Bible commends obedience to authority as a virtue. In the context of government, Christians often quote Romans 13:1-2:

> Everyone must submit himself to the governing authorities, for there is no authority except that which God has established. The authorities that exist have been established by God. Consequently, he who rebels against the authority is rebelling against what God has instituted, and those who do so will bring judgement on themselves.

When the Bible was written, "government" usually meant kings and emperors. It's true that the ancient Greeks experimented with democracy, and the Romans with a republic. But from the time of Christ until about 200 years ago, most nations were monarchies. Emperors reigned in China for over 2,000 years until 1911. The czars governed Russia until 1917; the Kaisers Germany until 1918. All the European countries—Spain, Italy, Portugal, Belgium, etc.—were once overseen by kings.

But where are all the monarchs now? Mostly gone or reduced to figureheads. The government forms of the two last centuries—republics, democracies, communism, socialism, fascism—were relatively new.

What type of government exists in heaven? Socialism? A democracy where we elect a new God every four years? Of course, it's a monarchy, under "God, the blessed and only Ruler, the King of Kings and Lord of Lords." (1 Tim 6:15)

Earthly monarchs could be very bad; some were notoriously cruel. Nevertheless, monarchy was the *form* of government most clearly structured on heaven's model.

Also: In Eden, how did Satan persuade Adam and Eve to disobey God and eat from the tree of the knowledge of good and evil? The Bible says:

> He said to the woman, "Did God really say, 'You must not eat from any tree in the garden'?"
> The woman said to the serpent, "We may eat fruit from the trees in the garden, but God did say, 'You must not eat fruit from the tree that is in the middle of the garden, and you must not touch it, or you will surely die.'"
> "You will not surely die," the serpent said to the woman. "For God knows that when you eat of it your eyes will be opened, and you will be like God, knowing good and evil."[84]

The core of the temptation was "you will be like God." The entire "power to the people" movement—from communism to democracy—involved a similar temptation. It's as though Satan said, "Did God say you should obey kings? He didn't mean that. Just get rid of those kings, and *you'll* have the political power, you'll *all* be kings! So, send King Louis to the guillotine! Murder the Czar and his family! Throw off King George! Power to the people, baby!"

Of course, I don't equate the American Revolution with the Russian Revolution. But God's model for government was monarchy. Had we not eliminated kings, Christians wouldn't face the problems they do today—abortion, banning of school prayer, etc. Christian monarchs would not have allowed these developments. However imperfect he may have been, the personal motto of Czar Nicholas II was: "Christ Above All." On older European coins, you'll see crosses and other Christian emblems. Many British coins, for example, were marked with the Latin "Fid def"—short for *fidei defensor*, "defender of the faith." Yes, kings could be tyrants, but could also uphold God's commandments.

Suppose that under Austrian emperor Franz Joseph, someone had proposed gay marriage. He would have said: "No! God shall not be mocked! By my royal decree, there shall be no homosexual marriage!" End of story. God wanted rulers with the power to enforce his laws.

But what happens in America? Let's say you're against pornography, so you visit your congressman. He says: "What can I do? You don't like it, but I've got other constituents who do. Tell you what. We'll get a committee together to study this issue. Get back to me in a couple of years." Two years and 50 million tax dollars later, the congressman tells you: "Sorry, but our legal counsel advised us that if we try to restrict pornography, we're violating the Constitution—free speech and all that, you know!"

While European monarchs inscribed crosses and "defender of the faith" on their coins, we Americans put Lady Liberty on ours. We have the Liberty Bell and the Statue of Liberty. Don't get me wrong—I'm for liberty, but when you make it a kind of *idol*, is it surprising that people eventually demand the liberty to have abortions, smoke marijuana, or redefine marriage?

Satan knew that once "democracy" replaced kings, he would only need 51% of the vote to dismantle Christian culture. And when you control the media, getting 51% is a cinch.

Another reason Satan sought to destroy monarchies: national sovereignty was strongly tied to kings—the heart and symbol of nationhood. While prime ministers and presidents are loyal to their *party* (if not *donors* and *lobbyists*), a king was loyal to the whole country. He was a unifying force behind whom the people would rally.

I am aware that a few royal families—most notably Britain's—have colluded with the satanic Establishment. But the latter's predominant policy on monarchs has been to remove them. Although the U.S. cites Iran as a world terrorist threat, few remember that the U.S. itself paved the way for the current Iranian regime, by deposing the pro-Western Shah during the Carter administration. Even the *Washington Post* frankly stated:

> On or about January 3, 1979, Air Force General Robert E. (Dutch) Huyser ... arrived in Teheran at the express direction of President Carter. . . . According to State Department and Pentagon sources the purpose of Huyser's mission was "to pull the rug out from under the Shah." These sources say Huyser's marching orders were: To tell the Shah his days were numbered . . . . To tell the Shah he should leave immediately. . . .To stop any pro-Shah military coup and clear the way for Khomeini's return by warning the U.S.-trained generals that if they moved to seize power, the United States would cut off all aid.[85]

The Carter administration cited "human rights" concerns as its reason for opposing the Shah. Yet fewer people were killed during the Shah's 38-year reign than during *Ayatollah Khomeini's first month*. On this fact, however, President Carter remained silent. Should our sons fight in a war against Iran, when U.S. meddling put the current regime there?*

[*For a full discussion of the betrayal of the Shah, see this author's 2009 article "Iran and the Shah: What Really Happened" at www.thenewamerican.com.]

The Shah's case is hardly unique. After World War I, the cartel's agents convened at Paris to restructure the globe's map and rulers. Du Berrier said of this gathering (which led to the CFR's founding):

> I would lead my readers back to a spring night in Paris many years ago. A group of men in the exuberance of victory, met in the Majestic Hotel on the evening of May 19, 1919, to discuss how they would reshape the world. They had mandates from no one and in that their aims were secret they could only be called conspiratorial. Intoxicated with slogans about saving the world for democracy, they condemned it to what has happened since. They sneered when General von Ludendorf

begged the victorious allies to let Germany retain her throne and the result was a Hitler and a Willy Brandt. Three empires, six monarchies and twenty-three duchies and principalities disappeared because leaders who had a stake in nationhood had been carried along in a losing tide. To the little group in the Paris hotel dining room, bent on reshaping the world, the age of permanent national interests was dead, and with missionary zeal they went about converting one-worlders, swearing the while that they were doing nothing of the sort.[86]

A similar process followed World War II. The Soviets eliminated the monarchs of the Balkans after their troops occupied that region. Meanwhile, the U.S. intervened to prevent King Leopold from resuming Belgium's throne, and kept King Victor Immanuel from returning to Italy's.

We've described the U.S. policies that caused the Vietnam disaster. Few people recall that, until 1954, Vietnam had an emperor, even during French colonization. The last was Bao Dai, whom the United States insisted step down in favor of "democracy." The CFR's choice for president was Ngo Dinh Diem, who, when he visited America, was brought to John D. Rockefeller Jr.'s home. Included at the meeting were David Rockefeller, John J. McCloy, and Dean Rusk, head of the Ford Foundation. The corrupt Diem seized the emperor's property for himself and his family, and ruthlessly suppressed all opposition. He thus antagonized the population, splitting it into factions and ripening it for communist takeover. Many Vietnamese have said that had Bao Dai remained in power, the country would have united behind him, the communists would have failed, and the Vietnam War would never have happened.

The emperor himself stated: "If your country had given me one-thousandth of the sum they spent to depose me, I could have won that war."[87] Bao Dai was a friend of Hilaire du Berrier, who wrote: "When the throne was destroyed, fragmentation resulted because only the man on the throne was above the regional, racial, and religious hatreds dividing the national family."[88] I believe this comment embodies a universal principle concerning monarchies.

Satan knew: without their kings, the world's people would become like sheep without shepherds. With no shepherd, a flock is easy prey for the wolf. By the way, along with kings, nations of both East and West once had a sub-royalty called *noblemen*. We've removed them, too, because in modern times we're told "all men are created equal." But the Bible says:

> But who are you, O man, to talk back to God? Shall what is formed say to him who formed it, Why did you make me like this? Does not the potter have the right to make out of the same lump of clay some pottery for noble purposes and some for common uses?[89]

I realize that the Bible also says God judges us without favoritism—regardless of race, sex, or social standing. But equal access to God's mercy and justice does not mean we are born with equal abilities or circumstances. The Tenth Commandment instructs us not to covet what others have. But largely through envy, men overthrew the world's kings and nobles.

Why did Satan tempt us to do this? During a battle, sharpshooters prioritize targeting the enemy's *officers*, because an outfit of privates will be disorganized and ineffective. In chess, if your only pieces were pawns—no knights, rooks, bishops, or queen—you'd quickly lose. Socialism and democracy are designed to reduce us to armies of privates or pawns, who would then be ruled by Satan's elite—the Rothschild-Rockefeller-CFR-Bilderberger clique.

CHAPTER 9
REVOLUTIONS, MARXISM & MERGER

While some kings were swept away by wars, and others compelled by diplomatic pressure to step down for "democracy," Satan's main tool for eliminating royalty has been *revolution*. The purpose of revolution is to overthrow authority. In fact, the Bible reports that Satan led one of his own in heaven:

> And there was war in heaven. Michael and his angels fought against the dragon, and the dragon and his angels fought back. But he was not strong enough, and they lost their place in heaven. The great dragon was hurled down, that ancient serpent called the devil, or Satan, who leads the whole world astray. –Rev 12:7-9

Revolution is characteristic of Satan's nature, not God's. Rebellion against the thrones of earth emulated the one against heaven's throne. That, I believe, is a very applicable context of Romans 13:1-2:

> Everyone must submit himself to the governing authorities, for there is no authority except that which God has established. The authorities that exist have been established by God. Consequently, he who rebels against the authority is rebelling against what God has instituted, and those who do so will bring judgement on themselves.

Figure 2 is the original title page of *Proofs of a Conspiracy against All the Religions and Governments of Europe*, a book published in 1798 by scholar John Robison.

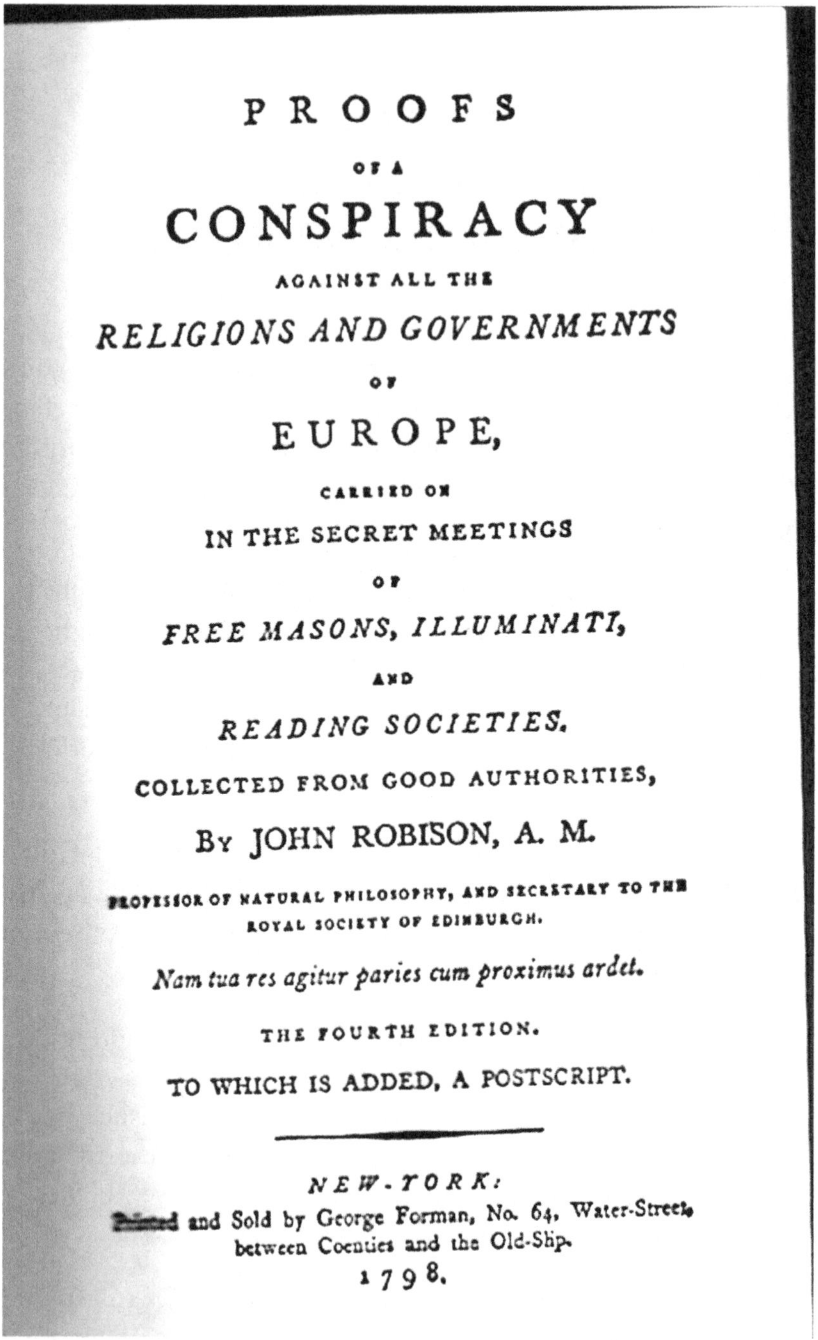

PROOFS

OF A

CONSPIRACY

AGAINST ALL THE

RELIGIONS AND GOVERNMENTS

OF

EUROPE,

CARRIED ON

IN THE SECRET MEETINGS

OF

FREE MASONS, ILLUMINATI,

AND

READING SOCIETIES.

COLLECTED FROM GOOD AUTHORITIES,

By JOHN ROBISON, A. M.

PROFESSOR OF NATURAL PHILOSOPHY, AND SECRETARY TO THE
ROYAL SOCIETY OF EDINBURGH.

Nam tua res agitur paries cum proximus ardet.

THE FOURTH EDITION.

TO WHICH IS ADDED, A POSTSCRIPT.

NEW-YORK:
Printed and Sold by George Forman, No. 64, Water-Street,
between Coenties and the Old-Slip.
1798.

Figure 2. Title Page of Robison's book.

☺ This guy Robison was obviously the conspiracy kook of his day. It just goes to show that there were always whack jobs around, even back then.

To the contrary, his book has proven prophetic. All the European governments then existing—the monarchies—are either gone now or rendered impotent. And Christian faith, which nearly personified Europe, has been shattered—huge cathedrals, that once held thousands of believers, draw only a handful on Sundays.

The kings were primarily destroyed through revolution. Standard history books present the French Revolution as a spontaneous event: they claim France's kings were tyrannical and/or inept, causing the people to suffer, so the masses reacted, seizing the government for themselves. This is a misrepresentation. All revolutions are planned, organized, and financed. Robison documented this for the French Revolution, as did Augustin Barruel in *Memoirs Illustrating the History of Jacobinism* (1797), Sir Walter Scott in *The Life of Napoleon Bonaparte* (1827), Nesta Webster in *The French Revolution* (1919), and others.

The French mob which marched on the Versailles Palace on October 5, 1789 was screaming for bread, *but their pockets were full of coins.*[90] They had been bribed to riot by agents of the same cartel we have been discussing.

The revolution was satanic—a million Frenchmen died during the Reign of Terror; the clergy were massacred and the church outlawed. A document attributed to the revolutionist Count Mirabeau declared:

> We must overthrow all order, suppress all laws, annul all power, and leave the people in anarchy. The laws we establish will not perhaps be in force at once, but at any rate, having given back power to the people, they will resist for the sake of their liberty which they will believe they are preserving. We must caress their vanity, flatter their hopes, promise them happiness . . . . we must necessarily use them as a support, and render hateful to them everything we wish to destroy and sow illusions in their path; we must also buy all the mercenary

pens which propagate our methods and which will instruct the people concerning their enemies whom we attack. The clergy, being the most powerful through public opinion, can only be destroyed by ridiculing religion, rendering its ministers odious, and only representing them as hypocritical monsters . . . . To exaggerate their riches, to make the sins of an individual appear to be common to all, to attribute to them all vices; calumny, murder, irreligion, sacrilege, all is permitted in times of revolution.[91]

The Rich and the Reds

The same cabal has funded nearly all revolutions—most prominently the Russian Revolution. Britain's Lord Alfred Milner, a Rothschild financial agent, distributed 21 million rubles in Russia for the Bolshevik cause.[92] Another major source was Kuhn, Loeb in New York, headed by Paul Warburg and Jacob Schiff. The *New York Journal-American* of Feb 3, 1949 reported:

Today it is estimated even by Jacob's grandson, John Schiff, that the old man sank about $20,000,000 for the final triumph of Bolshevism in Russia. Other New York banking firms also contributed.

This $20 million—given in gold—was in addition to another $50 million which, according to contemporary U.S. and British intelligence reports, Kuhn, Loeb placed in the Bank of Sweden for the revolution's leaders, Lenin and Trotsky.[93] When the Czar abdicated in 1917, Trotsky was actually living in New York City. That March, he and fellow revolutionaries sailed for Russia with Schiff's $20 million in gold, but the British Navy intercepted the ship. The British and Canadians detained Trotsky at Halifax, Nova Scotia, because they knew he intended to foment revolution in Czarist Russia—our ally in the raging First World War. The Bolsheviks had promised to pull Russia out of the war if the revolution succeeded. The British and Canadians realized what that meant: Germany would shift its troops from the Eastern to Western front, where they could kill more British, Canadians, and Americans. But at the bankers' behest, President Wilson personally intervened, and requested that Canada release Trotsky. The President thus placed Bolshevism's success above the lives of American soldiers.

As earlier noted, Wilson proposed the League of Nations at the 1919 Paris Peace Conference. That was the fourteenth of his famous Fourteen Points. Few remember the sixth:

> VI. The evacuation of all Russian territory [by then in communist hands] and such a settlement of all questions affecting Russia as will secure the best and freest cooperation of the other nations of the world in obtaining for her an unhampered and unembarrassed opportunity for the independent determination of her own political development and national policy and assure her of a sincere welcome into the society of free nations under institutions of her own choosing; and, more than a welcome, assistance also of every kind that she may need and may herself desire. The treatment accorded Russia by her sister nations in the months to come will be the acid test of their good will, of their comprehension of her needs as distinguished from their own interests, and of their intelligent and unselfish sympathy.

Wilson then helped fulfill these aspirations by sending the murderous Bolshevik regime $100 million from the Special Emergency War Fund.[94]

During World War II, Germany and her European allies invaded the USSR. Under Establishment direction, the United States rescued the Soviets with Lend-Lease: 15,000 aircraft, 7,000 tanks, 51,000 jeeps, 375,000 trucks, 130,000 machine guns, 2,000 locomotives, 11,000 freight cars, 200 torpedo boats, 350,000 tons of explosives, 4.5 million tons of food, and 15 million pairs of boots, among many other things.[95] Even Stalin admitted Russia would have lost the war without American help.

Likewise, communist victory in China would have been impossible without Establishment intervention. In Chapter 1 we recounted how the Soviet army, equipped by the U.S., entered

China during the last week of World War II. They turned over their American supplies, as well as surrendered Japanese munitions, to communist Mao Tse-tung for the overthrow of Chiang Kai-shek's Nationalist government. As to what happened next, I quote *The Shadows of Power*:

> In late 1945, President Truman dispatched General [George] Marshall to China as a special ambassador to mediate the conflict. Marshall had been an obscure colonel until the reign of FDR, who boosted him past dozens of senior officers to Chief of Staff. Marshall was never listed on the CFR's roster, but he was chronically in the company of its members, and once wrote the introduction to the Council's annual volume, *The United States in World Affairs*.
>
> In China, Marshall demanded that Chiang accept the Communists into his government or forfeit U.S. support. He also negotiated truces that saved the Reds from imminent defeat, and which they exploited to regroup and seize more territory. Finally, Marshall slammed a weapons embargo on the Nationalist government, as the Communists had been urging him to do.
>
> He returned home and was appointed Secretary of State. It became the official line of the CFR-dominated State Department that Chiang Kai-shek was a corrupt reactionary and that Mao Tse-tung was not a Communist but an "agrarian reformer." This propaganda was extensively disseminated to the public by the now-defunct Institute of Pacific Relations (IPR). The CFR was the parent organization of the IPR, which had no less than forty Council members in its ranks. The Institute, like the Council, was heavily funded by Establishment foundations. . . .
>
> The situation in China became desperate. Thanks to the U.S. embargo, the Nationalists were running out of ammunition, while the Communists remained Soviet-supplied. In 1948, Congress voted $125 million in military aid to Chiang. But the Truman administration held up implementation for nine months with red tape, while China collapsed. In contrast,

after the Marshall Plan had passed, the first ships set sail for Europe within days.

Chiang and the Nationalists fled to Taiwan. The IPR myth that he was the heavy and Mao the hero fell apart: Taiwan emerged as a bastion of freedom, and out-produced the world trade of the entire mainland; Mao, on the other hand, instituted totalitarian Communism, and slaughtered tens of millions of Chinese in purges lasting over two decades.[96]

For a full discussion of this subject, see the author's article "China Betrayed" at thenewamerican.com.

Ironically, there has always been a covert but powerful alliance between communists and their supposed archenemies: Establishment capitalists. John Lehman, Ronald Reagan's Secretary of the Navy, told the 1983 Annapolis graduating class:

> Within weeks, many of you will be looking across just hundreds of feet of water at some of the most modern technology ever invented in America. Unfortunately, it is on Soviet ships.[97]

How did the USSR acquire American technology? Not just from spying; most came through Establishment-engineered trade agreements. Ironically, America built the nation long regarded as its greatest enemy.

The reams of aid U.S. capitalists provided the Soviets were documented by Professor Antony Sutton, former research fellow at Stanford's Hoover Institution, in *Wall Street and the Bolshevik Revolution* and *The Best Enemy Money Can Buy*; and by Joseph Finder in *Red Carpet*. Of course, the Establishment press ignored these books.

In the 1920s, the Rockefellers—capitalism's icons—built the Soviets an oil refinery and sold bonds for them through their Chase Bank. Finder writes:

> The Chase National Bank was the Soviet government's leading lender almost from the time of the Revolution. During the twenties, it financed Soviet imports of American cotton. When

Amtorg [the Soviet trade mission in the U.S.] was established in 1924, Chase agreed to handle its promissory notes and letters of credit to aid the import from Russia of fur, timber, and precious metals. In 1926 Chase advanced the Soviet government revolving credit of thirty million dollars.[98]

During that same decade, the Ford Motor Company supplied the Bolsheviks with 24,000 trucks, and trained Russian mechanics.[99] Later Ford helped the Soviets build their huge Gorki motor vehicle plant—which produced trucks that rolled down Vietnam's Ho Chi Minh Trail, loaded with supplies to kill American GIs.

In the 1970s, Chase Manhattan financed construction of the Kama River plant—the world's largest truck factory—which the Soviets promptly converted to building vehicles for their invasion of Afghanistan. The communists awarded David Rockefeller's private plane landing rights in Moscow, and gave Chase Manhattan space for its Russian headquarters at 1 Karl Marx Square.[100]

Averell Harriman, founder of Brown Brothers Harriman, was a prototypal Wall Streeter. Yet the Soviets granted him a 20-year monopoly on mining their manganese; he formed a joint shipping firm with them and arranged to sell their government bonds.

Armand Hammer, chairman of Occidental Petroleum, made a fortune mining Russian asbestos, built factories for the Soviets, shipped them wheat, laundered their money, and organized numerous joint ventures. The Soviets gratefully gave him Czarist art treasures. Like David Rockefeller, he was permitted to land his private jet in Moscow.[101]

America industrialist Cyrus Eaton, who started out working for John D. Rockefeller, supplied the Russians with textiles, leather goods, and pharmaceuticals. The Soviets ultimately awarded him the Lenin Peace Prize.[102]

One cannot argue that profit alone motivated these capitalists. Most of their "deals" with the Reds lost them money. Chase even made a number of loans to the Soviets *below cost*—i.e., the loans were guaranteed to lose money. What American bank customer gets a bargain like that?

Sometimes the assistance extended to outright spying and treason. Du Berrier recounts the Stern family's activities:

> For over a decade Sarnoff's vice-president of NBC and chairman of NBC International was Alfred R. Stern, whose grandfather, Julius Rosenwald, is estimated to have donated over $18 million to Joseph Stalin. Rosenwald, like the Sterns, set up a tax-free foundation to finance communists, according to Congressman Eugene Cox's insertion in the Congressional Record of August 1, 1951. Alfred R. Stern was still chairman of NBC International in 1957 when his father, Alfred K. Stern, fled to Cuba with his second wife, the former Martha Dodd, to escape arrest as Soviet spies.[103]

In his ignored book *The Fifth Man*, Roland Perry identified Victor Rothschild, one of Britain's most powerful bankers, as the long-sought "Fifth Man" of the notorious Burgess-MacLean-Philby-Blunt spy ring. As an inspector for MI5 (Britain's equivalent of the FBI), Rothschild had complete authority over state security during World War II. He passed numerous government secrets to the Russians, including information on the atomic bomb. Former KGB officials confirmed Perry's identification of Rothschild, who evidently saw no contradiction in being both a wealthy banker and Soviet agent.

What was the Establishment's strategy behind helping communism? The Fabian Society's Nicholas Murray Butler encapsulated it in 1937: "Communism is the instrument with which the financial world can topple national governments and then erect a world government with a world police and a world money."[104]

Communism served Satan's plan by:

• overthrowing monarchies;

• generating divisive class hatred within nations (making them easier to conquer); and

• striving to eradicate religion (which Marx had denounced as the "opiate of the masses"), murdering millions of Christians and demolishing churches.

Although communism was packaged as a movement of "the people," it was actually their butcher and jailer. From Russia to Cambodia, genocide marked its arrival; then barbed wire and watchtowers ensured no one could escape the "workers' paradise." Communism was totalitarianism: complete government control. It was George Orwell's *1984* come true.

In reality, communists were the Establishment's hired thugs. They swept aside kings, noblemen, landowners and merchants who stood in its way. Although Marx proclaimed "capitalists" as the enemy, *communists did not go after the cartel's bankers.* For example, in the 1871 Paris Commune, the Reds burned down the city's most important buildings, but the House of Rothschild—France's highest emblem of capitalism—went untouched.[105]

Marxist governments nationalized industries, *appearing* to put them in the "people's" hands. But since communism doesn't work as an economic system, communist countries eventually went bankrupt. Then—in exchange for World Bank loans—they agreed to "privatize" those industries, *not* to the original owners, but to the Establishment's multinational corporations. Thus one object of communism was to seize the world's productive industries and ultimately transfer them to the capitalist clique that had funded the revolutions.

The Semantics of Socialism

How does *socialism* relate to communism? It is a watered-down version. Former communist Whittaker Chambers called it "communism with the claws retracted." Places like America and Britain wouldn't accept outright communist revolution. Along with strong Christian roots, they had a large middle class that saw no need to violently overthrow wealthier people. So the Establishment again used its timeworn principle: to boil a frog, put him in lukewarm water and gradually increase the heat. *If countries won't accept communism, we'll install it step by step.* This slowly warming water is called "Fabian" or "creeping" socialism:

• In communist states, religion was abolished; that was impossible in America, so the Supreme Court has destroyed religious freedom by degrees—in one case banning school prayer; in another outlawing display of the Ten Commandments; etc., etc.

• Whereas a communist government seizes control of the economy, socialism does it gradually, confiscating personal and business income through rising taxes, while burdening companies with mounting regulations related to the environment, safety, energy, hiring practices, wages, health insurance, etc.

• Communists usurped schools; in socialism the government increasingly directs public education, making it more "politically correct," and incrementally restricts home schooling until abolished.

Socialism's end result is EXACTLY the same as communism, but is achieved over many decades instead of through a single revolution. Satan is patient.

The Establishment plays with terminology. If the public perceives the word "socialism" as too radical, it's changed to "democratic socialism," and if people still can't stomach that, it's called "liberalism." Socialist Norman Thomas explained: "The American people will never knowingly, accept Socialism, but under the name of Liberalism, they will adopt every fragment of the Socialist program, until one day America will be a Socialist nation without knowing how it happened."[106]

East-West Merger

The following table (Figure 3) summarizes the strategy.

The plan was to overthrow monarchies, making them into either (1) communist dictatorships, or (2) republics that would gradually convert to socialism. Eventually, the communists would ostensibly *moderate* toward socialism, so that the two systems, now looking similar, could be merged into regional bodies (European Union, North American Union), paving the road for world government.

In 1972 Armand Hammer told London's *Times*: "In fifty-one years of dealing with the Soviets I've never known a better climate

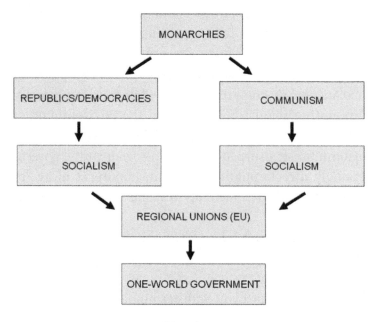

Figure 3

for growth. We're moving toward socialism, they toward capital-ism. Between us there's a meeting ground."[107]

Norman Dodd had unique insight into the gradual merger between the democratic West and communist East. In 1953 Congress formed the Special Committee to Investigate Tax-Free Foundations, also known as the Reece Committee. Dodd was its Director of Research. The following is from G. Edward Griffin's 1982 televised interview with him:

> **Dodd:** Rowan Gaither was, at that time, President of the Ford Foundation. Mr. Gaither had sent for me, when I found it convenient to be in New York. He asked me to call upon him at his office, which I did.
>
> Upon arrival, after a few amenities, Mr. Gaither said, "Mr. Dodd, we have asked you to come up here today, because we thought that, possibly, off the record, you would tell us why the Congress is interested in the activities of foundations such as ourselves."

And, before I could think of how I would reply to that statement, Mr. Gaither then went on, and voluntarily stated, "Mr. Dodd, all of us who have a hand in the making of policies here, have had experience either with the OSS during the war, or with the European Economic Administration after the war. We have had experience operating under directives. The directives emanate, and did emanate, from the White House. Now, we still operate under just such directives. Would you like to know what the substance of these directives is?"

I said, "Yes, Mr. Gaither, I would like very much to know." Whereupon, he made this statement to me, "Mr. Dodd, we are here to operate in response to similar directives, the substance of which is that we shall use our grant-making power so to alter life in the United States, that it can be comfortably merged with the Soviet Union."

Well, parenthetically, Mr. Griffin, I nearly fell off the chair. I, of course, didn't, but my response to Mr. Gaither then was, "Oh, Mr. Gaither, I can now answer your first question. You've forced the Congress of the United States to spend a hundred and fifty thousand dollars to find out what you have just told me." I said, "Of course, legally, you're entitled to make grants for this purpose. But, I don't think you're entitled to withhold that information from the people of this country, to whom you're indebted for your tax exemption. So why don't you tell the people of the country just what you told me?" And his answer was, "We would not think of doing any such thing."[108]

The Soviets' New Face

This merger necessitated a seeming *moderation of communism*, which began in 1989 when Soviet chief Mikhail Gorbachev introduced *glasnost* ("openness") and *perestroika* ("restructuring"). One possible factor in communism's decline: monarchies were now eradicated, so the Establishment no longer needed violent revolutions—few remaining governments required overthrow. Also, communism is atheistic, and Satan has no intention of ruling a purely secular culture—during the End Times, people will worship the Antichrist or "beast" as though he were God.

However, Satan might not be done with communism just yet. During the Cold War, Anatoly Golitsyn was the highest-ranking KGB officer to defect to the West. His revelations led to the arrest of over 200 Soviet spies. In 1984 he published an astonishing exposé, *New Lies for Old*, which predicted *glasnost* five years in advance.

In the KGB, Golitsyn had learned of a dramatic change in communist strategy. Experience had taught the Soviets that if they exhibited strength and unity, or made threats, the West responded by arming. But if they demonstrated *weakness, infighting, and eagerness for peace*, the West responded by *dis*arming. The new strategy: display these attributes at unprecedented levels. This, they believed, would prompt the West to disarm to the point where the communists could achieve decisive superiority. Golitsyn defected to reveal this strategy. What he wrote in 1984 was so remarkably foretelling that we will quote him extensively:

> The communist strategists are now poised to enter into the final, offensive phase of the long-range policy, entailing a joint struggle for the complete triumph of communism. . . . to engage in maneuvers and stratagems beyond the imagination of Marx or the practical reach of Lenin and unthinkable to Stalin. Among such stratagems are the introduction of false liberalization in Eastern Europe and, probably, in the Soviet Union and the exhibition of spurious independence on the part of the regimes in Romania, Czechoslovakia and Poland. . . .
>
> In the economic field reforms might be expected to bring Soviet practice more into line with Yugoslavia, or even seemingly, with Western socialist models. The party would be less conspicuous, but would continue to control the economy from behind the scenes as before. Political "liberalization" and "democratization" would follow the general lines of the Czechoslovak rehearsal in 1968. . . .The liberalization would be spectacular and impressive. Formal pronouncements might be made about a reduction in the communist party's

role; its monopoly would be apparently curtailed. An ostensible separation of powers between legislative, executive, and the judiciary might be introduced. . . .The KGB would be "reformed.". . .

Dissidents at home would be amnestied; those in exile abroad would be allowed to return, and some would take up positions of leadership in government. Sakharov might be included in some capacity in government or allowed to teach abroad. The creative arts and cultural and scientific organizations, such as the writers' unions and the Academy of Sciences, would become apparently more independent, as would the trade unions. Political clubs would be opened to non-members of the communist party. Leading dissidents might form one or more alternative political parties. Censorship would be relaxed; controversial books, plays, films, and art would be published, performed and exhibited. Many prominent Soviet performing artists now abroad would return to the Soviet Union and resume their professional careers. Constitutional amendments would be adopted to guarantee fulfillment of the provisions of the Helsinki agreements and a semblance of compliance would be maintained. There would be greater freedom for the Soviet citizens to travel. Western and United Nations observers would be invited to the Soviet Union to witness the reforms in action.

But, as in the Czechoslovak case, the liberalization would be calculated and deceptive in that it would be introduced from above. It would be carried out by the party through its cells and individual members of government, the Supreme Soviet, the courts, and the electoral machinery, and by the KGB through its agents among the intellectuals and scientists. . . .

"Liberalization" in Eastern Europe would probably involve the return to power in Czechoslovakia of Dubcek and his associates. If it should be extended to East Germany, demolition of the Berlin Wall might even be contemplated. Western acceptance of the new "liberalization" as genuine would create favorable conditions for the fulfillment of communist strategy for the United States, Western Europe, and even, perhaps, Japan. . . .

Pressure could well grow for a solution of the German problem in which some form of confederation between East and West Germany would be combined with neutralization of the whole and a treaty of friendship with the Soviet Union. . . . The European Parliament might become an all-European socialist parliament with representation from the Soviet Union and Eastern Europe. "Europe from the Atlantic to the Urals" would turn out to be a neutral, socialist Europe. . . .

One cannot exclude that at the next party congress or earlier, Andropov will be replaced by a younger leader with a more liberal image who will continue the so-called "liberalization" more intensively."[109]

Before *glasnost* happened, who besides Golitsyn predicted Soviet liberalization, the rise of a Gorbachev-like leader, or the Berlin Wall's fall? In his book, Golitsyn made 148 falsifiable predictions; by 1993, 139 had been fulfilled—a 94 percent accuracy rate. Although the U.S. media should have hailed Golitsyn as a political prophet, they ignored his book and assured us that Soviet reforms were spontaneous and genuine.

But Golitsyn said the changes would be *spurious* and calculated to *deceive*. In the end, the strategy calls for communism to resume its worst form:

In the new worldwide communist federation the present different brands of communism would disappear, to be replaced by a uniform, rigorous brand of Leninism. The process would be painful. Concessions made in the name of economic and political reform would be withdrawn. Religious and intellectual dissent would be suppressed. Nationalism and all other forms of genuine opposition would be crushed. . . . The last vestiges of private enterprise and ownership would be obliterated. Nationalization of industry, finance, and agriculture would be completed. In fact, all the totalitarian features familiar from the early stages of the Soviet revolution and the postwar Stalinist years in Eastern Europe might be expected to reappear, especially in those countries newly won for communism. Unchallenged and unchallengeable, a true communist monolith would dominate the world.[110]

If the USSR *really* collapsed, why weren't those who ran gulags, and who tortured and murdered for the KGB, ever tried for human rights violations (as was done to Nazis at Nuremberg after World War II)?

It is typically claimed the Soviet Union fell apart because, under Ronald Reagan, the U.S. successfully tested an anti-ballistic missile, demonstrating our capacity to put up the Strategic Defense Initiative (SDI). If implemented, this system, nicknamed "Star Wars," could have repelled a missile attack. The USSR allegedly collapsed because it couldn't meet the cost of competing with SDI.

However, let's compare U.S. and Soviet military capabilities at the time (1985). (Abbreviations: ICBM–Intercontinental Ballistic Missile; SLBM–Submarine-Launched Ballistic Missile; ABM–Anti-Ballistic Missile)

STRATEGIC NUCLEAR FORCES

	USSR	USA
ICBM launchers	1,850	1,000
Heavy ICBM launchers	820	0
Ready ICBM warheads	9,300	2,100
Total ICBM warheads	20,200	2,100
Ballistic missile submarines	101	35
Intercontinental range SLBMs	596	0
Intercontinental range SLBM warheads	2,000	0
Cruise missile submarines	220	3
Sea-launched nuclear cruise missiles	575	12
Intercontinental bombers	650	239
Predominant age of systems in years	5 or less	15

RESERVE STRATEGIC NUCLEAR FORCES

	USSR	USA
Modern stockpiled & reload ICBMs	3,350	0
Modern reload ICBM warheads	9,300	0
Stockpiled older ICBMs	1,500	100
Rail-mobile modern ICBMs	300	0
Covert intercontinental bombers	50	0

ANTI-NUCLEAR STRATEGIC DEFENSE FORCES

	USSR	USA
Surface-to-air missile launchers	13,800	0
Primary anti-ballistic missile launchers	100	0
Secondary anti-ballistic missile launchers	3,500	0
Modern interceptor aircraft	3,200	42
Air-defense radars	7,000	117
Anti-submarine warfare subs	280	99
Percentage of ICBMs defended by ABMs	33	0

TACTICAL NUCLEAR FORCES

	USSR	USA
Tactical nuclear missiles	800	0
Land-based tactical nuclear delivery aircraft	6,800	451

CHEMICAL & BIOLOGICAL FORCES

	USSR	USA
Modern chemical weapon production facilities	14	0
Biological weapon production facilities	8	0
Modern chemical weapons (in tons)	700,000	0
Biological weapons (in tons)	unknown	0
ICBMs for global chemical/biological weapons delivery	150	0

CONVENTIONAL FORCES

	USSR	USA
Ground combat divisions	195	16
Battle force ships	2,249	524
Merchant marine ships	1,800	12
Attack aircraft	6,750	2,606
Tanks	51,900	4,960
Armored personnel carriers	63,390	7,090
Artillery tubes	46,300	1,350[111]

Thus, in 1985, the Soviet Union led America in virtually every nuclear and conventional category. By contrast, in 1960 American military strength had been estimated as eight-to-one superior to the Soviets. If the communists didn't quit then, why do so when superior?

Regarding SDI: although the U.S. had successfully test-fired an anti-ballistic missile, Congress, then controlled by Ted Kennedy and the Democrats, vigorously opposed the program. They were only willing to fund research, *not* deployment. Why would the Soviets cave in to such an improbable threat?

According to Golitsyn, the Soviets intended *glasnost* and *perestroika* to deceive the West into disarming. One could argue that the plan succeeded. During the Cold War, the United States had a three-part nuclear deterrent: bombers on standby, land-based ICBMs, and nuclear submarines. Today, on the presumption that Russia will never attack us, we no longer have standby bombers, and have drastically reduced land-based missiles (the best, Reagan's MX "Peacekeepers," have all been dismantled). Our nuclear sub force remains, but sophisticated satellite technology may make it possible to detect and destroy those subs in a first strike.

When the USSR broke up, the American media heavily publicized the Soviets scrapping SS-18 missiles. However, those weapons were outdated anyway. The Russians have meanwhile continued upgrading their missiles. In recent years that have claimed that their SS-27 Topol M can evade any defense system.

Furthermore, they have stridden ahead in other forms of warfare, such as nanotechnology (super-microscopic) weapons, and scalar wave weapons—which can knock out a plane or missile with a concentrated blast of electromagnetic energy. The Russians are also building a vast nuclear-proof complex at Yamantau, underneath the Ural Mountains; it is 400 square miles (as big as Washington, DC) and employs 60,000 workers.[112] No foreigner has ever been allowed inside.

Contrary to prevalent claims, the Russian military is not defunct; it is seemingly preparing for war. I don't know what role it might play in the End Times, but it seems unlikely it would be no factor. While America exhausts its defense budget in the Middle East, is Moscow quietly advancing its first-strike capability? Coupled with Golitsyn's advance prediction of *glasnost*, the Russian threat cannot be ignored.

CHAPTER 10
SATAN'S CONTROL STRUCTURE

Let's start with a mini-comparison. The 1950s saw what was called "the Golden Age of Television." *Every* program was a family show. By design, there was no sex, gore, or foul language. If there had been, hardly anyone would have purchased a TV back then. So the programs were loaded with traditional values. Someone would say, "Hey, Joe, I just bought a TV and it's great! My children are learning the importance of honesty, patriotism, and obeying parents!" His friend would respond, "Gee, if that's what TV's like, I'm buying one for my kids too!" Then, about 1963, television approached saturation—over 90 percent of all American homes had one. Programming then began to change. That year, *Leave It to Beaver* and *Dobie Gillis* were cancelled. Like the boiled frog, content was gradually modified year-by-year until now you've got R-rated stuff: sex, gross violence, bizarre occult horror, foul language, "politically correct" propaganda. Ask a Christian how this happened, and he/she might say something like:

☺ Man has a sinful nature, and so his appetite required entertainment that was more and more sinful. The TV networks were simply responding to public demand.

But man already had a sinful nature in the 1950s. Sure, it allowed him to be taken in, but the equation above is missing something. In Eden, did Adam and Eve just sin, all by themselves? There was also a *tempter*, Satan. Television was no different. Someone plotted to put TVs into homes by starting with traditional values, then gradually changing the content without people knowing they'd been deceived. Who's that clever? Not some network executive. It was Satan. Let's examine his international hierarchy.

We have discussed how the Establishment rules the American government and its policies through the Council on Foreign Relations. But the CFR is not unique; it has dozens of foreign counterparts. Here is a sampling:

Britain: Royal Institute of International Affairs
Canada: Canadian Institute of International Affairs
Germany: German Society for Foreign Policy
France: French Institute of International Relations
Italy: Institute for International Affairs
Belgium: Royal Institute of International Relations
Austria: Austrian Association for Foreign Policy and International Relations
Russia: Institute of World Economics and International Relations
Norway: Norwegian Institute of International Affairs
Holland: Dutch Institute of Foreign Affairs
Poland: Poland Institute of International Affairs
Romania: Association of International Law and International Relations
China: Chinese Institute of International Relations
Japan: Japanese Institute of International Affairs
Australia: Australian Institute of International Affairs
New Zealand: New Zealand Institute of International Affairs
Pakistan: Pakistan Institute of International Affairs
Jordan: World Affairs Council
Nigeria: Nigerian Institute for International Affairs

These organizations influence foreign policy in their respective countries. Experts agree that Britain's Royal Institute of International Affairs (RIIA) outranks and dominates the others, including the CFR.

Supra-National Organizations

How do leaders of such organizations coordinate policy with each other? One venue is the *Bilderberger conferences*. Once a year, the world's elite from government, banking, industry and media hold an international summit at a five-star resort—a different locale every year, in Europe or North America. The name "Bilderberger" comes from the first hotel used in 1954—the Hotel de Bilderberg in the Netherlands. The conferences, which have no mandate from governments, are completely closed to the public and reporters. Even the hotel's employees are compelled to leave; the elite's private staffs temporarily run the facility. The funding source for these meetings has never been revealed. (An excellent resource on this group is *The True Story of the Bilderberg Group* by Daniel Estulin.)

Another coordination tool is the Trilateral Commission, which David Rockefeller founded in 1973. It has three regional divisions—North America, Europe and Asia—hence the name "Trilateral." Like the Bilderbergers, the Trilaterals meet for an annual conference. Former Arizona Senator Barry Goldwater called the Commission "David Rockefeller's newest international cabal," and said, "It is intended to be the vehicle for multinational consolidation of the commercial and banking interests . . . ."[113]

But the Bilderberger and Trilateral gatherings are dwarfed in significance by a permanent hierarchy that long predates them.

We referred earlier to John Robison's 1798 book *Proofs of a Conspiracy against All the Religions and Governments of Europe* (Figure 2, page 98). Its subtitle was *Carried on in the Secret Meetings of Free Masons, Illuminati, and Reading Societies.* Underscore *Illuminati*—they were the foundation for today's Establishment.

According to Robison and other investigators, the Illuminati were a powerful secret society founded in Bavaria by Adam Weishaupt in 1776, under the direction and financing of Mayer Amschel Rothschild. The Illuminati were exposed by what some called an act of God—in 1785, lightning struck one of their couriers riding horseback. On his dead body, the Bavarian police discovered papers revealing the Illuminati's plans for continent-wide revolutions. As a result, the Elector (prince) of Bavaria banished the sect and ordered its members arrested, but most escaped and went underground to continue their activities. The Bavarian authorities sent warnings to the other European governments—who failed to heed them.

Illuminati means "enlightened ones." They worshiped Lucifer (Satan), whose name translates to "light bearer."

In a somewhat typical Christian view, the world looks like this:

GOD

THE CHURCH

THE LOST (i.e., unsaved people outside the church)

But if that's all there is, why are Christians losing the culture war on every front? If we have God behind us, we're organized, have a plan, and know what we're doing, while the rest of the world is stumbling around, lost and clueless, *then Christians should be winning hands down.*

In response, some Christians might say:

☺ OK, you're right, Satan is a factor; we ought to add elements of spiritual warfare, including God's angels and Satan's fallen angels. A correct view of the world would be:

GOD   SATAN

ANGELS   DEMONS

THE CHURCH

THE LOST

But that still omits a big part of the picture—*Satan's church.* A more accurate chart would be:

GOD   SATAN

ANGELS   DEMONS

THE CHURCH   SATAN'S CHURCH

THE LOST

Figure 4

🙂 Satan's church? Oh, I get it. He does have worshipers, that's true. Scattered across the Earth there are a handful of witches and warlocks, and what they do is, they'll come out on Halloween and dance a few jigs to Satan. Sometimes the police even find the remains of small animals sacrificed during their rituals!

That's only a tiny part of it. People like that don't tell governments and TV networks what to do. I'm talking about *the Establishment.*

🙁 Come on now, Jim, it's one thing to criticize their policies, but to say they worship Satan! How do you know that?

From intelligence reports provided by such men as Ted Gunderson (FBI), Dr. John Coleman (Britain's MI6) and William

Guy Carr (Canadian Intelligence Service). The broad public doesn't know for the same reason they've never heard of the CFR and other matters discussed in this book—it's *concealed*. Christ's church is open, functioning in light. Satan's followers operate in the dark, worshiping secretly. The Establishment's top leaders are *not* atheists. Atheism is a useful tool for persuading people that God doesn't exist, but that's all.

Since 1873, America's elite have gathered annually at the Bohemian Grove in Northern California. The rituals there include dressing en masse in gothic, hooded robes and sacrificing a human being in effigy before a forty-foot tall concrete owl (Figure 4). Radio talk show host Alex Jones (www.infowars.com) succeeded in breaking through the Grove's tight security to videotape the bizarre nighttime ceremony. Bohemian Grove participants have included the Bushes, Bill Clinton, Dick Cheney, Colin Powell, Henry Kissinger, Walter Cronkite, Richard Nixon, top Bechtel executives, and many other "notables."

Satan exerts more control than most Christians seem to acknowledge. I often hear them say "God is in control." And while many Bible passages speak of God's power and sovereignty, we need to balance them with verses such as:

"The whole world is under the control of the evil one." (1 John 5:19)

"... Satan, who leads the whole world astray."* (Rev 12:9)

The Bible calls Satan:

"the prince of this world" (John 12:31, 14:30)
"the god of this age" (2 Cor 2:4)
"the ruler of the kingdom of the air" (Eph 2:2)

[*Isn't mass media one way he does this today?]

The Satanic Pyramid

How *does* Satan rule the world? Through a hierarchy—not just a spiritual one, but a chain of command using people on Earth.

What is this hierarchy's structure? Figure 5, a page from a 1787 German book, describes the Illuminati's organizational framework in the 18th century.

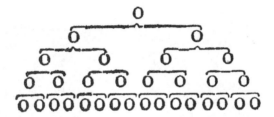

32

mit ich indeſſen ſpeculiren, und die Leute ge-
ſchickt rangieren kann; denn davon hängt alles
ab. Ich werde in dieſer Figur mit ihnen operieren.

Ich habe zwey unmittelbar unter mir, wel-
chen ich meinen ganzen Geiſt einhauche, und von
dieſen zweyen hat wieder jeder zwey andere, und
ſo fort. Auf dieſe Art kann ich auf die einfach-
ſte Art tauſend Menſchen in Bewegung und
Flammen ſetzen. Auf eben dieſe Art muß man
die Ordres ertheilen, und im Politiſchen operieren.

Es iſt ein Kunſt dabey, dem Pythagoras et-
was aus dem Ill. min. vorzuleſen. Ich habe
ihn ja nicht: ich habe keinen einzigen Grad in
Handen, nicht einmal meine eigene Auffätze.

Ich habe auch in des Philo Provinzen eine
Art von Eid, Verſicherung oder Betheuerung:
bey der Ehre des ⊙o: beym ⊙, einge-
führt. Man gebraucht ſie nur, um ſie nicht
zu profaniren, bey den wichtigſten Vorfällen.
                                        Wer

Diagram of Weishaupt's System. From *Nachtrag von weitern
Originalschriften der Illuminatensekte*, p. 32. München, 1787.

Figure 5

Each person had two people underneath him, each subordinate had two below *him*, and so on. Furthermore, a member only knew the identity of his immediate superior. He didn't know who was two levels up (his master's master). This concealed the leadership. If someone slipped up and revealed his superior's name, he still didn't know who was *two* tiers above, so the upper hierarchy was always protected.

Notice that, when extended, this diagram becomes a pyramid—that is the order's geometric shape. (Figure 6)

Figure 6

At the top is Satan. Through this structure, he exercises control and communicates his plans. He is real, literally operating on Earth.

The Bible recounts Satan's effort to tempt Jesus:

> Again, the devil took him to a very high mountain and showed him all the kingdoms of the world and their splendor. "All this I will give you," he said, "if you will bow down and worship me."
>
> Jesus told him, "Away from me, Satan! For it is written: 'Worship the Lord your God, and serve him only.'"[114]

Jesus refused the offer, but didn't deny that Satan could make good on it. Apparently the kingdoms were later offered to others who, unlike Jesus, yielded to temptation.

The pyramid today probably does not descend in perfect geometric doubling (1-2-4-8-16-etc.). According to William Guy Carr, there is a council of 33, and above that a supreme council of 13.[115] I have also seen reports of high councils numbering nine, seven, six and three. Sketching a completely accurate picture of the upper pyramid is probably impossible, since it is doubtful that any intelligence operative ever penetrated that high. The names of the men at these levels are unknown.

However, it is well-established that below the council of 33 is "the Committee of 300."

It has long existed; if a member dies or cannot continue, a designated person takes his place, so the committee always has 300 members. The book *The Committee of 300*, by former MI6 officer Dr. John Coleman, is the best resource on this international group and names its members, living and dead. David Rockefeller and Henry Kissinger are among those most familiar to Americans.

A few statesmen have publicly acknowledged the committee's existence. Walter Rathenau, a close associate of the Rothschilds, was once Germany's foreign minister. He stated:

> Only three hundred men, each of whom knows all the others, govern the fate of Europe. They select their successors from their own entourage. They have in their hands the means to put an end to the form of the State, which they find unreasonable.[116]

The Committee of 300 rules the world's governments, media, banks, foundations and global corporations. We've discussed the first four—let's touch on the latter.

Multinational Corporations

According to Dr. Coleman, the Committee controls over 400 of the "Fortune 500" companies[117]—IBM, Exxon, Citibank, Bechtel, Halliburton, British Petroleum, etc.

Politically, world government is formed by progressively merging countries (as into the European Union and North American Union). But *corporately* a similar process is happening through business mergers: Time, Inc. merged with Warner Brothers, then Time Warner merged with America Online. J. P. Morgan & Co. merged with Chase Manhattan Bank, then J. P. Morgan Chase merged with BankOne. The corporate world has "merger mania." We are increasingly run by corporations *larger in size* but *fewer in number.*

As the huge multinationals grow, they destroy small businesses. CVS knocks out the local pharmacy, Home Depot the local hardware, Wal-Mart the local department store, Dunkin Donuts the local coffee shop. Consumers, despairing from tax and inflation, seek cheaper goods, and are herded into these corporate stores.

☺ Hey, growth and mergers are just a normal part of being a business. You see, Jim, it's all about the *bottom line.* Big corporations are motivated solely by *profits.* And one way to improve profits is mergers. No need to put a goofy conspiracy spin on this!

When I was a hippie, we'd complain that big business was driven exclusively by greed and profits; of course, that's the Marxist slant. It has a *degree* of truth. Satan desires money pouring into his cartel, making it richer and stronger. Therefore he wants his corporations to make profits, and is unlikely to tolerate slackers that don't. However, it's about more than profits.

Christians tend to assume most businessmen are conservatives who share their values. The logic might run something like this:

–America's Founding Fathers were Christians;
–the Founding Fathers established free enterprise;
–therefore businessmen, who practice free enterprise, will embrace Christian values.
Furthermore:
–Karl Marx opposed both free enterprise and religion;
–consequently, businessmen will be pro-religious and will share our values.

Nevertheless, Christians are regularly surprised by the political correctness of big corporations—for example, they see the gay agenda pushed by IBM, Ford, Wal-Mart, McDonald's and Allstate. They're shocked as Macy's, Lowe's and Target replace "Christmas trees" with "holiday trees."

Let's sort this out. Under free enterprise, people can:
- create their own business;
- run it without burdensome government regulations;
- enjoy the fruits of their labor without onerous taxation.

Free enterprise generates prosperity, as has been proven by nations who embraced it, such as America, Hong Kong and Singapore. It is consistent with Biblical principles like individual responsibility, rewards for work, and respect for personal property. Communist and socialist economies, on the other hand, have failed. Among the reasons:
- when government takes over businesses, personal initiative is stifled; and
- centralized bureaucracies cause rampant waste and inefficiency.

If governments receive increased powers, they typically abuse them and subjugate the population—validating Lord Acton's famous dictum, "Power corrupts, and absolute power corrupts absolutely." In reality, America has been steadily moving from free enterprise toward a hybrid with socialism, as evidenced by the dramatic increase in taxes and government regulation over the past century.

A few Christians and conservatives, however, take these observations to an extreme conclusion: that *government is inherently bad* and *private enterprise inherently good*. However, private enterprise, unchecked by morality, can rival government in abuses. The Bible has no shortage of verses denouncing wealth's corrupting nature.

Satan knows his kingdom requires money, and that free enterprise can generate it. As an autocrat, his governing style is that of a communist like Lenin or Stalin; but as a pragmatist, he realizes he needs the capitalism of Rockefeller and Rothschild.

Most small businessmen *are* conservative, with a strong work ethic and family values rooted in religious faith. However, the global multinational corporations are quite different, because the Establishment—specifically the Committee of 300—controls them.

When Christians see such corporations enforcing pro-gay guidelines, or banning the word "Christmas," they may think along these lines:

☹ Hm! Why are they doing that? I shouldn't think a bunch of liberal hippie types, dressed in blue jeans, could have gotten an audience with IBM's board of directors—but apparently they did! Not only that, the board agreed with them! I guess we Christians just don't lobby as well as the gays and atheists. If we did, these corporations would see things *our* way. After all, they're conservative businessmen! So here's what we'll do. We'll email the chairman of IBM and say "We won't buy IBM products unless you change your tune!" And they'll listen because, after all, profits are all that matter to these guys!

Christians boycotts can have some effect, especially at a corporation's local store. But the bottom line for these global companies is *not* profits. If it was, they would never take anti-family, anti-Christian positions in the first place. The reason they advance politically correct agendas is *not* because grassroots liberals lobbied the board. They don't take orders from the bottom, but from the top—from those who put them on the board. And while the Satanic hierarchy considers profits very important, it is willing to strategically sacrifice them at times for political objectives.

A Note on Drugs

Like other global business sectors, the drug industry has long been ruled by the Establishment: not only pharmaceutical giants like Merck, but illegal operations too. Well over a century ago, the cartel ran the British East India Company, the most powerful commercial concern of its time. It harvested opium in India, then

sold it in China, turning millions into addicts. The cartel still runs illegal drugs today—that's why we never win "the war on drugs." They occasionally let a minor heroin smuggler be caught at an airport—the headlines make people think we're doing something about drugs—but the big boys upstairs are never touched.

Chapter 11
FREEMASONRY

We have briefly discussed the pyramid's top, but who's at the bottom level of Figure 6? These are the cartel's shock troops, most of whom don't know who they're really working for. They have included street revolutionaries, environmental activists, pro-choice demonstrators, drug runners, and—in *certain contexts*—low-ranking Freemasons.

How does Masonry fit into the picture?

In every American city, and many towns, you'll notice a Masonic Lodge. There are about two million Freemasons in the U.S. today. As you may know, Masonry is a secret society with secret rituals, handshakes, and recognition phrases.

Why do men join? One reason: to be in a brotherhood. If you're in trouble, fellow Masons are supposed to aid you. It also represents advancement opportunities: in business, another Mason may favor you for transactions or promotions.

Masonry has a hierarchy of 33 degrees. Progressing to the next degree requires participation in a secret ritual. One cannot advance at his own discretion—only if invited by higher-ranking Masons.

The vast majority of Masons belong to the three lower degrees (Entered Apprentice, Fellow Craft, and Master Mason). It is very clear that their activities in America mostly involve innocent socialization and charitable activities. But low-ranking Masons know almost nothing about the upper levels because tight secrecy protects the latter. As ex-Mason Copin Albancelli noted: "I did not suspect the nature of the association in which I had become an active member. How skillfully things are devised to deceive those who are Masons as well as those who are not."[118] Masons take oaths of absolute loyalty, vowing never to reveal the brotherhood's secrets. For example, first degree Masons swear (the wording may vary somewhat among lodges):

> If I should in the very least degree violate my oath, may my head be cut off, my heart, my teeth and my entrails be torn out and thrown into the sea, may my body be burnt and the ashes cast to the winds so that nothing may remain of me or of my thoughts among men or among my brother Masons.

What would happen to a first-degree Mason who violated his oath by revealing what he knew? Probably nothing—because he knows nothing significant. But this vow establishes a pattern. As one rises through Masonry, the oaths become more severe and enforceable.

Why pledge loyalty to something shrouded in secrecy, that one doesn't understand? And if Masonry is just a philanthropic brotherhood, why does it require severe bloody oaths?

The Bible generally associates secrecy with evil; for the most part, only acts that are evil require concealment by darkness. Christianity, in contrast, is very open about its beliefs.

In reality Masonry has been a recruiting ground for the Illuminati for over 200 years. Members are carefully screened. At the lowest ranks, one is told that a Mason "must believe in God"; but some of the select few who rise to high levels begin to learn that Masonry's God is Satan. For example, reportedly part of the 19th degree's oath is: "War on the Cross of Jesus Christ. Adopt the cult of Lucifer of fire and of flesh."[119] In the 30th degree ritual, one tramples on the cross of Christ. What if the Mason *refuses* to trample on the cross? His fellow Masons applaud; he's awarded the degree and thinks he's done the right thing—but never advances further in Masonry.[120] Thus one purpose of these ceremonies is to weed out those who might retain scruples about opposing Christ.

The description of rituals I have given here is based on the testimony of ex-Masons. Yet I have also spoken to sincere ex-Masons of high rank, who *deny* these elements existed in the rituals they went through. As I do not wish to demean the honesty of witnesses on either side, I am going to suggest the possibility that there is more than one brand of Freemasonry, with more than one existing ritual for a particular degree. Perhaps some 33rd degree Masons unwittingly serve as innocent fronts for a darker strain of Masonry.

Origins of Freemasonry

The word "assassin" comes from the Hashashin, an Islamic cult begun in the 11th century by Hassan-I Sabah. Known as "The Old Man of the Mountain," he commanded his ruthless forces from an impregnable mountain fortress. He was a satanic figure who possessed such loyalty among his followers that they would instantly slit their own throats or jump off a cliff if so ordered.

How did he induce this loyalty? He would select young men whom he thought would make good assassins. He told them that he was on equal footing with the prophet Mohammed, and could send anyone to Paradise whom he chose. These youths were then drugged with opium. When they awoke, they would be in a valley where Hassan owned several palaces. Surrounded by beautiful women and every imaginable pleasure, they were told this was Paradise. After four or five days, they were drugged again and removed from the valley. Upon waking, they were told they could return to this Paradise forever if they would obey Hassan's every command—which most did.

There were certain similarities between the Assassins and Masons—the Assassins had a hierarchy of degrees, secret signals, and oaths of absolute obedience. Also, on reaching the top of the Assassin hierarchy, members were told the Koran was a lie, just as some high-ranking Masons are told the Bible is a lie. The Assassins were Islam's Masonry, loosely the forerunners of the today's Shiite suicide bombers.

Masonry is historically connected to the Assassins. During the early Crusades, the Knights Templar were assigned to guard pilgrims going to the Holy Land. However, they became increasingly corrupt and given to plundering. At one point they were supposed to battle the Assassins, but the Old Man of the Mountain offered them huge amounts of gold. Instead of fighting the Assassins, the knights made a truce with them, fellowshipped with them, and adopted many of their rituals. When they returned to Europe, they brought back these rituals, which became the occult beginnings of Freemasonry.

Enter the Illuminati

By the late 18th century, the Illuminati controlled Masonry on the European continent, as Robison, Barruel and others then documented. The Illuminati were in turn directed by Weishaupt, who answered to the Rothschilds.

Because Freemasonry enjoys legalized secrecy, its lodges have historically served as a venue for subversive activities. We previously commented that the French Revolution was not a "spontaneous uprising." It was carefully organized through France's 2,000 Masonic lodges, each having a revolutionary committee. When the National Assembly took over the government in 1789, many of its members were Masons. Bonnet, orator of the Convent of the Grand Orient Lodge of France, declared in 1904:

> During the 18th century the glorious line of the Encyclopedistes found in our temples a fervent audience, which, alone at that period, invoked the radiant motto, still unknown to the people, of "Liberty, Equality, Fraternity." The revolutionary seed germinated rapidly in that select company. Our illustrious brother masons d'Alembert, Diderot, Helvetius, d'Holbach, Voltaire and Condorcet, completed the evolution of people's minds and prepared the way for a new age. And when the Bastille fell, freemasonry had the supreme honor to present to humanity the charter which it had friendly elaborated. . . .

> On August 25, 1789, the Constituent Assembly, of which more than 300 members were masons, finally adopted, almost word for word, such as it had been for long elaborated in the lodges, the text of the immortal declaration of the Rights of Man.

At that decisive hour for civilization, French masonry was the universal conscience . . . .[121]

Freemasons were also behind the 1910 revolution which overthrew King Manuel of Portugal and brutally suppressed the Catholic Church there. The revolutionary government even printed new banknotes bearing the Masonic symbols of the square and compass.[122] Furnemont, grand orator of the Grand Orient of Belgium, said in 1911:

> Do you recall the deep feeling of pride which we all felt at the brief announcement of the Portuguese revolution?
>
> In a few hours the throne was brought down, the people triumphed and the republic was proclaimed. For those who were not initiated, it was a flash of lightning in a clear sky. But we, my brothers, we understood, we knew the marvelous organization of our Portuguese brothers, their ceaseless zeal, their uninterrupted work. We possessed the secret of that glorious event.[123]

The "Young Turk" revolution, which induced the fall of the Ottoman Empire's Sultan, was likewise a Masonic event. In 1909, 45 Turkish lodges formed the "Grand Orient Ottoman."[124] The French Masonic review *Acacia* explained:

> A secret Young Turk Committee was founded, and the whole movement was directed from Salonika, as the town which has the greatest percentage of Jewish population in Europe— 70,000 Jews out of a total population of 110,000—was specially qualified for this purpose. Besides, there were many Freemason lodges in Salonika in which the revolutionaries could work undisturbed. These lodges were under the protection of European diplomacy, the Sultan was defenceless against them, and he could not any more prevent his own downfall.[125]

Freemasons were the backbone of Europe's other revolutions, such as the Italian insurrections under Mazzini and Garibaldi.

Leon Trotsky was a 33rd degree Mason.[126] Lenin, his cohort in leading the Russian Revolution, belonged to a Swiss lodge.[127]

History books present Archduke Ferdinand's 1914 assassination—immediate trigger of World War I—as an act of Serbian nationalism. However, the trial of the conspirators established that several were Freemasons, and that a Masonic edict had condemned the Archduke to death. One of the assassins, 19-year old Nedeljko Cabrinovic, bluntly explained: "In Freemasonry it is permitted to kill." One reason Freemasons have made such dependable revolutionaries: their oaths bind them to absolute, unquestioning obedience to orders.

☹ Hold it, Jim. Masons are certainly *not* engaged in violent revolutionary stuff here in America. In fact, I know a Freemason; he's a World War II vet, grandfather, big baseball fan—a regular good Joe! So why are you spreadin' all this venom about Masons?

I myself have known fine Freemasons, and have even been a guest on radio shows hosted by them. My maternal grandfather was a Freemason; in her youth, my mother belonged to the Freemasonic Order of the Eastern Star. Many observers have noted a distinction between *Scottish Rite Masonry*, practiced in England and North America, and *Grand Orient Masonry*, observed on the European continent. They see the former as relatively benign, while the latter has a long history of subversive activity. It is obvious that the overwhelming majority of American Freemasons are certainly *not* involved in any sinister activity.

However, one reason American Freemasonry is not now engaged in violent revolution: *our revolution ended over 200 years ago. We have no monarchy to overthrow.* And while most Masons, who never pass beyond the third degree, undoubtedly *are* good Joes, a few high-ranking ones have contributed to the piecemeal conversion of our Republic into socialism. Some lower Masons may prove unwitting tools in this process; their vows of obedience can make them helpful in carrying out subordinate tasks.

The Supreme Court, in wrecking religious liberty over the past sixty years, has been dominated by Freemasons such as

Hugo Black, William O. Douglas, Earl Warren, Potter Stewart and Thurgood Marshall. Why did these men undermine the U.S. Constitution? Was it perhaps because their *secret oaths* to the brotherhood far outweighed their *public oaths* to uphold the Constitution? Didn't their Masonic membership help put them in these lofty positions? One can properly understand their controversial decisions *not* as innocent "misinterpretations" of the Constitution, but as following orders privately received. Violating these orders might have resulted in their own destruction, whereas violating the Constitution only resulted in a few verbal criticisms from conservatives and Christians, which were drowned out by cheers from the Establishment media anyway.

Federal Reserve architect Paul Warburg was a 33rd degree Mason, as were his lieutenants Edward Mandell House and Nelson Aldrich. At least 14 Presidents have been Freemasons, as well as innumerable Senators and congressmen. Listings may be found online.

The Great Seal of the United States did not appear on the dollar bill (Figure 7) until 1935, when Franklin D. Roosevelt, a 33rd degree Mason, ordered our currency changed to include it. The seal is loaded with Masonic imagery.

Figure 7

On the left is a pyramid—a Masonic, not American, symbol. Above the pyramid is the all-seeing eye, a universal Masonic emblem. It reportedly reflects Satan's promise to Adam and Eve to open their eyes so they would be like God. The inscription "Annuit

Coeptus Novus Ordo Seclorum" means "Announcing the Birth of a New Order of the Ages," which the pyramid represents—Satan's world order. The pyramid is unfinished. When completed, connecting to Satan's eye, he will reign.

The six-pointed star (Figure 8) is used in Satan worship, which can be verified by checking satanic books and websites.

Figure 8

Placed over the pyramid (Figure 9), it brackets Satan's eye on top while the other five points spell "Mason."

Figure 9

☹ Dude, there's a word for that—"coincidence."

Then inspect the bill's right side (Figure 10).

Figure 10

The cluster of stars above the eagle also forms a six-pointed star. The eagle has 32 feathers on the right wing, 33 on the left, signifying Masonry's two highest degrees.

America is great in many ways. The Bill of Rights, appended to the Constitution, is a significant barrier to the rule of Antichrist. I don't wish to pursue much controversy over the American Revolution's merits. But to affirm the Masonic role in it, visit the Museum of our National Heritage (Lexington, Mass.), run by the Freemasons. The Sons of Liberty, who held the famous "Boston Tea Party" in 1773, were mostly members of the same Masonic Lodge that met at the Green Dragon Tavern. Freemason Paul Revere, who stirred the citizenry against Britain, went on to become Grand Master of the Grand Lodge of Massachusetts. Many other Masons helped lead the Revolution, including Benjamin Franklin, John Hancock, Ethan Allen and—perhaps with less zeal for the brotherhood than others—George Washington. In many respects, it's reasonable to call the revolution Masonic.

CHAPTER 12
ENVIRONMENTALISM

We will treat this subject very briefly.

Report from Iron Mountain was published in 1967 as the leaked findings of a private three-year study commissioned by the U.S. government. The *Report* made shocking Orwellian recommendations, some of which are now becoming reality. The Establishment press denounced the report as a hoax; five years later, the late Leonard C. Lewin said he had written it as a satire on government think tanks.

However, economist John Kenneth Galbraith, writing under a pseudonym in *Washington Post Book World*, said he had been asked to join the study, but had declined due to other commitments. "I would put my personal repute behind the authenticity of this document," he wrote. If the *Report*, as Lewin claimed, was "satire," it was strangely devoid of humor. Many wonder if the "hoax" charge was issued for damage control.

The study chiefly discussed the implications of the world moving from the system of war—which nuclear weapons were making impractical—to disarmament. The report cited many advantages to war, not the least of which was allegiance by citizens to their government:

> In general, the war system provides the basic motivation for primary social motivation. In doing so, it reflects on the societal level the incentives of individual human behavior. The most important of these, for social purposes, is the individual psychological rationale for allegiance to a society [read: government] and its values. Allegiance requires a cause; a cause requires an enemy. This much is obvious; the critical point is

that the enemy that defines the cause must seem genuinely formidable.[128]

The report noted that if wars disappeared, a new "enemy" would be required to induce allegiance. Among the solutions proposed were threats to the environment:

> Nevertheless, an effective political substitute for war would require "alternate enemies," some of which might seem equally farfetched in the context of the current war system. It may be, for instance, that gross pollution of the environment can eventually replace the possibility of mass destruction by nuclear weapons as the principal apparent threat to the survival of the species. Poisoning of the air, and of the principal sources of food and water supply, is already well advanced, and at first glance would seem promising in this respect; it constitutes a threat that can be dealt with only through social organization and political power. But from present indications it will be a generation to a generation and a half before environmental pollution, however severe, will be sufficiently menacing, on a global scale, to offer a possible basis for a solution.
>
> It is true that the rate of pollution could be increased selectively for this purpose; in fact, the mere modifying of existing programs for the deterrence of pollution could speed up the process enough to make the threat credible much sooner.[129]

Was this the "green" movement's beginning? In the report's wake, numerous environmental scares were raised—global warming, acid rain, overpopulation, ozone depletion, toxic waste, deforestation, endangered species, etc. Establishment foundations began pouring billions of dollars into environmental groups. (For a sample, see Appendix II.) When I was a young man leafing through newspaper "help wanted" sections, I saw plenty of ads from environmental organizations. The jobs required no experience, but offered excellent pay. I wondered: "How can grass-roots groups afford to pay salaries like that?" Little did I know they were riding the Establishment gravy train!

What are the true purposes of environmentalism?

According to Dr. John Coleman, one key motivation is the Committee of 300's fanatical concern for preserving natural resources, which they believe will be personally needed for their reign during world government.[130]

Concerning America, there is another factor. The Club of Rome is an important European think tank. Its famous 1972 report *The Limits to Growth*, which sold over 30 million copies, proposed massive environmental controls. In 1980, one of the Club's leaders, Étienne Davignon, called for the United States to deindustrialize.[131] Supposedly we were overdeveloped, consuming too many natural resources, polluting the environment, etc. In reality, the cartel feared America was too strong for world government to contain. Essential to their strategy is that *no nation must ever be too powerful*. As we saw earlier, part of America's deindustrialization came through trade agreements (NAFTA, GATT), which crippled our manufacturing. The other means to deindustrialization was *environmentalism*. The well-financed eco-groups are trying to shut down U.S. industry: we see lumber companies hamstrung over spotted owls, factories closed due to smokestack emissions, offshore oil drilling banned to protect sea creatures, etc. Follow the money; these developments are rooted in Davignon's strategy, not the humane concerns of grass-roots activists.

Yet perhaps the most important reason for environmentalism is *furnishing governments with an excuse to regulate individuals*. An excellent reference on this is Steve Malloy's book *Green Hell*. The core environmental "danger" greens currently discuss is global warming, allegedly caused by man-made carbon dioxide. Many scientists have refuted global warming's existence. Over 30,000 scientists have signed a petition denying the claims of global warming (www.petitionproject.org). Furthermore, as the "Climategate" scandal proved, statistics used to prove global warming have been grossly falsified. Carbon dioxide is a naturally occurring substance required by plants, and man's contributions to carbon dioxide levels are negligible.

Nevertheless, Al Gore and other green spokespersons ignore reality and continue to push the "fact" of global warming. Greens argue that each human has a "carbon footprint"—the amount of carbon emissions their lifestyle creates by driving cars, using electricity, etc. If a person's carbon footprint is deemed too great, radical greens want government to impose penalties. This, if the greens prevail, would entail energy rationing—even government remote control of home thermostats has been proposed.

Energy is required for all activity. By opposing all effective forms of energy development, from offshore drilling to nuclear power, greens are creating an artificial energy shortage, drastically increasing the cost of energy, and providing an excuse for the government to micro-regulate every home in Orwellian fashion. And, since global warming is seen as a "global" threat, it is also being used as an excuse for world government. Former French President Jacques Chirac said in a speech advocating the Kyoto Protocol:

> For the first time, humanity is instituting a genuine instrument of global governance, one that should find a place within the World Environmental Organization which France and the European Union would like to see established.

The UN's main tool for environmental dictatorship is Agenda 21. It mandates sweeping regulation of human activity in the name of "sustainable development," and is being implemented in the United States right down to the level of local government. I have not written more on this because (as you will find if you Google "Agenda 21") so many authors and organizations have already provided excellent resources exposing it.

CHAPTER 13
ZIONISM

The Rothschilds have long been the Establishment's dominant financial power. They have supported three major goals: *world government* (League of Nations and UN), *revolution* (e.g., funding Lenin and Trotsky), and *Zionism*—the movement to establish the modern state of Israel. Why the last?

Figure 11 is a Perloff family picture from around 1900.

Figure 11

My paternal ancestors were Russian Jews. My great-grandfather's name was Abraham Perlovsky. People who criticize Zionism (as I'm about to do) are frequently accused of being motivated by *anti-Semitism*. Since I'm half-Jewish myself, I hope it's clear that *such feelings do not impel me.* And lest this book be quoted out of context, let me state that *I am unequivocally opposed to racism in any form.*

A typical Christian view of present-day Israel might run something like: "Israel is a marvelous example of God's sovereignty. He preserved his chosen people, the Israelites, for all these years, and miraculously restored them to the Holy Land, recreating Israel as a nation."

The Nature of Zionism

Israel's flag (Figure 12) bears what may legitimately be called a satanic six-pointed star.

Figure 12

Though called "the Star of David," it has no Biblical basis. If desired, Israel could have used a more familiar Jewish image, such as a menorah (the seven-branch candelabrum described in the book of Exodus). *Wikipedia* said of the Star of David in 2008: "Its usage began in the Middle Ages. Exact origins of the symbol's relation to Jewish identity are unknown. Several theories were put forward."

Satan tries to counterfeit the things of God. The Bible says the Antichrist will do signs and wonders, and amaze the world because he was wounded yet lived. That sounds like Christ. It also says he will rule for 3 and ½ years—the same amount of time theologians ascribe to Christ's earthly ministry.

Christianity teaches the *Trinity*—Father, Son and Holy Spirit. The relationship of Satan to the Antichrist and false prophet (described in the book of Revelation) has been called an *unholy* trinity—with Satan counterfeiting God the Father, Antichrist a counterfeit Christ, and the false prophet counterfeiting the Holy Spirit.

Contrary to the widely held Christian view, I suggest the modern political state of Israel is not the rebirth of Biblical Israel, but a satanic counterfeit. I stress that I say this in a political context; I do not for a moment deny the sincere faith of many of the professing followers of Judaism now living in Israel.

How did that state begin? Israel received the land from the British, but how did *they* acquire it? Historically, Britain never had interests in Palestine.

In 1916, when Britain was facing likely defeat in World War I, leading Zionists intimated they could bring America into the war, *provided that Britain would secure the Jewish people a national homeland in Palestine.* The British government consented, resulting in the Balfour Declaration, named for its purported author, Foreign Secretary Arthur Balfour, a 33rd-degree Mason.

Samuel Landman, secretary of the World Zionist Organization, wrote that

> the only way (which proved so to be) to induce the American President to come into the war was to secure the cooperation of Zionist Jews by promising them Palestine, and thus enlist and mobilize the hitherto unsuspectedly powerful forces of Zionist Jews in America and elsewhere in favour of the Allies on a *quid pro quo* contract basis. Thus, as will be seen, the Zionists having carried out their part, and greatly helped to bring America in, the Balfour Declaration of 1917 was but the public confirmation of the necessarily secret "gentleman's" agreement of 1916 . . . . [132]

Here is the Balfour Declaration's full text:

November 2nd, 1917.

Dear Lord Rothschild,

I have much pleasure in conveying to you, on behalf of His Majesty's Government, the following declaration of sympathy with Jewish Zionist aspirations which has been submitted to, and approved by, the Cabinet:

"His Majesty's Government view with favour the establishment in Palestine of a national home for the Jewish people, and will use their best endeavours to facilitate the achievement of this object, it being clearly understood that nothing shall be done which may prejudice the civil and religious rights of existing non-Jewish communities in Palestine, or the rights and political status enjoyed by Jews in any other country."

I should be grateful if you would bring this declaration to the knowledge of the Zionist Federation.

Yours sincerely,
Arthur James Balfour

This declaration was issued to Walter Rothschild, a private banker holding no government position. Furthermore, it pledged that the British would "use their best endeavours" to found a Jewish homeland in Palestine, even though Britain had no position or authority there whatsoever. Although Balfour signed the declaration, its wording evolved from numerous consultations between Zionists and the government. The phrase about "the rights of existing non-Jewish communities" was not in original drafts, but was eventually appended to deter critics.[133]

How did Britain gain control of Palestine to fulfill this pledge? Palestine had been under Ottoman (Turkish) control for 400 years. During World War I, the Ottoman Empire was a German ally; on this pretext, the British invaded Palestine, though it had little strategic significance. The famous film *Lawrence of Arabia* portrayed the exploits of T. E. Lawrence, the British officer who led the Arabs against the Turks. The Arabs were promised Palestine in return for helping Britain defeat the Ottoman Empire. They did not know that, behind their backs, the Balfour Declaration would secretly pledge the land to the Jews.

One reason many Arabs hate modern Israel: they bled for Palestine, but by broken agreements, much of it was given instead to the Jews, few of whom partook in the combat. T. E. Lawrence was so upset by the betrayal that he refused to accept his war medals, changed his name, and attempted to live in anonymity as an RAF airman.

Even before the Balfour Declaration, the Rothschilds were purchasing Palestinian land for Jewish settlements. French banker James de Rothschild spent about $50 million; today Israel honors him with his portrait on its 500 shekel note.

Jerry Golden is a Messianic Jew living in Israel. Look on his website, www.thegoldenreport.com, for the article "The Roots of Evil in Jerusalem." You will see an aerial photograph of the Israeli Supreme Court building, built by the Rothschilds. Notice the Masonic pyramid on its roof. Entering the building, one walks on an inverted cross—the Masonic tradition of trampling the cross of Christ. One then comes to a painting (also viewable on the website) of Lord Rothschild and Israeli leaders examining an architect's model of the building.

What were they after? What is Zionism's true purpose? I believe the answer is in the Bible's description of the Antichrist. Jesus said (Matthew 24:15) the End Times would occur "when you see standing in the holy place [God's temple in Jerusalem] 'the abomination that causes desolation,' spoken of by the prophet Daniel." 2 Thessalonians 2:3-4 says:

> Don't let anyone deceive you in any way, for that day will not come until the rebellion occurs and the man of lawlessness is revealed, the man doomed to destruction. He will oppose and exalt himself over everything that is called God or is worshipped, so that he sets himself up in God's temple, proclaiming himself to be God.

I suggest Zionism is not Godly or Biblical; its goal is to establish Satan's rule in God's city, Jerusalem. Modern Israel is a counterfeit. Here are two principles:

• Satan wants to rule the world (purpose of world government)
• He wants to rule it from a throne in Jerusalem (purpose of Zionism)

Understand those principles, and you can understand most world events. Jerusalem is the Bible's holiest city: the center of ancient Israel, Solomon built God's temple there; Jesus was crucified there. Satan wants to *reign, as a counterfeit Christ-Messiah, from a rebuilt Jerusalem temple,* thumbing his nose at God as if to say, "Look! I rule your Earth, from your own temple in your own city!"

Christian Aid is a leading Christian charity and missionary organization. Founded in 1945, it works in about 60 countries, focusing on the world's poorest. Here is an extensive but informative quote from Bob Finley, Christian Aid's founder and CEO:

> Since the state of Israel proclaimed its existence within a small portion of Palestine in 1948, many events have transpired in that region which have had devastating effects on tens of thousands of evangelical Christians living in 29 Islamic countries from Morocco to Indonesia. Their continued suffering weighs so heavily upon the missionary staff of Christian Aid that we can no longer maintain silence. We must speak up on behalf of our fellow believers whose very lives have been put in jeopardy by the endorsement of Zionism by evangelical Christians in America.
>
> Christian support for the Zionist movement began in England a century ago when a few Bible teachers began to interpret certain Old Testament prophecies regarding the ancient Hebrews as being applicable to the present day Jewish people. Apparently those teachers did not know that (according to the Universal Jewish Encyclopedia) the Ashkenazi, or Yiddish, majority of Jewish people originally came from the empire of Khazaria in Southern Russia and are not biologically related to Abraham. So when a few Ashkenazi Zionists began trying to take over parts of Palestine through acts of terrorism about 70 years ago, some Christians started saying it signified the fulfillment of some obscure Old Testament prophecies.

Christians today fail to realize how such statements have had a destructive effect on our fellow believers in many parts of the world, so Christian Aid has begun to call attention to these facts. Since 1940 the Zionists have killed, driven out or displaced over two million of the original residents of Palestine. Their lands, houses and businesses have all been stolen, and most of their personal property as well. Hundreds of thousands of Palestinians fled to refugee camps in surrounding countries over a 20-year period. Yet all the while, unbelievably, some Christians in America were cheering for the Zionists, and proclaiming their atrocities as being blessed of God.

In the eyes of Palestinians and their neighbors, what the Zionists have been doing is the equivalent to what the Nazis did to 600,000 Jews in Germany 60 years before. How, then, could Christians endorse such things? Our thoughtless expressions of approval have been destructive in three ways.

1. What we have done to our fellow Christians in Islamic Lands.

When Americans speak favorably about Zionist aggression in Palestine, we bring needless persecution on multiplied thousands of our fellow believers now living in Islamic countries. Christian citizens of those countries are suspected of being in agreement with what the Americans are saying, though not one in a thousand of them are. When Muslims hear of Baptists in America praising Zionist atrocities, what are they to think of the Baptist churches in their countries? Or the Pentecostals? Or Presbyterians? How can we expect them not to retaliate against those who favor killing their fellow Muslims?

2. What we have done to missionary work among the Muslims.

Fifty years ago millions of Muslims were open to the gospel. There was a great missionary opportunity for reaching them for Christ. Muslims make up the largest segment of unreached peoples on earth, and they were very open until American Christians began to praise Zionist conquests in Palestine. Since most of the violence has been against Muslims, it is to be expected that Muslims in other countries would be sympathetic toward the victims and resentful toward the Christians who support Zionist expansion. This political development has served to cut off millions of Muslims from their previous receptivity to the gospel. For a Muslim to become a Christian today has come to mean that he would have to endorse Zionist atrocities against innocent victims. To them that's the equivalent of a Jew approving Hitler. Not one in a million would be willing to accept such a seemingly vile and evil persuasion. So accepting Christ is no longer a reasonable alternative for millions of Muslims. Our missionary opportunity among them has been ruined.

3. What Zionism has done to our churches.

Until 50 years ago most Christians accepted events recorded in the book of Joshua as something special for that particular time. We believed that the coming of the Saviour brought a New Covenant under which we no longer resort to violence to advance the kingdom of God. But when the Zionist movement began in Palestine around 1920, some Christians started to disregard New Testament principles. We would say it's wrong for us to kill our neighbor and steal his property, but if Jewish people did it in Palestine, then it was O.K. First it was thousands, then tens of thousands, and eventually hundreds of thousands of Palestinians who were driven from their homes. All of their property was stolen by the Zionists. Forty percent of the victims were professing Christians, many of whom were born again believers. Yet, to our everlasting shame, many Christians in America have stood on the sidelines and cheered for the murderers. It's all O.K., we say, because Zionism is a fulfillment of prophecy. It is hard to imagine how any Bible believer with reasonable intelligence could endorse such things, particularly when so many thousands of conscientious Jews the world over have objected strenuously to Zionist aggression in Palestine.

Some of our faithful friends in Christ have told us that if we dare to say anything about the tragedies that have resulted from Christians endorsing Zionist atrocities we may lose some financial support as a result. That doesn't bother me. My Bible says, "We must obey God rather than men." (Acts 5:29)

Faithfully yours in Him,
Bob Finley
Chairman and CEO[134]

I disagree with Finley only when he says American evangelicals have "endorsed Zionist atrocities." I would instead say they endorsed Zionism without conscious *knowledge* of the atrocities, which the U.S. media suppressed. We will discuss those atrocities momentarily, but let's first address Finley's remark: "the Ashkenazi, or Yiddish, majority of Jewish people originally came from the empire of Khazaria in Southern Russia and are not biologically related to Abraham."

The Khazar Connection

According to the Bible, the Hebrews, who inhabited ancient Israel, were descended from Abraham. Jews today are widely considered their descendants. Arthur Koestler was a Jewish Pulitzer Prize-winning author. In his book *The Thirteenth Tribe*, he demonstrated that the vast majority—perhaps 90 percent—of those now calling themselves Jews are descended from Khazaria, not the ancient Hebrews.

How can this be? Khazaria (Figure 13) was a kingdom just north of the Black and Caspian seas, in what is now southern Russia.

The Khazars were pagans, but in 740 AD the kagan (ruler) of Khazaria converted the entire nation to Judaism. You can look this up in *Wikipedia*. It wasn't a matter of personal, individual conversions; Judaism became the state religion. Details on how this happened are sketchy. Quoting Koestler:

Figure 13

At the beginning of the eighth century the world was polarized between the two super-powers representing Christianity and Islam. Their ideological doctrines were welded to power-politics pursued by the classical methods of propaganda, subversion and military conquest. The Khazar Empire represented a Third Force, which had proved equal to either of them, both as an adversary and an ally. But it could only maintain its independence by accepting neither Christianity nor Islam—for either choice would have automatically subordinated it to the authority of the Roman Emperor or the Caliph of Baghdad.

There had been no lack of efforts by either court to convert the Khazars to Christianity or Islam, but all they resulted in was the exchange of diplomatic courtesies, dynastic inter-marriages and shifting military alliances based on mutual self-interest. Relying on its military strength, the Khazar kingdom, with its hinterland of vassal tribes, was determined to preserve its position as the Third Force, leader of the uncommitted nations of the steppes.

At the same time, their intimate contacts with Byzantium [Christianity] and the Caliphate had taught the Khazars that their primitive shamanism was not only barbaric and outdated compared to the great monotheistic creeds, but also unable to confer on the leaders the spiritual and legal authority which the leaders of the two theocratic world powers, the Caliph and the Emperor, enjoyed. Yet the conversion to either creed would have meant submission, the end of independence, and thus would have defeated its purpose. What could have been more logical than to embrace a third creed, which was uncommitted towards either of the two, yet represented the venerable foundation of both?[135]

According to one ancient account, Khazaria's king received envoys from both Constantinople and the Caliph. As paraphrased by Koestler:

He convokes the discutants separately. He asks the Christian which of the other two religions is nearer the truth, and the Christian answers, "the Jews." He confronts the Muslim with the same question and gets the same reply. Neutralism has once more carried the day.[136]

Though details are imprecise, it is indisputable that Khazaria converted to Judaism. Rabbis were brought from abroad to teach the people the Judaic religion and traditions. A number of Jews, fleeing persecution elsewhere, immigrated to the kingdom, bringing further influence.[137]

What became of Khazaria? Over centuries, the empire gradually crumbled due to invasions, culminating with the Mongol onslaught in the 1200s. The Khazarians, still calling themselves Jews, fled eastward and settled in Eastern Europe, especially Poland, becoming most of whom we call the modern European Jews. They spoke Yiddish and became ethnically identified as *Ashkenazi* Jews. Light skinned, they contrast to *Sephardic* Jews, a minority among Jews today. Sephardim, whom many consider the Israelites' real descendants, are darker skinned and more resemble

Arabs, as one might expect, since true Jews and Arabs both have Abraham as their ancestor.

Some genetic studies have validated this distinction between Ashkenazi and Sephardic. For example, in 2003 the *New York Times* reported:

> A team of geneticists studying the ancestry of Jewish communities has found an unusual genetic signature that occurs in more than half the Levites of Ashkenazi descent. The signature is thought to have originated in Central Asia, not the Near East, which is the ancestral home of Jews. The finding raises the question of how the signature became so widespread among the Levites, an ancient caste of hereditary Jewish priests.
>
> The genetic signature occurs on the male or Y chromosome and comes from a few men, or perhaps a single ancestor, who lived about 1,000 years ago, just as the Ashkenazim were beginning to be established in Europe. Ashkenazim, from whom most American Jews descend, are one of the two main branches of Jews, the other being the Sephardim, whose ancestors were expelled from Spain.
>
> The new report, published in the current issue of the American Journal of Human Genetics, was prepared by population geneticists in Israel, the United States and England, who have been studying the genetics of Jewish communities for the last six years. They say that 52 percent of Levites of Ashkenazi origin have a particular genetic signature that originated in Central Asia, although it is also found less frequently in the Middle East. The ancestor who introduced it into the Ashkenazi Levites could perhaps have been from the Khazars, a Turkic tribe whose king converted to Judaism in the eighth or ninth century, the researchers suggest.[138]

However, there are also genetic studies suggesting that Ashkenazim trace their ancestry to the Middle East, not Asia. A website that quotes many scientific journal articles, on both sides of the debate, is www.khazaria.com/genetics/abstracts-diseases.html.

Perhaps a factor in the contradictory findings is that Jews lived among the Khazars, probably leading to some genetic mixing.

Before proceeding, let me make it clear: No one calling themselves Jewish should ever be doubted as to whether they are a "true Jew." Aside from the fact that proving or disproving someone's ancient lineage would be difficult if not impossible, this book has not the remotest intention of raising such personal questions.

However, the confluence of Khazaria and Zionism may have significant historical and Biblical implications. The prophetic book of Revelation says:

> I know the slander of those who say they are Jews and are not, but are a synagogue of Satan. (Rev 2:9)

> I will make those who are of the synagogue of Satan, who claim to be Jews though they are not, but are liars—I will make them come and fall down at your feet and acknowledge that I have loved you. (Rev 3:9)

Some Bible expositors relate these verses to comments made by Paul, the Jewish Apostle, who spoke of Jews who were circumcised in the flesh, but not in heart—i.e., Jews ethnically, but not spiritually. In Romans 2:28 he said:

> A man is not a Jew if he is only one outwardly, nor is circumcision merely outward and physical. No, a man is a Jew if he is one inwardly; and circumcision is circumcision of the heart, by the Spirit, not by the written code.

However, could Revelation have *literally* referred to people claiming to be Jews who are not? From a Biblical perspective, who were the Khazars?

In *The Thirteenth Tribe*, Koestler notes: "A Georgian chronicle, echoing an ancient tradition, identifies them with the hosts of Gog and Magog."[139]

Ibn Fadlan, a 10th century Arab traveler, wrote: "Some are of the opinion that Gog and Magog are the Khazars."[140]

The ninth century Westphalian monk Christian Druthmar

recorded: "There exist people under the sky in regions where no Christians can be found, whose name is Gog and Magog; among them is one, called the Gazari [Khazars], who are circumcised and observe Judaism in its entirety."[141]

Josephus, the famed first century Jewish historian, wrote: "Magog founded those that from him were named Magogites, but who by the Greeks are called Scythians."[142] *Webster's New World Dictionary* defines "Scythia" as "Ancient region centered about the north coast of the Black Sea" (i.e., Khazaria).

Biblically, Gog and Magog figure prominently in two books—Revelation and Ezekiel. Revelation 20:7-8 states that, in the final days, they will surround Jerusalem:

> When the thousand years are over, Satan will be released from his prison and will go out to deceive the nations in the four corners of the Earth—Gog and Magog—to gather them for battle. In number they are like the sands of the seashore. They marched across the breadth of the earth and surrounded the camp of God's people, the city he loves. But fire came down from heaven and devoured them.

According to Ezekiel 39:1-2, ancient Gog and Magog were north of Israel:

> "Son of Man, prophesy against Gog and say: 'This is what the Sovereign Lord says: I am against you, O Gog, chief Prince of Meshech and Tubal. I will turn you around and drag you along. I will bring you from the far north and send you against the mountains of Israel.'"

Over recent decades, pop theologians like Hal Lindsey interpreted Gog and Magog as the Soviet Union. After all, it was north of Israel, had state-mandated atheism, and, as a weapons supplier to Arab countries, was Israel's purported enemy. What more logical nation to fulfill Biblical prophecies? Would it not produce the Antichrist, invade Israel, and ultimately be vanquished by God? With the Soviet Union's fall, many Christians began doubting this theory, but most remain convinced that Biblical Israel has been restored, while speculation continues on Gog and Magog's identity.

I'll make a controversial suggestion: the prophecy of Revelation 20:7-8 has already been fulfilled. Satan, freed from his prison, went out to deceive the nations, *through the very means and events this book has been describing.* And Israel's invasion has already occurred, under the noses of theologians awaiting it. Gog and Magog are the Khazarians' descendants, whom Zionism gathered from around the Earth to occupy Israel.

I realize this raises many questions. Very intelligent objections, based on Scripture, can be made against my suggestion. We will address some of those later (especially in Appendix IV), but for now let's put them on hold to keep our narrative moving.

Israel in the International Arena

Many assume that Jews worldwide support Zionism and modern Israel. This is not the case. For example, Neturei Karta (www.nkusa.org) is an organization of Orthodox, Torah-believing Jews resolutely opposed to them. In the *New York Times* it declared:

> Far from being a cause of celebration, the birth of the Zionist state is to be deplored, a state which we know to be conceived in atheism, based on materialism, nurtured by antisemitism, led by Marxism, ruled by chauvinism, trusting in militarism.[143]

We typically view Israel as the underdog of the Middle East. Here's this tiny country, surrounded by hostile states, that somehow survives. But Israel is no more an underdog than six men, armed with submachine guns, would be if they invaded a wedding banquet. New Jersey's *Star-Ledger* reported in 2002:

> Israel can field 19 divisions of ground troops; the United States boasts 13 divisions worldwide. Israel's Air Force, which flies souped-up U.S. F-15 and F-16 fighters, can generate 3,000 sorties, or combat missions, per day. The United States can sustain about 1,600 per day. "We have created an 800-pound gorilla," says Kenneth Browser, a

military consultant in Washington, assessing decades of US military aid to Israel.[144]

Due to its involvement in Middle East wars, U.S. military strength has increased since the above enumerations, but the comparison remains apt. Israel has about 4,000 tanks and 400 combat aircraft. When did you last hear of Palestinians piloting tanks or warplanes? The U.S. media consistently play up stories of suicide bombers crossing into Israel, but never mention that the unarmed Palestinians have few other means of fighting back against Israel's state-of-the-art weapons, funded by American taxpayers. Since 1976, Israel has been the single largest recipient of U.S. military aid, currently about $3 billion annually.

The United States went to war with Iraq over weapons of mass destruction (WMDs) that were never found. Now there's talk of war with Iran over mere *potential* WMDs (based on Iran's enrichment of plutonium). President Bush cited Iraq and then Iran for violating UN regulations and refusing UN weapons inspections. But *Israel has hundreds of nuclear weapons and refuses to let the UN inspect them.* The American government looks the other way.

☺ That's OK, Jim, because Arabs are *bad guys* and our *terrorist enemies*, whereas Israelis are *good guys* and our *peace-loving friends*.

That's how the media have stereotyped them. I submit that the reality is different.

Why do many Arabs hate the Israelis? First, as we discussed, the Arabs fought for the land during World War I, only to discover that Britain had secretly promised it to the Zionists.

When Israel was officially created in 1948, the UN set strict boundaries on its territory. But it has since occupied the Gaza Strip and West Bank. (See Figure 14.)

It acquired this territory by *force*. For documentation of this, and of the countless atrocities and massacres committed against the Palestinians, I urge readers to consult *The Encyclopedia of the Palestinian Problem*, written by Palestinian Christian Issa Nakhleh. It is available online.

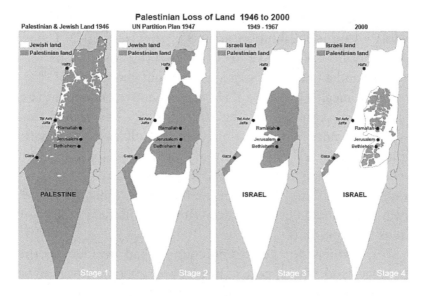

Figure 14

☹ But the Arabs won't recognize Israel's right to exist!

Israel gained recognition when she signed the Oslo Accords; in return she agreed to withdraw from the occupied territories. As du Berrier notes:

> It appears to have dawned on no one that Jordan, Egypt, Morocco and Syria, who wanted to destroy Israel when the nation was founded, agreed in Oslo to recognize Israel's right to exist. Other Moslem states were ready to follow. All Israel had to do to make acceptance general and peace permanent was to cease colonizing and pull her settlements out of the Golan Heights, the West Bank and the Gaza Strip.[145]

But when Benjamin Netanyahu became prime minister, he discarded the Oslo Accords, re-igniting Arab hostility toward Israel.

The United States has repeatedly demanded that Iraq and Iran comply with UN resolutions. President Bush cited UN Security Council Resolution 1441 as his legal justification for the Iraq War. On October 31, 2002, he declared in a speech: "America will be making only one determination: is Iraq meeting the terms of the Security Council resolution or not?"[146] Before the UN General Assembly he asked: "Are Security Council resolutions to be honored and enforced, or cast aside without consequence?"[147]

Yet ironically, while the UN has frequently condemned Israel for violating agreements, the United States has vetoed those resolutions more than forty times, consistently as the *only* nation siding with Israel. For a summary of these vetoes, see www. jewishvirtuallibrary.org/jsource/UN/usvetoes.html. This flagrant double standard, together with the billions in military aid we've given Israel, should help Americans understand the hostility some Arabs feel toward us.

If we Americans heard one country had invaded another, seizing its land, we'd oppose it. In 1991 we supposedly went to war to save Kuwait from Iraq. Yet Israeli invasions and conquests hardly bother anybody in America—especially Christians. Why?

☺ Jim, the Israelis are God's chosen people—Abraham's seed. In the Old Testament, God promised them this land. Who are we to defy God?

The old Covenant was superseded by the new one under Christ; furthermore, most of these people are apparently *not* descendants of Abraham, but of the Khazars, and therefore have no conceivable claim to the land.

☺ But the Bible sometimes mentions people converting to Judaism. If the Khazars converted …

So let me get this straight. An Irishman goes to Palestine. He finds an Arab's house and vineyard attractive. So he says, "I hereby convert to Judaism. Give me your house and your land, or I'll blow your head off with God's blessing."

☺ But Jim, I've been on trips to the Holy Land. Israel is so nice to us Christians!

Sure—and largely for political motives. Christians constitute a powerful voting bloc. The *Jerusalem Post* observed in 1983:

The real Zionists in the U.S. are not the American Jews but the Christian evangelicals since these Christians feel that we are coming closer to a critical period in history and they want the Jews to fulfill prophecies and thus hasten the Second Coming of the Messiah. The evangelicals affect 20 million people a day in America. They are a great asset *and must be used as such.*[148]

Jack Bernstein, an American Jew who lived in Israel, wrote:

Tourism is one of Israel's main sources of income. The largest group of visitors are American Jews. But, there are also many American Christians who want to visit the holy shrines and to see the land of "God's Chosen People." These Christians come away very impressed and filled with religious fervor.

While in Israel, Jews and Gentiles alike are carefully watched so that they do not stray and happen to see the sordid side of Israel—the true Israel. Like in Soviet Russia and other communist countries, visitors to Israel are taken on carefully planned guided tours. They are shown the religious sites, the universities, the lush orchards, the technical accomplishments, the arts, and to stir sympathy, they are taken to visit the Holocaust Museum.

But, kept from the eyes of the tourists are the ghettos, the prisons where political prisoners, mostly Arabs and Sephardic Jews, are subjected to the most inhumane forms of torture. The tourists do not see the widespread crime activities and the corruption and cooperation between organized crime bosses and government and police officials. The tourists do not learn of the true inner workings of Israel's Marxist/Fascist government; nor do they see Israel's racism.

I met one American tourist who couldn't help telling me about the wonderful religious feeling she had from being in Israel—the Holy Land. I remarked to her, "Just try giving a Bible to a local Jew and you will see how much religion and religious freedom there is in Israel. If seen by the police, you will be arrested."[149]

Palestinian scholar Sami Hadawi, former director of the Institute of Palestine Studies in Beirut, commented:

> For succor they [the Israelis] turned their attention to evangelical Christians and found support among some who were willing to sell their soul to the devil for thirty pieces of silver. Dangling fame and the dollar before their eyes with free trips to the Holy Land, the honor of being photographed with Israeli leaders as well as adequate financial means to maintain a comfortable way of life for themselves, the misguided and corrupt among them have turned Christianity into a lucrative business . . . . and conduct tours of the Holy Land under the guise of visiting holy sites but the real purpose behind these is to influence Christians in favor of Israel.[150]

Friendship Israel offers America is pragmatic. The history of Israeli tactics reveals it is more enemy than ally.

The False Friend

After World War II, the British continued governing Palestine, with their administrative, military and police headquarters in Jerusalem's King David Hotel. Zionists wanted Britain to exit Palestine so they could proclaim Israel a nation. In 1946, members of Irgun, an Israeli terrorist group, entered the King David *dressed as Arabs*. They brought in explosives, concealed in milk cans, and blew up the hotel, leaving 91 dead and many others mutilated. This was one of numerous Zionist terrorist acts against the British, who got the message and departed.

The USS *Liberty* was an American reconnaissance ship, unarmed except for four 50-caliber machine guns, serving with the U.S. 6th fleet in the Mediterranean. During the 1967 Six Day War between Israel and her Arab neighbors, it was stationed in international waters off the Egyptian coast. Israel's air force and navy attempted to sink the *Liberty*. First their unmarked planes (bearing no Israeli insignia) hammered the ship with rockets, cannons, and napalm. They especially targeted the *Liberty*'s communication antennas; after destroying these, they sent in torpedo boats to finish the job. Five torpedoes were launched; one struck the ship, which had taken evasive action. In the meantime, *Liberty* crew members patched together some communications equipment, and got off a message to the 6th fleet that they were under attack. The aircraft carrier *Saratoga* replied that warplanes were on the way. The Israelis, apparently having overheard the communications, ceased attacking and fled. However, unknown to both the *Liberty* and her assailants, U.S. warplanes were *not* on their way. Defense Secretary Robert McNamara had ordered Rear Admiral Geis, commander of the task force which included the *Saratoga*, to recall them. As John E. Borne relates in *The USS Liberty: Dissenting History vs. Official History*:

> The first rescue flight was canceled on direct orders by radio from Secretary of Defense McNamara, who ordered a 90-minute delay before any further flights. When the second flight took off at 1550 (having waited 90 minutes as ordered) Geis notified McNamara, who again ordered the recall of the flights. Any officer who doubts the wisdom of an order he has received has the prerogative to ask that the order be confirmed by a yet-higher officer, and Geis availed himself of that right. Since he was questioning the order of the Secretary of Defense, the only man superior to the Secretary was the President. President Johnson himself came on the radio and ordered Geis to recall the flights because "we are not going to embarrass an ally."[151]

The attack left 34 Americans dead and 173 wounded. The Israelis announced that they had misidentified the *Liberty* as an Egyptian transport ship, *El-Quseir*. This was implausible. The planes made many passes over the ship before commencing the assault. *Liberty* was approximately twice the size of *El-Quseir*; its markings were in English, not Arabic; and it flew an American flag. When that flag was shot down, the crew raised a huge ceremonial America flag.

Admiral Thomas H. Moorer, former Chief of Naval Operations and Chairman of the Joint Chiefs of Staff, stated:

> Despite claims by Israeli intelligence that they confused the *Liberty* with a small Egyptian transport, the *Liberty* was conspicuously different from any vessel in the Egyptian navy. It was the most sophisticated intelligence ship in the world in 1967. With its massive radio antennae, including a large satellite dish, it looked like a large lobster and was one of the most easily identifiable ships afloat.[152]

Nevertheless, the United States government rubber-stamped Israel's explanation. As *Liberty* survivor Richard Sturman relates:

> Disgracefully, before awarding the Congressional Medal of Honor to our Commanding Officer for his heroic deeds our government first asked the government of the State of Israel if they had any objections. The Medal of Honor was then presented in a Washington, D.C. Naval Shipyard by the Secretary of the Navy. Hours later, then-President Lyndon Johnson awarded similar Medals of Honor at the White House with all the pomp and circumstance accorded the recipient of our country's highest award for valor. Furthermore, Captain McGonagle is the only recipient of the Congressional Medal of Honor in United States history who has not been accorded White House recognition. So not to embarrass the State of Israel for their attacking the USS *Liberty*, there is no mention in Captain McGonagle's Medal of Honor Citation or in any Citation awarded the USS *Liberty* and her crew as to the identity of our attackers. A practice unheard of in American military awards.[153]

Also unprecedented for an attack of this magnitude: Congress never investigated the incident. The Navy's investigation was limited to one week. The following is excerpted from the 2004 declaration of Ward Boston, Jr., chief counsel to the Naval Court of Inquiry; for the full text see http://www.ussliberty.org/bostondeclaration.pdf.

Declaration of Ward Boston, Jr., Captain, JAGC, USN (Ret.)

I, Ward Boston, Jr. do declare that the following statement is true and complete:

For more than 30 years, I have remained silent on the topic of USS *Liberty*. I am a military man and when orders come in from the Secretary of Defense and President of the United States, I follow them.

However, recent attempts to rewrite history compel me to share the truth.

In June of 1967, while serving as a Captain in the Judge Advocate General Corps, Department of the Navy, I was assigned as senior legal counsel for the Navy's Court of Inquiry into the brutal attack on USS *Liberty*, which had occurred on June 8th.

The late Admiral Isaac C. Kidd, president of the Court, and I were given only one week to gather evidence for the Navy's official investigation into the attack, despite the fact that we both had estimated that a proper Court of Inquiry into an attack of this magnitude would take at least six months to conduct. . . .

Despite the short amount of time we were given, we gathered a vast amount of evidence, including hours of heartbreaking testimony from the young survivors.

The evidence was clear. Both Admiral Kidd and I believed with certainty that this attack, which killed 34 American sailors and injured 172 others, was a deliberate effort to sink an American ship and murder its entire crew. Each evening, after hearing testimony all day, we often spoke our private thoughts concerning what we had seen and heard. I recall Admiral Kidd repeatedly referring to the Israeli forces responsible for the attack as "murderous bastards." It was our shared belief, based on the documentary evidence and testimony we received first hand, that the Israeli attack was planned and deliberate, and could not possibly have been an accident.

I am certain that the Israeli pilots that undertook the attack, as well as their superiors, who had ordered the attack, were well aware that the ship was American.

I saw the flag, which had visibly identified the ship as American, riddled with bullet holes, and heard testimony that made it clear that the Israelis intended there be no survivors.

Not only did the Israelis attack the ship with napalm, gunfire, and missiles, Israeli torpedo boats machine-gunned three lifeboats that had been launched in an attempt by the crew to save the most seriously wounded—a war crime. . . .

I know from personal conversations I had with Admiral Kidd that President Lyndon Johnson and Secretary of Defense Robert McNamara ordered him to conclude that the attack was a case of mistaken identity despite overwhelming evidence to the contrary.

Admiral Kidd told me, after returning from Washington, D.C. that he had been ordered to sit down with two civilians from either the White House or the Defense Department, and rewrite portions of the court's findings.

Admiral Kidd also told me that he had been ordered to put the lid on everything having to do with the attack on USS *Liberty*. We were never to speak of it and we were to caution everyone else involved that they could never speak of it again.[154]

Air Force intelligence analyst Steven Forslund stated in a formal declaration:

On the day of the attack on the *Liberty*, I read yellow teletype sheets that spewed from the machines in front of me all day. We obtained our input from a variety of sources including the NSA [National Security Agency]. The teletypes were raw translations of Israeli air-to-air and air-to-ground communications between jet aircraft and their ground controller. I read page after page of these transcripts that day as it went on and on. The transcripts made specific reference to the efforts to direct the jets to the target which was identified as American numerous times by the ground controller. Upon arrival, the aircraft specifically identified the target and mentioned the American flag she was flying. There were frequent operational transmissions from the pilots to the ground base describing the strafing runs. The ground control began asking about the status of the target and whether it was sinking. They stressed that the target must be sunk and leave no trace.[155]

Air Force intelligence analyst James Ronald Gotcher, also on duty that day, has testified:

> We received a CRITIC message, informing us that USS *Liberty* was under attack by Israeli aircraft. Shortly thereafter, we began receiving rough translations of the Israeli air to air and air to ground communications. . . . It was clear from the explicit statements made by both the aircraft crews and the controllers that the aircraft were flying a planned mission to find and sink USS *Liberty*. My understanding of what I read led me to conclude that the Israeli pilots were making every effort possible to sink USS *Liberty* and were very frustrated by their inability to do so. Approximately ten days to two weeks later, we received an internal NSA report, summarizing the Agency's findings. The report stated in, in no uncertain terms, that the attack was planned in advance and deliberately executed. The mission was to sink USS *Liberty*. A few days after the report arrived, another message came through directing the document control officer to gather and destroy all copies of both the rough and final intercept transmissions, as well as the subsequently issued report. After the destruction of these documents, I saw nothing further on the subject.[156]

Navy communications technician Harold Cobbs has testified:

> I arrived in Morocco, July of 1967. I was young and new to the NSG world. While performing my duties on base, I was a witness to the collection and order to destroy ALL traffic regarding the attack on the USS *Liberty*. Not wanting to

believe what I had just seen and heard, I made the comment to comm officer, Lieutenant Rogers, "That's just not right!" Upon making the above comment I received a severe lecture regarding the following of direct orders.[157]

The *Liberty*'s survivors maintain a website, www.gtr5.com, which I urge you to visit.

Now the paramount question: Why attack the *Liberty*? This was to be another *Maine*, another *Lusitania*, Pearl Harbor, Tonkin Gulf. The plan was to sink the *Liberty* with no survivors. That's why the Israelis even machine-gunned the inflatable lifeboats. They flew in unmarked planes because, if successful, the attack would have been blamed on the Arabs. The intention was probably to then bring the U.S. into the Six Day War on Israel's side, guaranteeing victory.

In 1986, U.S. soldiers were frequenting a Berlin discotheque called *La Belle*. One night a bomb tore through it, killing two American servicemen and wounding over 50 others. U.S. intelligence then intercepted radio messages, originating in Libya, that congratulated alleged perpetrators of the crime. The incident outraged many Americans. I myself called the White House opinion line and said, "How long will the United States tolerate this kind of thing?" President Reagan sent bombers which struck Libya. The adopted daughter of Libyan leader Muammar al-Gaddafi was killed in those raids.

Victor Ostrovsky is a former agent of the Mossad, Israel's intelligence service. In his book *The Other Side of Deception*, Ostrovsky revealed that the Mossad originated the radio signals from Libya, completely deceiving U.S. intelligence:

> A Trojan was a special communication device that could be planted by naval commandos deep inside enemy territory. The device would act as a relay station for misleading transmissions made by the disinformation unit in the Mossad, called LAP [LohAma Psicologit—psychological warfare], and intended to be received by American and British listening stations. Originating from an IDF navy ship out at sea, the prerecorded

digital transmissions could be picked up only by the Trojan. The device would then rebroadcast the transmission on another frequency, one used for official business in the enemy country, at which point the transmission would finally be picked up by American ears in Britain.

The listeners would have no doubt they had intercepted a genuine communication, hence the name Trojan, reminiscent of the mythical Trojan horse. Further, the content of the messages, once deciphered, would confirm information from other intelligence sources, namely the Mossad. The only catch was that the Trojan itself would have to be located as close as possible to the normal origin of such transmissions, because of the sophisticated methods of triangulation the Americans and others would use to verify the source.[158]

After detailing how the Mossad succeeded in planting a Trojan in a Tripoli apartment in 1986, Ostrovsky describes the results:

> By the end of March, the Americans were already intercepting messages broadcast by the Trojan, which was only activated during heavy communication traffic hours. Using the Trojan, the Mossad tried to make it appear that a long series of terrorist orders were being transmitted to various Libyan embassies around the world . . . . As the Mossad had hoped, the transmissions were deciphered by the Americans and construed as ample proof that the Libyans were active sponsors of terrorism. What's more, the Americans pointed out, Mossad reports confirmed it. . . .
>
> Heads of the Mossad were counting on the American promise to retaliate with vengeance against any country that could be proven to support terrorism. The Trojan gave the Americans the proof they needed.
>
> The Mossad also plugged into the equation Qadhafi's lunatic image and momentous declarations, which were really only meant for internal consumption. . . .
>
> Ultimately, the Americans fell for the Mossad ploy head over heels, dragging the British and the Germans somewhat reluctantly in with them. Operation Trojan was one of the

Mossad's greatest successes. It brought about the air strike on Libya that President Reagan had promised . . . . [159]

In the 1946 King David Hotel bombing, the 1967 *Liberty* incident, and the 1986 Libyan Trojan operation, we see a clear pattern to Israeli strategy: deceive America and Britain into thinking *Arabs* had attacked them. And the worst was yet to come.

CHAPTER 14
9-11

Zionism: The Link Continues

On the day of the World Trade Center bombings, CNN reported that a group of Middle Eastern-looking men had been spotted celebrating the attack. They were dancing, high-fiving each other, and photographing themselves against the backdrop of the burning buildings. They then took off in a white van. Neighbors wrote down the license number and gave it to police. An all-points bulletin was put out for the vehicle. Later that day, CNN reported that the men in the van had been apprehended. And then ... nothing more was said. The American media dropped the story. However, Scotland's *Sunday Herald* did not. It reported:

> There was terror and ruin in Manhattan, but, over the Hudson River in New Jersey, a handful of men were dancing. As the World Trade Centre burned and crumpled, the five men filmed the worst atrocity ever committed on American soil as it played out before their eyes.
>
> Who do you think they were? Palestinians? Saudis? Iraqis, even? Al-Qaeda, surely? Wrong on all counts. They were Israelis—and at least two of them were Israeli intelligence agents, working for Mossad, the equivalent of MI6 or the CIA.[160]

The FBI detained the men, but since they were from "friendly" Israel, and the crime was attributed to Al-Qaida, they were deported back to Israel after less than two months.

But a critical question had been left unanswered. On 9-11, we didn't yet know who had attacked us—the FBI announced that two days later. So why were Mossad agents *already celebrating* on the day of the tragedy? At the very least, it means they knew about the attacks, and knew that America was therefore about to deepen its alliance with Israel. At the most, it means Mossad was directly involved with the 9-11 atrocities.

There are coincidences related to 9-11; any one, by itself, would mean little. Collectively, they raise serious concerns.

Supported by funds from Israel's government, Zim Israel Navigational was the world's ninth largest shipping firm. The only Israeli company operating in the World Trade Center, it had its American headquarters there—*until one week before 9-11*. Zim then moved its offices, with all 200 employees, to a new building, claiming rent was cheaper there. This could be dismissed as lucky coincidence if it stood alone—but it doesn't.

When police detectives try to solve a murder, among the first questions they ask is: Who benefitted from the crime? In 9-11's case, Middle Eastern Muslim extremists did not benefit—the U.S. is making war on them. America did not benefit—we're suffering the casualties and other costs of wars in Iraq and Afghanistan. The true *beneficiary* is Israel—her enemies were neutralized, courtesy America, with Iran reputedly next on the hit list.

The Iraq war was foreseen before 9-11. Syndicated columnist Pat Buchanan was an advisor to Presidents Nixon, Ford and Reagan, and was himself the Reform Party's Presidential candidate in 2000. He wrote in 2004:

> In 1996, in a strategy paper crafted for Israel's Benjamin Netanyahu, Richard Perle, Douglas Feith and David Wurmser urged him to "focus on removing Saddam Hussein from power" as an "Israeli strategic objective." Perle, Feith, Wurmser were all on Bush's foreign policy team on 9-11.
>
> In 1998, eight members of Bush's future team, including Perle, Wolfowitz and Rumsfeld, wrote President Clinton urging upon him a strategy that "should aim, above all, at the removal of Saddam Hussein."
>
> On Jan. 1, 2001, nine months before 9-11, Wurmser called for U.S.-Israeli attacks "to broaden the [Middle East] conflict

to strike fatally ... the regimes of Damascus, Baghdad, Tripoli, Teheran and Gaza ... to establish the recognition that fighting with either the United States or Israel is suicidal."

"Crises can be opportunities," added Wurmser.

On Sept. 11, opportunity struck.[161]

Consider some of the men Buchanan mentioned:

In 1970, the National Security Agency caught Richard Perle spying on the U.S. for Israel. Unlike Jonathan Pollard, who got life imprisonment for very similar espionage, Perle was not even prosecuted, and allowed to keep working for the U.S. government, ultimately serving as chairman of George W. Bush's Defense Policy Board.

Douglas Feith, Bush's Undersecretary of Defense Policy, is an ardent Zionist; the Zionist Organization of America has honored him with its prestigious Louis D. Brandeis award.

Paul Wolfowitz, another Zionist—he spent a year in Israel as a teenager—was Bush's Deputy Secretary of Defense. He went on to head the World Bank, not an uncommon destination for top government officials after compliantly serving the Establishment.

Perle and Wolfowitz took part in the Project for a New American Century. In September 2000—one year before 9-11—it issued a paper entitled "Rebuilding America's Defenses," which called for an increased U.S. military presence overseas, especially the Middle East. But, it warned: "The process of transformation, even if it brings revolutionary change, is likely to be a long one, absent some catastrophic and catalyzing event—like a new Pearl Harbor."[162]

So we know that, before 9-11, these men wanted to remove Saddam, intimidate other Muslim nations, and bolster Israel; and that they believed a "crisis" or "new Pearl Harbor" would avail these goals. But does any evidence show 9-11 was more than what the government said?

What Brought Down the Towers?

An outstanding video on the 1995 Oklahoma City bombing is *A Noble Lie*, available at www.anoblelie.com. Shortly after the 1995 Oklahoma City bombing, numerous eyewitness reports affirmed the discovery and removal of unexploded bombs from the Alfred P. Murrah building. These reports include affidavits from witnesses, emergency personnel, and Murrah building employees, as well as transcripts of police, FEMA and Defense Department reports. Copies of these are online at http://whatreallyhappened. com/RANCHO/POLITICS/OK/bombs/bombs.html. An extremely strong case has been made that the car bomb attributed to Timothy McVeigh and Terry Nichols could not possibly have done all the destruction. It was assisted by planted explosives; the failure of some of these to detonate explains why the Murrah building damage was asymmetrical. Many think this relevant to 9-11, because evidence also exists that the Twin Towers did not collapse from the planes alone.

Ted Gunderson, former senior special agent-in-charge of the FBI's Los Angeles office, stated: "I have witnesses who saw and heard systematic, simultaneous explosions on the top floors of the World Trade Center towers before they collapsed."[163] Let's quote a few witnesses who were at the scene:

• "It seemed like on television, they blow up these buildings. It seemed like it was going all the way around like a belt, all these explosions." –Rick Banaciski, New York City Fire Dept.

• "I figured it was a bomb, because it looked like a synchronized deliberate kind of thing." –Kennith Rogers, New York City Fire Dept.

• "Do you ever see professional demolition where they set the charges on certain floors and then you hear, 'Pop, pop, pop, pop, pop'? That's exactly what—because I thought it was that." –Daniel Rivera, paramedic, Battalion 31.

• It was weird how it started to come down. It looked like it was a timed explosion . . . ." –Dominick Derubbio, New York City Fire Dept.[164]

The original, official government explanation for the Twin Towers' collapse was that burning jet fuel melted the buildings' steel beams, causing the floors to "pancake" down on each other. In 2005, a report of the government's National Institute of Standards and Technology amended this, saying the buildings core columns had "failed."

According to the report, WTC 1 collapsed in approximately 11 seconds; WTC 2 in nine. By contrast, if a billiard ball had been dropped from the top of WTC 1 (1368 feet), falling in a vacuum (without even wind resistance), it would have hit the pavement in 9.22 seconds. In other words, the Twin Towers collapsed at approximately the speed of gravity. Many experts find this not credible, since the buildings' powerful steel structures should have slowed the falls.

John Skilling, the World Trade Center's chief structural engineer, said the buildings were designed to absorb the impact of a Boeing 707 (not much smaller than the 767s that actually struck them).[165] In January 2001, World Trade Center construction manager Frank A. Demartini said:

> The building was designed to have a fully loaded 707 crash into it. That was the largest plane at the time. I believe the building could probably sustain multiple impacts of jetliners because this structure is like the mosquito netting on your screen door—this intense grid—and the jet plane is just a pencil puncturing that screen netting. It really does nothing to the screen netting.[166]

To melt, steel must reach a temperature of about 2800 degrees Fahrenheit. Jet fuel burns at a maximum of 1500 degrees, and most experts concur that the World Trade Center flames probably didn't exceed 500-600 degrees. Exposure to such flames wouldn't melt the buildings' steel any more than your stove's gas flames will melt your pots and pans.

What *would* cause steel to melt would be detonation of the military explosive *thermite*, which reaches 4500 degrees in seconds.

It would also explain why the building's concrete pulverized into dust instead of falling in large chunks.

With over 1,700 building professionals in its ranks, Architects & Engineers for 9/11 Truth (www.ae911truth.org) <u>has documented</u> <u>overwhelming evidence that the Twin Towers' collapse resulted</u> <u>from controlled demolition,</u> which they have summarized as follows:

(1) Rapid onset of destruction

(2) Destruction occurred at near free-fall pace

(3) Destruction followed path of greatest resistance

(4) Perimeter column steel ejected laterally up to 500 feet

(5) Blast waves blew out windows in buildings 400 ft away

(6) 118 first responders report explosions at onset of destruction

(7) Numerous eyewitness reports of flowing molten metal in rubble

(8) Mid-air pulverization of concrete with *outward* arching plumes

(9) Rapid expansion & pyroclastic flow of enormous dust clouds

(10) Squibs: explosive ejections 40 stories below impact zone

(11) Total dismemberment of steel core column structures

(12) 1200 ft diameter symmetrical debris field

(13) Chemical evidence of thermate on steel and in dust samples

(14) FEMA steel analysis: sulfidation, oxidation & intergranular melting

(15) No precedent for steel frame highrise collapse caused by fire

Even if burning jet fuel did cause the Twin Towers' implosion, that theory goes out the window for Building No. 7. Part of the WTC complex, <u>this 47-story steel frame building also collapsed,</u> <u>even though no airplane touched it.</u> The government says that Twin Towers debris damaged Building No. 7, making it fall. But damage was superficial, and the building's smooth descent, which took only 6.6 seconds, looks very much like controlled demolition.

☹ But how could anyone put explosives in the World Trade Center without being detected?

This quotation may help shed light:

> My name is Scott Forbes and I still work for Fiduciary Trust. In 2001 we occupied floors 90 and 94-97 of the South Tower and lost 87 employees plus many contractors.
>
> On the weekend of 9/8, 9/9 there was a "power down" condition in WTC tower 2, the south tower. This power down condition meant there was no electrical supply for approximately 36 hours from floor 50 up. I am aware of this situation since I work in IT and had to work with many others that weekend to ensure that all systems were cleanly shut down beforehand ... and then brought back up afterwards. The reason given by the WTC for the power down was that cabling in the tower was being upgraded . . . . Of course without power there were no security cameras, no security locks on doors and many, many "engineers" coming in and out of the tower. I was at home on the morning of 9/11 on the shore of Jersey City, right opposite the Towers, and watching events unfold I was convinced immediately that something was happening related to the weekend work . . . .
>
> I have mailed this information to many people and bodies, including the 9/11 Commission, but no one seems to be taking and registering these facts. What's to hide?[167]

9-11 Oddities

Who *owned* the World Trade Center? On July 24, 2001, less than two months before the attacks, it came under new management for the first time in its history. Larry Silverstein and his partners purchased a 99-year lease for $124 million. After the tragedy he received an insurance payout of nearly $5 billion. He even successfully sued the insurers, saying the attacks should be treated as two separate incidents instead of one. Silverstein, incidentally, is a Zionist; the friend of three Israeli prime ministers, he has extensive business holdings in Israel. The company in charge of security for the WTC: Securacom. The President's brother, Marvin Bush, was a director and part owner of Securacom until 2000.

Another 9-11 anomaly was the failure of the Air Force to promptly scramble fighters. Once a commercial jet deviates off course or radio contact is lost, the FAA (Federal Aviation Administration) is supposed to immediately notify NORAD (North American Aerospace Defense Command), so it can scramble fighters to intercept it. That was standard operating procedure long before 9-11.

The first tower was struck at 8:46 AM. In just three minutes, CNN picked up the story. At 8:54, American Airlines Flight 77—which would ultimately hit the Pentagon—deviated off course and at 8:56 turned off its transponder (the device which emits an identifying signal for air traffic controllers). The second WTC tower was impacted at 9:03. At that point, everyone knew the first crash was no accident. Flight 77 did not hit the Pentagon until 9:38. Why were no fighters waiting to intercept it? The government had known America was under attack for at least 35 minutes, and it had been 44 minutes since Flight 77 veered off course for Washington. Andrews Air Force Base, with two squadrons of fighters always on alert, was only 10 miles from the Pentagon.

Government apologists have said that Flight 77 was hard to track because its transponder was off. But surely NORAD, with its ultra-sophisticated radar and satellite systems, was capable of detecting the flight. (If not, does this mean that should Russia send planes to bomb Washington, NORAD won't be able to spot them unless the Russian pilots cooperatively keep their transponders on?)

But let's assume NORAD really couldn't locate the plane. With America under attack, shouldn't fighters have been deployed *anyway* over Washington, the nation's highest defense priority? At best this was incompetence—yet no one in NORAD was demoted or reprimanded for what happened that day. Many believe the Air Force was ordered to *stand down*.

Questions also abound concerning the hijackers. The FBI positively named them just three days after the attack, though no one survived the crashes to identify them. Yet several alleged hijackers were soon found to be alive. London's *Telegraph* reported on Sept. 23, 2001:

> Their names were flashed around the world as suicide hijackers who carried out the attacks on America. But yesterday four innocent men told how their identities had been stolen. The men—all from Saudi Arabia—spoke of their shock at being mistakenly named by the FBI as suicide terrorists. None of the four was in the United States on September 11 and all are alive in their home country. The Telegraph obtained the first interviews with the men since they learned they were on the FBI's list of hijackers who died in the crashes. All four were outraged to be identified as terrorists. One has never been to America and another is a Saudi Airlines pilot who was in Tunisia at the time of the attacks. Saudi Airlines said it was considering legal action against the FBI for seriously damaging its reputation and that of its pilots.[168]

In all, at least six on the hijacker list turned up alive. As summarized with full documentation at the *9-11 Research* website (http://911research.wtc7.net/):

Abulaziz Alomari

Abulaziz Alomari was identified by the FBI as the hijacker who accompanied Mohammed Atta from the connecting flight from Portland and helped him hijack and pilot Flight 11 into the North Tower. Abulaziz told the London-based *Asharq Al-Aswat* newspaper: "The name [listed by the FBI] is my name and the birth date is the same as mine, but I am not the one who bombed the World Trade Center in New York." Saudi Embassy officials in Washington defended the innocence of Alomari, saying that his passport was stolen in 1996 and that he had reported the theft to police.

Saeed Alghamdi

Saeed Alghamdi, a Saudi Airlines pilot, was identified by the FBI as being a hijacker of Flight 93, which crashed in

Pennsylvania. Alghamdi was "shocked and furious" to learn this three days after the attack, noting that his name, place of residence, date of birth, and occupation matched those described by the FBI. "You cannot imagine what it is like to be described as a terrorist—and a dead man—when you are innocent and alive," said Alghamdi, who considered legal action against the FBI.

Salem Al-Hamzi

Al-Hamzi was identified by the FBI as one of the hijackers of Flight 77, thought to have crashed into the Pentagon. Al-Hamzi said: "I have never been to the United States and have not been out of Saudi Arabia in the past two years."

Ahmed Al-Nami

Al-Nami was identified by the FBI as one of the hijackers of Flight 93. Al-Nami said: "I'm still alive, as you can see. I was shocked to see my name mentioned by the American Justice Department. I had never heard of Pennsylvania where the plane I was supposed to have hijacked. [sic]"

Waleed Alsheri

Waleed Alsheri, a Saudi Arabian pilot, was identified by the FBI as one of the hijackers of Flight 11. Alsheri turned up in Morocco after the attack where he contacted both the Saudi and American authorities to tell them he was not involved in the attack.

Abdulrahman al-Omari

Abdulrahman al-Omari, a Saudi Airlines pilot, was identified by the FBI as one of the hijackers of Flight 11. After learning this, he visited the US consulate in Jeddah to demand an explanation.[169]

On September 21, 2001, CNN reported: "FBI director Robert Mueller has acknowledged that some of those behind last week's terror attacks may have stolen the identification of other people."[170] However, the FBI issued no corrections, nor did the 9-11 Commission investigate the controversy surrounding the hijackers' identities. Also, Arab terrorists stealing the identities of other Arabs, to pin the blame on Arabs, seems most unlikely. *Israelis* stealing them is far more credible, especially considering Israel's history of attempting to frame Arabs for atrocities against Western states.

Evidence supporting the Arab terrorist hypothesis is very limited. The government claimed it had evidence that Osama Bin Laden was the culprit, but never publicly produced it. The media mentioned "phone intercepts." But as we have seen, in 1986 the United States was deceived into attacking Libya by intercepting false messages from an Israeli Trojan.

One can imagine the sort of message Mossad would send via Trojan on 9-11: "Hello! This is Osama Bin Laden speaking! Congratulations to my fellow Al-Qaida terrorists! You have successfully carried out my orders, and destroyed the World Trade Center by flying jumbo jets into it! As you know, my fellow Muslims, the reason we committed this act of terrorism was to vent our rage over all the freedoms that Americans have!"

Here is what Bin Laden actually told the Islamic press, as reported in the Pakistani newspaper *Ummaut*, on September 22, 2001:

> I was not involved in the September 11 attacks in the United States nor did I have knowledge of the attacks. There exists a government within a government within the United States. The United States should try to trace the perpetrators of these attacks within itself; to the people who want to make the present century a century of conflict between Islam and Christianity.[171]

With the case against Bin Laden very weak, on December 13, 2001 the U.S. released a video which purported to be Bin Laden confessing to 9-11. The tape's sound was faint and garbled; Arabic experts challenged the government's translation. And the man in the tape did not look much like Bin Laden. Where did this video come from? Without providing details, the government reported that U.S. forces "found" it in a house in Jalalabad, Afghanistan—a convenient chance discovery indeed. This "evidence" had the hallmarks of being contrived and planted by an intelligence service.

Another key clue was Mohammed Atta's passport, found intact and unburned outside the WTC. Supposedly it somehow survived the explosion unscathed and floated to the ground. A far more credible explanation: it was planted. Atta had reported his passport stolen in 1999.

Also, a car attributed to the hijackers was found at Boston's Logan Airport. Inside: a Koran and a flight training manual. What were investigators to conclude from these clues?

☹ A Koran. Hmmm … These guys were Muslims!

☺ A flight training manual … Aha! Flight training *school*!

☺ Now, a Koran *with* a flight training manual … Eureka! These were Muslims *at* a flight training school!

I suggest that these were more planted clues, calculated to produce specific conclusions.

In Germany, Atta was a shy architectural student; according to his family, he was timid around girls and hated to fly. But a very different Atta appeared in America. According to eyewitnesses, on the Friday before 9-11 Atta and two other alleged hijackers went to Shukum's Oyster Bar in Hollywood, Florida, where they drank heavily, played video games and cursed. They argued with the manager over their bill, which Atta paid with a $100 bill, saying, "Of course I can pay the bill. I'm an airline pilot."[172] U.S. journalist Daniel Hopsicker, in his book *Welcome to Terrorland*, cites testimony that "Atta," in Florida, was a party animal who loved to drink, snort cocaine, and listen to rock 'n' roll.

On Sept. 14, 2001, CBS News reported:

> Three men spewed anti-American sentiments in a bar and talked of impending bloodshed the night before the terrorist

attacks on New York and Washington, a Daytona Beach strip club manager interviewed by the FBI said Thursday.

"They were talking about what a bad place America is. They said 'Wait 'til tomorrow. America is going to see bloodshed,'" said John Kap, manager of the Pink Pony and Red Eyed Jack's Sports Bar. . . .

In Daytona Beach, Kap said he told FBI investigators the men in his bar spent $200 to $300 apiece on lap dances and drinks, paying with credit cards. Kap said he gave the FBI credit card receipts, photocopied driver's licenses, a business card left by one man and a copy of the Quran—the sacred book of Islam—that was left at the bar.[173]

We were consistently told that Atta and his fellow hijackers were Islamic fundamentalists, motivated to die for their faith. Yet their lifestyle completely contradicted this thesis. What devout Muslim brings his Koran to a strip club? What operatives on a secret mission call attention to themselves by loudly arguing over bills and leaving behind their business cards? These facts do not fit the official story—they do, however, fit someone planting a trail of misleading evidence.

Rudi Dekkers ran the Florida flight school where Atta trained. In an interview with a Florida television station he said:

> When Atta was here, and I saw his face on several occasions in the building, I know that they're regular students and then I try to talk to them, it's kind of a PR. . . . I tried to communicate with him. I found out from my people that he lived in Hamburg and he spoke German. So one of the days that I saw him—I speak German myself, I'm a Dutch citizen—and I started telling him in German, "Good morning. How are you? How do you like the coffee?" and he looked at me with cold eyes, didn't react at all, and walked away.[174]

☹ Oh, it's obvious why Atta didn't respond to the greetings—he was a ruthless, cold-blooded killer.

Maybe—or perhaps this was *not* Atta, but a Mossad agent impersonating him, someone who looked the part *but couldn't understand German*—a predicament the Mossad hadn't anticipated.

Another problem: how did these "Arab terrorists" fly the planes with such accuracy? The *New York Times* profiled alleged Flight 77 terrorist Hani Hanjour:

> Mr. Hanjour, who investigators contend piloted the airliner that crashed into the Pentagon, was reported to the [Federal] aviation agency in February 2001 after instructors at his flight school in Phoenix had found his piloting skills so shoddy and his grasp of English so inadequate that they questioned whether his pilot's license was genuine. . . .
>
> Staff members characterized Mr. Hanjour as polite, meek and very quiet. But most of all, the former employee said, they considered him a very bad pilot. "I'm still to this day amazed that he could have flown into the Pentagon," the former employee said. "He could not fly at all."[175]

Hanjour was supposedly assisted by Khalid al-Mihdar and Nawaq al-Hamzi, who took flying lessons at Sorbi's Flying Club in San Diego. Sorbi's instructor Rick Garza stated: "It was like Dumb and Dumber. I mean, they were clueless. It was clear to me they weren't going to make it as pilots."[176]

Many experienced airline pilots have said they themselves could not have made the maneuver into the Pentagon—that only an ace fighter pilot could have executed it. Stan Goff, a former West Point instructor in military science, said:

> A pilot they want us to believe was trained at a puddle-jumper school for Piper Cubs and Cessnas, conducts a well-coordinated downward spiral descending the last 7,000 feet in two and a half minutes ... and flies the plane with pinpoint accuracy into the side of the Pentagon at 460 nauts. When the theory about learning to fly this well at the puddle jumper school began to lose ground, it was added that they received further training on a flight simulator. This is like saying you

prepared your teenager for her first drive on I-40 at rush hour by buying her a video driving game.[177]

The plane came in just level to the ground, yet without hitting it, at 530 miles per hour, and slammed into *the side of the Pentagon which luckily had low occupancy due to renovations.*

There were other anomalies:

When a hijacking is attempted, pilots are trained to immediately type in a 4-digit code that alerts air traffic control. None of the pilots did that.

Furthermore, there is no record of any pilots sending distress messages to air traffic control, such as "May Day!" "We're being hijacked!" or "One of our crew has been stabbed!"

Cockpits have voice recorders in their *black boxes*, but the two from the WTC were never found and flight 77's was mysteriously blank. Only flight 93's was recovered, and it has never been made public.

Also, how did the hijackers gain control of all the cockpits so easily? *Wikipedia*, summarizing news accounts of Flight 77, said: "Passenger Barbara K. Olson called her husband, United States Solicitor General Theodore Olson at the Department of Justice twice to tell him about the hijacking and to report that the passengers and pilots were held in the back of the plane ... and asked him 'What should I tell the pilot?'"[178]

We are thus led to believe the pilots meekly turned their aircraft over to hijackers, who were armed only with box cutters. Why so compliant? Six of the eight pilots had military experience, and all were in good physical condition.

One American military commentator, Colonel Donn de Grand-Pre said:

Absolutely nobody, whether armed with a razor knife, is going to take the controls away from these guys, much less overpower two of them. The absolute best defense: roll the plane over. Use the 8-click "barrel rill"; at the 4th click, you are inverted; at the 8th click you are once again upright and straight and level, total time 10 seconds.[179]

A Possible Explanation

A scenario has been proposed that resolves these anomalies: a number of analysts believe the planes were *remoted* into their targets.

The U.S. military can fly planes purely by remote control. For example, *BBC News* reported on April 24, 2001:

> An unmanned high-altitude spy plane has made aviation history by completing the first non-stop, robotic flight across the Pacific from California to Australia, US defense officials said on Tuesday. . . . The Global Hawk flies along a pre-programmed flight path, but a pilot monitors the aircraft via a sensor suite which provides infra-red and visual images.[180]

Though it is generally unpublicized, U.S. Boeing 757s and 767s were equipped to be flown by remote control. The late British aeronautical engineer Joe Vialls wrote:

> In the mid-seventies America faced a new and escalating crisis, with US commercial jets being hijacked for geopolitical purposes. Determined to gain the upper hand in this new form of aerial warfare, two American multinationals collaborated with the Defense Advanced Projects Agency (DARPA) on a project designed to facilitate the remote recovery of hijacked American aircraft. Brilliant both in concept and operation, "Home Run" [not its real code name] allowed specialist ground controllers to listen in to cockpit conversations on the target aircraft, then take absolute control of its computerized flight control system by remote means.
>
> From that point onwards, regardless of the wishes of the hijackers or flight deck crew, the hijacked aircraft could be recovered and landed automatically at an airport of choice, with no more difficulty than flying a radio-controlled model plane. The engineers had no idea that almost thirty years

after its initial design, Home Run's top secret computer codes would be broken, and the system used to facilitate direct ground control of the four aircraft used in the high-profile attacks on New York and Washington on 11th September 2001. . . .

In order to make Home Run truly effective, it had to be completely integrated with all onboard systems, and this could only be accomplished with a new aircraft design, several of which were on the drawing boards at that time. Under cover of extreme secrecy, the multinationals and DARPA went ahead on this basis and built "back doors" into the new computer designs. There were two very obvious hard requirements at this stage, the first a primary control channel for use in taking over the flight control system and flying the aircraft back to an airfield of choice, and secondly a covert audio channel for monitoring flight deck conversations. Once the primary channel was activated, all aircraft functions came under direct ground control, permanently removing the hijackers and pilots from the control loop.

Remember here, this was not a system designed to "undermine" the authority of the flight crews, but was put in place as a "doomsday" device in the event the hijackers started to shoot passengers or crew members, possibly including the pilots. Using the perfectly reasonable assumption that hijackers only carry a limited number of bullets, and many aircraft nowadays carry in excess of 300 passengers, Home Run could be used to fly all of the survivors to a friendly airport for a safe auto landing. So the system started out in life for the very best of reasons, but finally fell prey to security leaks, and eventually to compromised computer codes. In light of recent high-profile CIA and FBI spying trials, these leaks and compromised codes should come as no great surprise to anyone.

Activating the primary Home Run channel proved to be easy. Most readers will have heard of a "transponder," prominent in most news reports immediately following the attacks on New York and Washington. Technically a transponder is a combined radio transmitter and receiver which operates automatically, in this case relaying data between the four aircraft and air traffic control on the ground. The signals sent provide a unique identity for each aircraft, essential in crowded airspace to avoid mid-air collisions, and equally essential for Home Run controllers trying to lock onto the correct aircraft. Once it has located the correct aircraft, Home Run "piggy backs" a data transmission onto the transponder channel and takes direct control from the ground. This explains why none of the aircraft sent a special "I have been hijacked" transponder code, despite multiple activation points on all four aircraft. Because the transponder frequency had already been piggy backed by Home Run, transmission of the special hijack code was rendered impossible. This was the first hard proof that the target aircraft had been hijacked electronically from the ground, rather than by (FBI-inspired) motley crews of Arabs toting penknives.[181]

Ten years before 9-11, when British Airways learned that autopilots had been installed on their Boeings, they successfully demanded their removal. The British did not want any possibility of someone overriding pilot control. American Boeings, however, kept the systems. We must add that, if the planes on 9-11 were really hijacked, these devices could have, and should have, been used to *rescue* them.

Vialls noted that Home Run would override the black box, which has a tape that records cockpit conversation for 30 minutes on a continuous loop. "If Home Run is active for more than thirty minutes," he wrote, "there will therefore be no audible data on the Cockpit Voice Recorders." Is this not why Flight 77's tape was mysteriously blank?

Remote control destruction of the aircraft could explain many oddities:

• Why the planes were flown into their targets with pinpoint accuracy, despite known flying incompetency of the "hijackers"

• Why none of the pilots typed in a hijacking alert code

• Why none of the pilots sent distress messages

- Why the government has never publicly produced a cockpit tape from any of the flights
- How the hijackers took over the planes so easily (perhaps they never did)
- Why, in violation of protocols, fighters were inexplicably delayed getting airborne, preventing them from intercepting any of the aircraft (had they done so, and flown alongside, they might have seen something in the cockpits very different from what the government has told us).

Perhaps there were no Arabs, or if there were, they may have been dupes with no idea they were on death flights. A mission like this could never be trusted to a hijacker—who could lose his nerve, fail to take the cockpit, or miss his target. This way, success was guaranteed.

Not a single person survived any of the four flights, eliminating the possibility of a witness who could testify about what really happened. One reason the WTC had to be collapsed—besides maximizing psychological impact on Americans—may have been to obliterate the crime scene.

A project of this magnitude would require a trial run. And there may have been one. On October 31, 1999, Egypt Air Flight 990 left New York for Egypt. Thirty minutes out it suddenly nose-dived into the Atlantic, killing all 217 on board. The Western media speculated that the copilot, Gameel el-Batouty, deliberately crashed the plane to commit suicide—after all, he was a Muslim, and therefore supposedly prone to that kind of thing. To back this assertion, they pointed out that the cockpit recorder showed he was praying during the plane's dive; they implied that he sought Allah's help in committing suicide.

However:

- Although the media has conditioned Americans to view Muslims as "suicide bombers," committing suicide is strictly contrary to Egyptian cultural beliefs.
- Egypt Air Flight 990 was a Boeing 767, equipped with one of the *remote control recovery systems* we have been describing.

• Yes, the copilot was heard praying. But suppose you were a pilot, and your plane was heading straight down, out of your control? When you had exhausted every pilot action, what would be your final resort? Most people would *pray*.

The remote control system on the Boeings was developed by System Planning Corporation. Earlier we mentioned the Project for a New American Century, which published an article calling for increased U.S. military presence overseas, warning this might require "a new Pearl Harbor." One of the article's co-authors was Zionist Dov Zakheim, CEO of System Planning Corporation's International Division. Earlier in his career, he was instrumental in arranging a deal whereby Israel would purchase F-16s. He is also an Israeli citizen, holding dual citizenship in America and there. And what was Dov Zakheim doing on 9-11? He was George Bush's Under Secretary of Defense, and comptroller of the Pentagon, i.e., in charge of the Pentagon's budget!

9-11 appears to have resulted from collusion between Mossad and figures in our government. The U.S. probably carried out the high-tech aspects, while Mossad's role was perhaps to supply the phony Arabs who would attend flight school, make noise at bars, and otherwise leave a trail of incriminating evidence. For those who doubt that the two governments could commit such an atrocity, remember that:

• The *Maine*, *Lusitania* and Pearl Harbor demonstrated that Illuminists in our government have no scruples about allowing the mass-murder of our own citizens to involve us in wars; and

• The King David Hotel bombing, attack on the *Liberty*, and Libyan "Trojan" established an Israeli pattern of falsely blaming Arabs for atrocities against the West.

☹ Nice try, Jim. But one thing shoots down this whole "remote control" theory. People on those planes, especially Flight 93, made cell phone calls describing the hijackings. Some called *family members*, and there's absolutely no way to fake something like that.

I have no evidence that those calls weren't genuine; I do not wish to insult the deceased, or their families. However, there is debate over the technical feasibility of the calls, given the state of technology in 2001. For example, one NSA-trained employee wrote:

> I am a National Security Agency trained Electronic Warfare specialist, and am qualified to say this. My official title: MOS33Q10, Electronic Warfare Intercept Strategic Signal Processing/Storage Systems Specialist, a highly skilled MOS which requires advanced knowledge of many communications methods and circuits to the most minute level. I am officially qualified to place severe doubt that ordinary cell phone calls were ever made from the aircraft.
>
> It was impossible for that to have happened, especially in a rural area for a number of reasons. When you make a cell phone call, the first thing that happens is that your cell phone needs to contact a transponder. Your cell phone has a max transmit power of five watts, three watts is actually the norm. If an aircraft is going five hundred miles an hour, your cell phone will not be able to
>
> 1. Contact a tower,
>
> 2. Tell the tower who you are, and who your provider is,
>
> 3. Tell the tower what mode it wants to communicate with, and
>
> 4. Establish that it is in a roaming area before it passes out of a five watt range.
>
> This procedure, called an electronic handshake, takes approximately 45 seconds for a cell phone to complete upon initial power up in a roaming area because neither the cell phone or cell transponder knows where that phone is and what mode it uses when it is turned on. At 500 miles an hour, the aircraft will travel three times the range of a cell phone's five watt transmitter before this handshaking can occur. Though it is sometimes possible to connect during takeoff and landing, under the situation that was claimed the

calls were impossible. The calls from the airplane were faked, no if's or buts.[182]

However, some calls came from air phones (installed on the aircraft), which of course transmit reliably during flights.

Intelligence services sometimes go to extreme lengths to create deception. Victor Ostrovsky, the aforementioned Mossad agent, gives an example in *By Way of Deception*. The Mossad learned a Syrian officer was traveling to Brussels to purchase furniture for the Syrian air force's headquarters. So the Mossad bought a building in Brussels, and transformed it into a furniture store, complete with their agents posing as employees. They ensured that the Syrian was directed to the store. He was taken around it and given great deals. Before shipping the furniture to Syria, the Mossad rigged it with tiny microphones, so they could monitor the Syrian air force's conversations.[183] Deception is the *modus operandi* of intelligence work.

In the case of 9-11, the phone calls were essential to proving the government's explanation of events, since none of the pilots sent alerts to air traffic control, and not a single passenger survived the crashes to describe what happened. It would not be very difficult to fake a call to an operator, who doesn't know the person or where the message really originated; but what about calls to family members?

Shoppers surfing the Web will quickly discover an array of voice changers. For as little as $30, you can buy a device which, at a button's touch, changes a woman's phone voice to a man's, or an old man's to a little girl's. $500 high-end versions provide an array of voices. You can answer a call as "Mary the receptionist," then switch to "Joe in sales," and finally become "Mr. Nerdlinger, the manager," yet it's all you.

Intelligence agencies have technology light years ahead of this. They can make a *voice print* from your phone conversations and feed it into a computer. An agent can then impersonate you over the phone so well that your own mother wouldn't know the difference.

How, then, could the 9-11 calls have been faked?

(1) The intelligence service invades the airline's computerized reservations system, and notes who is booked on the targeted flight.

(2) It then eavesdrops on, and records, cell phone calls of selected passengers. These reveal how the individuals converse with family members, pet names used, etc. Voice prints are made.

(3) On 9-11, an agent, who has carefully studied the passenger's taped conversations, calls the victim's home, speaking through a voice print: "Honey, it's me, Rick! My plane's been hijacked! They look like Muslims! I don't what's gonna happen, but I just wanted to say I love you!" If anything goes wrong,—i.e., the wife asks something he can't answer—he says, "I gotta go now!"

The 9-11 calls exhibited a number of oddities and discrepancies, which could be explained as flubs by agents, but just as easily as the results of the real passengers' anxiety. We won't review the details here, but there is ample discussion online.

I certainly don't insist the calls were fabricated. Some came from passengers who had booked the flights during the preceding 24 hours; to stage such an undertaking would be complicated and risky; and I find it hard to doubt the lengthy recorded call attributed to Flight 11 attendant Betty Ong.

If the calls were authentic, the planes may still have been remoted to their targets, with Mossad volunteers as the hijackers, knowing—or not knowing—that death was their own destiny.

Some Final Questions

Why demolish Building No. 7? It may not be coincidental that the CIA's New York headquarters were in it. Some suggest the operation was directed from Building No. 7; when all work was completed, the perpetrators exited and clicked a remote. *Kaboom*— the building imploded, and all evidence was buried in rubble.

What happened to Bin Laden? Despite its space-age surveillance technology, the U.S. took nearly ten years to find him—

probably because it never wanted to. To do so would have ended any justification for the subsequent wars.

Of course, the U.S. has claimed that Bin Laden was killed on May 2, 2011 by a team of Navy Seals. There are many reasons to doubt this story's credibility:

(1) Allegedly Bin Laden was the head of the world's largest terror network. If true, capturing Bin Laden *alive* should have been top priority. A living Bin Laden would have been a goldmine of information about terrorist operations. Instead, he was simply shot dead. In the original government version of his death, Bin Laden used a woman as a shield—a cliché that seems to have been borrowed from the climaxes of old Hollywood westerns like *High Noon*. Eventually the government retracted the "woman shield" story, as it did many details of the alleged shoot-out.

(2) Unbelievably, within a day of the incident, the U.S. announced it had dumped Bin Laden's body into the ocean—which guaranteed that the body could not be viewed and its identity critically examined. The government alleged it had "DNA evidence" that the body was Bin Laden's. The word "DNA" generates a specter of objectivity, but the source, control, and analysis of this "DNA evidence," if it existed at all, was entirely in the political hands of the government.

(3) "Leaked" photos of Osama's bullet-ridden body quickly surfaced on the Internet, but analysis demonstrated that these were old pictures of Bin Laden that had been Photoshopped. There are adages such as: "Seeing is believing" and "Pictures don't lie." However, I hope no one adheres to these ideas unswervingly in the era of Adobe Photoshop.

(4) The incident's timing suggests it was part of a campaign to boost President Obama's critically sagging ratings in the polls, which had reached an all-time low in April 2011. Less than two weeks before the Bin Laden incident, the White House released a purported long version of the President's birth certificate. A number of Obama's critics had charged that he was not an American citizen by birth, which would have disqualified him from the Presidency. It was highly suspicious that the President of the

United States, with all the powers at his disposal, could not produce a full birth certificate over a span of three years—something most average citizens can obtain in a day or two. Former Adobe engineer Gary Poyssick and others have charged that the President's birth certificate is a computer forgery.[184]

When the President made the announcement of Bin Laden's "death," huge crowds were gathered outside the White House, even though it was after midnight and few residences are near the White House. The image of the President saying "God Bless America" as hundreds of demonstrators chanted "USA!" had a smell of an orchestrated media event designed to boost the President's pre-election image as a patriot.

And the purposes of 9-11? At least two are evident:

(1) *To create the National Homeland Security Agency* as a "Big Brother" apparatus that will incrementally spy on, and oppress, the American people, based on ever-widening definitions of the word "terrorist." As discussed in Chapter 6, the Agency was proposed before 9-11. According to Ted Gunderson, when the 1993 government-arranged *initial* bombing of the WTC failed to bring about the desired anti-terrorist legislation, they upgraded to Oklahoma City. When that failed to produce Homeland Security, they resorted to 9-11.

(2) *To generate the Middle East wars* sought by Wolfowitz, Feith, Perle and Israel. This leads to another question: Why did we go to war in Iraq?

Chapter 15
PURPOSES OF THE IRAQ WAR

There appear to be three:

(1) Destroy the regime of Saddam Hussein, whose military posed the most credible threat to the Zionist stronghold of Israel.

(2) Obtain control of Iraq's oil reserves—second in the world only to Saudi Arabia's.

As to the third, insight may be gained by citing Albert Pike, Satanist and Grand Commander of North American Masonry in the late 19th century. He is reputed to have predicted three world wars, the last ending with the reign of Lucifer. Controversy has long swirled over a letter allegedly written by Pike on August 15, 1871, to Giuseppi Mazzini, revolutionary, Satanist, and head of Italian Freemasonry. William Guy Carr said of this letter in 1957:

> Pike's letter also confirmed what I had published regarding the Illuminati's plan to make Zionists and Moslems destroy each other as world powers in a war that would involve many other countries. If the war between Political Zionists and Islam, as now being fomented, is permitted to break out ONLY Atheistic-Communism and Christendom will remain as WORLD POWERS when it is ended.[185]

Pike's letter predicted:

> We shall unchain the Nihilist and Atheist revolutionaries, and we shall provoke a formidable cataclysm which will show clearly to the nations, in all its horror, the effect of the absolute heresy, mother of savagery, and of the most bloody disorder. Then citizens everywhere, obliged to defend themselves against an enraged minority of revolutionaries, will

exterminate those destroyers of civilization, and the mul-
titude—disillusioned with Christianity whose deistic spirit
will be from that moment without direction and anxious for
an ideal—without knowing where to put their worship, will
receive the true light through the universal manifestation of
the pure Luciferian doctrine, finally made public; a manifestation which will raise a general movement of reaction, which
will follow the destruction of Atheism and of Christianity,
both conquered and exterminated at the same time.[186]

When Pike said the world would "receive the true light
through the universal manifestation of the pure doctrine of
Lucifer," he was referring to the Antichrist's arrival. He also said
Christianity *and* atheism would be destroyed. Again, Satan does
not desire an atheistic culture, because he wants to be worshiped.
To him, atheism, though useful for destroying faith in God, is
only a temporary tool.

We may understand the Iraq war's third purpose as:

(3) Initiate WW III—the final war Pike predicted—beginning
as conflict between Zionism and Islam, and culminating as war
between Christianity and atheism (America and Russia?*). Out
of the ashes of this final war, which no nation wins, the Antichrist
would emerge.

[*Perhaps the reborn communist Russia that defector Golitsyn
predicted?]

In this context, it is widely claimed that the Temple of Solomon
lies in Jerusalem underneath the Dome of the Rock (Figure 15),
one of the holiest Muslim shrines.

This idea is a complete fabrication, advanced to the Christian
community through a 1963 article in *Biblical Archeological Review.*
According to Dr. John Coleman, what the journal's readers didn't
know was that the article's author, Asher Kaufman, was a member
of the highest and most secretive of all Freemasonic lodges—the
Grand Mother Lodge Quatuor Coronati.[187] There has long been
a plot in Israel to destroy the Dome of the Rock and rebuild

Solomon's temple on the site. Figure 16 shows an old Zionist depiction of this.

Figure 15

Many Christians buy into the idea. But if built, it would be *a temple for Satan*; furthermore, any attempt to destroy the Dome of the Rock would touch off a world war with Islam, the very goal of the Illuminati.

Figure 16

Nor is the provocation one-sided. We previously discussed the relationship of Masonry to the ancient Muslim faction called the *Assassins*. Today, a number of sects within Islam resemble Masonry, with hierarchies of degrees and secret rituals. Just as Masonry was behind Europe's revolutions, look to these sects to be the main driving force behind Islamic fanaticism and violence.

Let's now look at world wars, and how they progressively serve(d) the purposes of the Antichrist.

	WORLD GOVT	COMMUNISM	ZIONISM
WORLD WAR I	LEAGUE OF NATIONS	CONQUEST OF RUSSIA	BALFOUR DECLAR-ATION
WORLD WAR II	UNITED NATIONS	EASTERN EUROPE, CHINA	FOUNDING OF ISRAEL
WORLD WAR III	WORLD GOVT	COMMUNIST-STYLE RULE	THRONE OF ANTICHRIST

Figure 17

• *World Government* was first established by World War I (the League of Nations); was strengthened by World War II (United Nations), and would presumably be fulfilled by World War III (all-powerful world government).

• *Communism* is a tool to overthrow kings and religion. World War I established the first communist state; World War II empowered communism and spread it over half the globe; World War III would not end in communism *per se*, but would establish totalitarian rule surpassing communism's worst excesses.

• *Zionism*: World War I generated the Balfour Declaration, and seizure of Palestine for a "Jewish homeland"; World War II led to establishment of the political state of Israel; World War III would result in the Antichrist reigning from a rebuilt temple in Jerusalem.

Chapter 16
THE ARTS

How does someone like Britney Spears reach the top of the charts?

☺ Jim, there are good reasons for that. You see, the music industry is a democracy, just like our country. And so, the most talented people naturally gravitate upwards. Britney Spears went to the top of the charts because she's so talented and beautiful! But more than that— the American people *wanted* her there! They *demanded* Britney! You know, Jim, for many of us, the most important news story we heard over the last few years came the day that Britney decided to shave her head. We Americans just can't get enough Britney!

In Chapter 2, we described how Jimmy Carter was picked at the top, then packaged and sold to Americans. There was no spontaneous demand for Carter; the media simply inundated the public with his image, artificially inducing votes. A similar process controls pop culture.

Let's start with a rather innocent example. In 1955 Disney released the film *Davy Crockett*. Suddenly, coonskin caps became the rage; 10 million were sold in eight months. Every kid in America seemed to want one. But a year later, stores were hard pressed to sell even one; all interest had vanished. In other words, there was nothing *inherently desirable* about coonskin caps. Though harmless, this episode demonstrated how marketing and conformity can convince the public it wants something.

A far more significant example: the Beatles. They were the musical icons of the 1960s, but more importantly, the center of that decade's cultural revolution. They first seized America's attention on the *Ed Sullivan Show* in 1964. That television broadcast received such a publicity buildup, it seemed like everybody in my 7th grade English class watched it. The next day, our teacher asked what we thought. We talked mostly, *not* about the music, but the reaction of the girls in the audience. They were screaming, weeping, and hysterical.

Figure 18

After that, "Beatlemania" swept America. Young men emulated the Fab Four, wearing their hair long. But it went much further: the Beatles helped start the psychedelic culture—drugs, free sex, revolution. Their lyrics were filled with drug code words. "Lucy in the Sky with Diamonds" stood for LSD.

We were led to believe that, somehow, four lads from Liverpool had taken the world by storm *on their own*. They were characterized as "anti-Establishment," but the truth is, the Establishment created them. *Life* and *Newsweek* emblazoned them on their covers. LSD was manufactured by Sandoz, a Warburg pharmaceutical firm. In reality, the Beatles worked *for* the Establishment.

Former MI6 officer Dr. John Coleman has revealed that the Beatles were a set-up. When they first appeared on *Ed Sullivan*, they could only play four basic chords. According to Coleman, although Lennon and McCartney eventually wrote some of their own songs, the music on their first albums was created at the Tavistock Institute in Sussex, England.[188]

☹ That's absurd! I've never even heard of Tavistock!

And for the same reason most people never heard of the Council on Foreign Relations—the media doesn't discuss it. Tavistock Institute is the cartel's center for mass brainwashing and cultural manipulation. It does not work alone, but networks with think tanks such as the Rand Corporation, Hudson Institute, and Stanford Research Institute. Ed Sullivan spent six weeks at Tavistock being schooled on how to promote the Beatles. The hysterical girls were also orchestrated. As Ed Wallace noted in the Fort Worth *Star-Telegram*:

> It is widely believed that [Beatles manager] Brian Epstein hired the girls who showed up at JFK International and screamed uncontrollably as the Beatles arrived on their first US visit. Other historians have discovered that some girls were paid to perform the same screaming act during the Beatles' appearance on the *Ed Sullivan Show*.[189]

Why *did* young men start imitating the Beatles? Because they were led to think that's the kind of guy pretty girls wanted—long-haired dope-smoking revolutionaries.

Not long after Coleman's revelations, John David Chapman fired five bullets into John Lennon. The strange assassin had previously been living in Beirut, close to a CIA training camp. Why was Lennon targeted? Perhaps because he was the Beatles' outspoken, bar-brawling "big mouth." If any of the foursome was to speak up and admit how the Beatles were really created, it would have been Lennon.

Coleman also says Tavistock originated *Harry Potter* and, very probably, *The Da Vinci Code*.

Included in this, the moral decadence of the "stars"—their affairs, drug use, arrests, etc.—is played up to encourage imitation. After all, Mom, if Britney does crazy stuff, why can't I?

CHAPTER 17
THE WAR ON FAITH

Producing a One-World Religion: A Three-Step Plan

Although Karl Marx denounced religion as the "the opiate of the people," and communist states attempted to abolish it, Illuminists knew that man has a spiritual nature which cannot be fully eradicated. They therefore deemed it more practical to *infiltrate and control* religion than try and destroy it outright.

The basic mechanism underlying the satanic New World Order: *consolidation*. In the context of nations, this has meant ending national sovereignty—bringing Europe from the Common Market to the European Union, and North America from NAFTA to the proposed North American Union, eventually merging these regional structures into a one-world government. As we have also seen, *corporately* a similar process is happening through business mergers.

The Illuminati also want consolidation of religions. The technical word for this is *ecumenism*, which comes from the Greek word "oikoumene" meaning "world" and "earth." All avenues of life must be consolidated for the Antichrist to rule, and religion is no exception. British globalist historian Arnold Toynbee stated in his book *Experiences*: "I believe that, in the field of religion, sectarianism is going to be subordinated to ecumenicalism, that in the field of politics, nationalism is going to be subordinated to world government . . . ."[190]

Of the many tasks to which the Rockefellers committed their vast fortune, one was ecumenical religion, which apparently required three steps:

(1) *Degrade Christianity as a unique faith*; this necessitated providing loans to major churches in exchange for doctrinal

change, and funding seminaries that would produce "Modernist" ministers who would undermine the faith. The subsequent weakening of Christianity would ultimately ripen it for consolidation with other religions.

(2) *Specific organizations (such as the National Council of Churches) would be formed* as the framework by which various denominations—and ultimately various religions—could be brought together under the ecumenical banner.

(3) To give churches *motive* for unification, *social causes*, acceptable within the morals of most denominations and religions, would be promoted as rallying points for "united action."

THE EARLY YEARS

Degrading Christianity

The Illuminati understood that Christianity would be difficult to incorporate into a world ecumenical movement, because Christianity has always been unique among religions—offering salvation not by good deeds, but faith in Jesus Christ through His finished work on the cross. An Illuminati goal, then, was to attack the authority and historicity of the Bible.

To this end, the Rockefellers heavily funded seminaries that would question the Gospel, the most notorious probably being Union Theological Seminary in New York City. It was Presbyterian theologian Charles Briggs—both a graduate and a professor of Union Theological—who, in the late 19th century, prominently introduced into America "Higher Criticism," claiming the Bible was full of errors, and denying that many of its books were actually written by the attributed authors.

In 1922, Baptist pastor Harry Emerson Fosdick, another graduate of Union Theological Seminary, delivered a controversial sermon called "Shall the Fundamentalists Win?" at the First Presbyterian Church of New York. In it, he cast doubts on: the Bible being God's Word; the Virgin Birth; the Second Coming of Christ; and even Christ's death on the cross serving as atonement for sins. And he denounced Fundamentalists—who held these beliefs—as "intolerant."

The sermon sparked outrage. The General Assembly of the Presbyterian Church demanded an investigation of Fosdick, who was forced to resign his pastorship. However, he was then immediately hired as pastor of Riverside Church—the church attended and built by John D. Rockefeller, Jr. at a cost of $4 million. Rockefeller paid for 130,000 copies of Fosdick's notorious sermon to be printed and distributed to Protestant ministers. Significantly, Fosdick's brother Raymond was president of the Rockefeller Foundation for twelve years. The views expressed by theologians like Briggs and Fosdick were called "Modernism," which also included denying Christ's divinity, miracles and resurrection. In short, Modernism was not merely a quibbling over some gray area in a passage of scripture; *it was a complete repudiation of the faith's major tenets.* And with Rockefeller backing, it made its way into seminaries, Christian colleges and churches across America. Modernism did not simply "happen"; it was an orchestrated, financed agenda.

Christians who discerningly opposed this movement were called "Fundamentalists" because they stood by the fundamental doctrines the Modernists were assaulting.

Forming an Ecumenical Structure

In the Illuminati's long view, once Modernism had sufficiently degraded Christianity into "just another religion," it could be bonded with other faiths. But before achieving this last step, Christian denominations themselves had to be united.

The Federal Council of Churches (later called National Council of Churches) was founded in 1908. Heavily funded by the Rockefellers, it was to become the structural core of the drive to consolidate American Christianity. The man chosen to spearhead ecumenism was John Foster Dulles, an in-law of the Rockefellers. Dulles was the attorney who defended Harry Emerson Fosdick during his heresy investigation, and he served as chairman of the trustees of the Rockefeller Foundation, where Emerson's brother Raymond was president.

At the 1919 Paris Peace Conference, which formed the League of Nations—first step toward world government—John Foster Dulles was legal counsel to the United States delegation. A founding member of the Council on Foreign Relations, Dulles contributed articles to the CFR's journal *Foreign Affairs* beginning with its very first issue in 1922. An inveterate globalist, he eventually helped write the preamble to the United Nations Charter (which makes no mention of God). Dulles also chaired the Carnegie Endowment for International Peace, where his choice for president of that institution was Alger Hiss, the notorious communist spy who was secretary-general at the UN's founding conference in 1945.

Part of Dulles's religious agenda was to persuade American churches to accept world government. In 1937, he wrote in the magazine *Religion in Life*: "Where then does the solution lie? A theoretical solution lies in the abolition of the entire concept of national sovereignty and the unification of the world into a single nation. All boundary barriers are thus automatically leveled . . . ."[191]

Dulles served on the executive committee of the Federal (later National) Council of Churches. In 1942, he chaired a meeting of 30 religious denominations brought together by the Federal Council of Churches, and *Time* (March 16 of that year) reported they adopted a program calling for "a world government of delegated powers," "strong and immediate limitations on national sovereignty," "a universal system of money," and many other globalist measures.

Since the Illuminati ambition was not merely to consolidate churches in America, but throughout the planet, in 1948 the World Council of Churches was formed. John Foster Dulles attended the founding conference in Amsterdam. The conference's director of research was John C. Bennett—member of the Council on Foreign Relations and president of Union Theological Seminary. Also attending was Reinhold Niebuhr (CFR, Union Theological). Funding for the World Council of Churches came from the Rockefeller and Carnegie foundations.

The Social Gospel:
A Method for Implementing Ecumenism

Although the National and World Council of Churches provided structures for consolidation, the question remained of how to *motivate* churches to unite. Christian denominations often differ over various theological issues. But they generally agree on values (helping the poor and sick, for example). The strategy for unification, therefore, was to encourage them to collaborate where they *did* agree. This took the form of an action-oriented program known as "the Social Gospel."

Walter Rauschenbusch, a Baptist minister trained at Rochester Theological Seminary—also funded by the Rockefellers—became a socialist and was known as "Father of the Social Gospel." In 1893—about the time Charles Augustus Briggs was initiating the U.S. Modernist movement—Rauschenbusch declared that "the only power that can make socialism succeed, if it is established, is religion." He said that "Christianity is in its nature revolutionary," denied that Christ died in substitutionary atonement for our sins, and said the Kingdom of God "is not a matter of getting individuals to heaven, but of transforming the life on earth into the harmony of heaven."[192]

Perhaps the most notorious "Social Gospel" pusher was Rockefeller-backed Reverend Harry F. Ward, who taught for 23 years at Union Theological Seminary. Ward was also founding chairman of the American Civil Liberties Union (ACLU)—an ironic position, since the organization has been a dedicated opponent of religious displays on public property. Ward also chaired the American League against War & Fascism, which was founded by the Communist Party, USA. Manning Johnson, a former Communist Party official, told Congress in 1953 that Ward "has been the chief architect for communist infiltration and subversion in the religious field." Union leader Samuel Gompers, founder of the American Federation of Labor, called Ward "the most ardent pro-Bolshevik cleric in this country." (Note the irony of a clergyman supporting communism, an ideology that denounces religion as "the opiate of the people" and has slaughtered millions of Christians.)

Ward's Social Gospel was a push for ecumenism. He helped found, in 1908, the Methodist Federation for Social Service (now called the Methodist Federation for Social Action). Ward was its secretary for 33 years. In the Federation, the Gospel of Christ took a back seat to the Social Gospel, which called for Christians to fight for things like social justice, better labor conditions, and "world peace." Not surprisingly, these were the same goals proclaimed by Marxists. Christians were thus to be united into a cheap volunteer work force for a socialist new world order.

Missionary work was not neglected. In 1930, at John D. Rockefeller, Jr.'s request, and with his financial support, a group of Baptist laymen persuaded seven denominations to participate in the "Laymen's Foreign Missions Inquiry." Their report, *Re-Thinking Missions: A Laymen's Inquiry after One Hundred Years*, recommended that missionaries de-emphasize Christian doctrine and seek to ally themselves with other religions in doing good works.

The denominations distanced themselves from the report. However, Pearl Buck, author and former missionary to China, praised it in *The Christian Century*, saying every Christian should read it. In articles published in *Harper's* and *Cosmopolitan*, Buck rejected the doctrine of Original Sin, and said that belief in the divinity—and even historicity—of Christ was unessential to the faith. She criticized the typical missionary as "narrow, uncharitable, unappreciative, ignorant."[193] In place of evangelization, she recommended that missionaries help with agricultural, educational, medical and sanitary work (i.e., the Social Gospel). In short, Pearl Buck's pronouncements fit perfectly with the Rockefellers' scheme for a "modernized" ecumenical Christianity. It should not be overlooked that, subsequent to praising Rockefeller's missionary inquiry, her novel *The Good Earth* was awarded the Nobel Prize in Literature and was turned into an Oscar-nominated movie.

RECENT YEARS:
THE THREE-STEP PLAN CONTINUES

Degrading Christianity

The process begun by Charles Briggs, introducing "Modernism" with its attack on every fundamental of Christianity and the Bible, continues today.

One prominent assault on the Bible's authenticity has been the Jesus Seminar, begun in 1985 by the late Robert Funk, with backing from the Westar Institute, whose financial supporters are not publicized. Funk packed his seminar with liberal "scholars"—more than a dozen had studied at Union Theological Seminary, and about half came from three liberal Establishment schools: Harvard and Vanderbilt (both of whose divinity schools were heavily funded by the Rockefellers) and the openly ecumenical Claremont School of Theology.

The Jesus Seminar used a system of colored beads to vote on whether something was really said or done by Jesus. A red bead meant "definitely yes," a pink bead "probably yes," a grey bead "probably no," and a black bead "definitely no." In short, the Bible's historical accuracy was to be determined by votes, based on personal opinions of people living two thousand years after the original eyewitnesses to the events.

The seminar concluded that over 80 percent of the sayings attributed to Jesus were not actually said by Him, and that only 2 percent were *definitely* accurate. Likewise, the seminar followed Modernist tradition by denying the miracles, divinity and resurrection of Jesus. Funk, who himself held these views, had hand-picked his seminar's participants; thus its outcome was no surprise. Nonetheless, the media touted the proceedings as a "scholarly" refutation of most of the New Testament.

Additionally, a slew of "documentaries" aimed at casting doubts on the Bible have aired on cable TV. These typically spend most of their air time interviewing Modernist theologians rather than conservative ones. The documentaries have aired prominently on:

• the History Channel (owned by A & E Television Networks, a joint venture of groups with CFR fingerprints: Disney-ABC Television Group, NBC International, and the Hearst Corporation);

• the National Geographic Channel (owned by CFR member Rupert Murdoch's Fox Cable Networks and National Geographic Television); and

• the Discovery Channel (which, in 2005, hired as its managing editor Ted Koppel—former CFR member and good friend of CFR heavyweight Henry Kissinger).

Perhaps the most ambitious strike at the Bible has been Dan Brown's 2003 novel *The Da Vinci Code*. As of 2009, it had sold over 80 million copies, making it the best-selling English language novel of the 21st century. It was also made into a film, released in 2006, which grossed over $200 million.

Although *The Da Vinci Code* is cast in the mold of an historical mystery—much like the "Indiana Jones" movies—its punch line is an assault against Christian faith. It is rife with false assertions regarding the early church. Despite thorough refutation by church historians, many people, caught up in the hype, accepted *The Da Vinci Code*'s disinformation as fact. At the heart of its message: Jesus was not divine, was never resurrected, and married Mary Magdalene and had children by her.

Lo and behold, within months of the film's release, the Discovery Channel aired a documentary claiming a tomb had been found containing the bones of Jesus and Mary Magdalene. This was not a chance sequence. Media events are being orchestrated to deceive the public.

The Ecumenical Structures Grow

The National Council of Churches (encompassing 37 Christian faith groups) and World Council of Churches (representing 349 churches, denominations and Christian fellowships) continue today. They have been reinforced by such organizations as Christians Uniting in Christ (established in 2002) and Christian Churches Together in the USA (formed in 2006).

Not to be missed is the Tony Blair Faith Foundation. Yes, the former British Prime Minister—a consummate insider—has formed another ecumenical organization. Blair might be compared to John Foster Dulles, the globalist politician who helped form the World Council of Churches. On the foundation's website, Blair states:

> I launched the Tony Blair Faith Foundation to promote respect, friendship and understanding between the major religious faiths . . . . I have always believed that faith is an essential part of the modern world. As globalisation pushes us ever closer it is vital it's not used as a force for conflict and division. . . . Rather, faith is something that has much to give and to teach a world in which economic globalisation and political change is offering many opportunities but also presenting many dangers.[194]

Note Blair's emphasis on globalization and his desire for unity among all faiths. Behind the fuzzy talk about "respect, friendship and understanding" is an aim for one-world religion—which the Antichrist will require to rule the globe. In fact, the Antichrist probably couldn't have said it much better.

The New Social Gospel: Today's Methods for Implementing Ecumenism

What means is used to motivate today's churches to unite? As before, it's social action. Just as Marxist pastor Harry F. Ward headed the Methodist Federation for Social Action, the website for Tony Blair's Faith Foundation has a section called "Social Action Projects." Viewers are asked to sign a declaration which states: "I commit to working together with people of all faiths to fight against disease and poverty."

In short, it's not about what you believe—social action should transcend your faith, so that it can be melded with all the others.

In America, the push for ecumenical social action is spearheaded by Rick Warren, pastor of Saddleback Church in Lake

Forest, California. He is perhaps best known for his book *The Purpose Driven Life*, which has sold over 30 million copies. Many churches were persuaded to join Warren's "Purpose-Driven" movement because his book topped the *New York Times* bestseller list and he was featured on mainstream media shows such as *Good Morning America*. After all, didn't this prove Warren was anointed by God? Somehow, where other evangelical spokesmen had failed, Warren had penetrated the anti-religious bias of America's leftist media. CNN even called him "America's Pastor," and Barack Obama invited him to give the invocation at his inauguration.

The true reasons for Warren's bursting on the scene suggest something besides God's anointing. Warren is a member of the Council on Foreign Relations. He has distinct ties to media tycoon Rupert Murdoch, whose empire includes the *Wall Street Journal* and England's *The Times*. Warren's book *The Purpose Driven Life* was published by Zondervan, now a division of HarperCollins, which has been owned by Murdoch's News Corporation since 1989. Murdoch also controls Fox, which produces the viciously anti-Christian TV show *Family Guy*; and he owns pornographic channels in Europe. Yet Rick Warren claimed in a *New Yorker* interview that he is Rupert Murdoch's pastor. If so, Christians have been asking, why does he not influence Murdoch away from his anti-faith, anti-family programming?

Once one realizes that Rick Warren is intimately connected to a man who is arguably the world's most powerful media magnate, and that both are CFR members, Warren's rising star becomes more fathomable.

While many Christians have criticized Warren for his theology and for his use of questionable Bible translations, his most disturbing attribute may be ecumenism. In 2008, helped by a $2 million donation from Murdoch, Warren launched the PEACE Coalition. *Time* magazine reported the initiative with the headline "RICK WARREN GOES GLOBAL." The coalition's website states that "The plan is a massive effort to mobilize 1 billion Christians to attack the five global, evil giants of our day—spiritual emptiness, self-centered leadership, extreme poverty, pandemic disease and illiteracy/education." Once again, behind idealist language lies a plan for an ecumenical world. Would it be healthy for Rick Warren to preside over an empire of a billion Christians?

Warren's PEACE coalition is an obvious complement to the Tony Blair Faith Foundation. Not surprisingly, Warren is on the Religious Advisory Council of Blair's foundation. On the latter's website, Warren states: "The vision and values of the Tony Blair Faith Foundation are desperately needed when every major issue in our world is influenced for good or harm by faith factors."

As America's point man for ecumenical social action, Rick Warren might be called the Harry F. Ward of today. Unlike Ward, Rick Warren does not openly praise communism—which, as an ideology, is considered passé. But like Ward, he is forging churches into a volunteer (i.e., unpaid) army in the service of the globalist, socialist new world order.

Adding yet more fuel to the ecumenical fire is the 2009 Manhattan Declaration. Though intended to appeal to conservative Christians, with its anti-abortion, traditional-marriage, religious-freedom proclamation, it is highly ecumenical. The declaration states: "We, as Orthodox, Catholic, and Evangelical Christians, have gathered together in New York on September 28, 2009, to make the following declaration . . . ." One of the three men on the declaration's drafting committee was Robert George—a CFR member who serves the UN on UNESCO'S World Commission on the Ethics of Scientific Knowledge and Technology. A signer of the Declaration is Richard Land—President of the Southern Baptist Convention's Ethics & Religious Liberty Commission—and a CFR member. A major ecumenist, Land also signed the 1994 document Evangelicals and Catholics Together, and is a member of the Leadership Group on U.S.-Muslim Engagement—a role he shares with several other CFR members, such as Stephen Heintz, president of the Rockefeller Brothers Fund.

An Analogue in Catholicism

The Rockefellers, as "Baptists," made non-Catholic churches their zone of influence. However, parallels exist in Catholicism, on whom pressures tend to emanate more from European than American sources.

The Catholic Church has had its own experience with attempts to degrade faith through Modernism: pressures to reject the authority of Scripture, to compromise with evolution (as prominently advocated by the priest Pierre Teilhard de Chardin), to accept abortion, and to ordain women and homosexuals as priests.

Like the non-Catholic church, the Catholic Church has recently seen major ecumenical developments, such as: the signing of the Joint Declaration on the Doctrine of Justification by Lutheran and Catholic representatives (1999); dialogue with Eastern Orthodox churches, resulting in the Common Declaration of Pope Benedict XVI and Ecumenical Patriarch Bartholomew I (2006); an unprecedented Catholic-Muslim summit at the Vatican (2008); and visits of Pope Benedict XVI to Israel and to the Great Synagogue of Rome (2009).

And Catholicism has experienced its own "social action" movement—comparable to the tactics of Harry F. Ward and Rick Warren—as in the doctrine of liberation theology, which was seen especially in Latin America beginning in the 1950s and 60s, where the Gospel took a back seat to fighting poverty and social injustice via Marxist precepts.

Unity and Discernment

Unity is a complex matter. The Apostle Paul did tell us to be "Endeavoring to keep the unity of the Spirit" (Ephesians 4:3) and "to be likeminded one toward another according to Christ Jesus" (Romans 15:5).

Furthermore, we know that a satanic strategy is to "*divide and conquer*." At the signing of the Declaration of Independence, Benjamin Franklin warned his peers that "We must all hang together, or assuredly we shall all hang separately."

So has Satan's goal been to unite the church or divide it? It appears that he has employed both strategies, but that essentially division was the *first* phase and ecumenism the *second*.

Intelligence analysts have cogently argued that:

• The Illuminati were behind nearly every major split in the Christian church—beginning with the Catholic-Orthodox division of 1054.

• Illuminati infiltrators in the Catholic Church spawned the Inquisition to deliberately alienate Christians from their faith.

• This infiltration was also responsible for the 16th-century Papal corruptions—such as selling indulgences and squandering the church budget—that resulted in the Protestant split. Martin Luther, while himself a sincere reformer, was encouraged by Illuminati seeking church division.

• The Protestant church was in turn infiltrated to split it into smaller and smaller denominations, ostensibly over doctrinal issues—some less essential to the Gospel than others. Unquestionably, many of those who argued for division were sincere in their beliefs, and truths can probably be found on both sides of most doctrinal rifts. But Satan held the long view: divide to conquer.

As part of its strategy to divide Christianity, the cartel was also reportedly behind the formation of major cults—including Jehovah's Witnesses and Mormonism. (I mention this while having the greatest respect for the morality and sincerity of many of the followers of these two sects.) Jehovah's Witnesses deny Christ's divinity, His physical resurrection, and the existence of hell. Mormons believe in multiple gods, that Jesus is a created being—Lucifer's brother—and treat the Book of Mormon as holy scripture, equal or even senior to the Bible.

Charles Taze Russell, founder of the Witnesses, and Joseph Smith, founder of the Mormons, were both Freemasons. Early issues of *The Watchtower*—the Witnesses' official publication—bore the Freemasonic cross on their covers. Russell is buried next to the greater Pittsburgh Masonic Center. A pyramid, displaying a Masonic cross, marks his grave.[195]

Masonic symbols also adorn Mormon temples. An all-seeing eye crowns the entrance to the Salt Lake City temple. According to some researchers, initial funding for both the Jehovah's Witnesses and Mormons originated with Kuhn, Loeb. These cults did not "just happen," but were created to confuse and splinter the Christian church.

From the perspective of the twenty-first century, it appears that the strategy of division has now essentially completed its season. With the church successfully fragmented, and confused by Modernism, it appears ripe for the Illuminati's final phase: ecumenism—the uniting of all Christian denominations, in turn to be merged with other faiths, to create a one-world religion over whom Antichrist can rule.

However, this does not mean churches should never stand together. For example, if several local pastors, from different denominations, wish to engage in a joint protest against abortion, nothing is inherently wrong with this. Discernment is called for. Is unity for the purpose of serving God—or of serving Satan's ecumenical goal? Examine the hearts and motives of those calling for unity. And follow the money: efforts tied to Warren-Murdoch-Blair-Rockefeller initiatives should be absolutely avoided.

For further discussion of faith issues—including Cyrus Scofield and the millennial controversy—see Appendix IV.

CHAPTER 18
THE MOST HIDDEN BOOK

Aside from the Bible, what is the world's most suppressed book?

I doubt if that question has a provable answer, but one candidate is *The Protocols of the Learned Elders of Zion*. Many efforts have been made to ban its sale. In the old Soviet Union, owning a copy was punishable by death.

I always heard the *Protocols* were a forgery. Supposedly, the Czar's secret police, the Okhrana, fabricated them to justify persecution of Jews. I assumed this was the case, and if someone mentioned the *Protocols*, I would say, "They were a forgery—everyone knows that!"

But since so many other events turned out differently from what the Establishment press claimed, I eventually asked myself: "Is it just possible the *Protocols are* true, and are suppressed to prevent us from reading them? Maybe I'll actually *look* at them, what the hey?" So I began reading the *Protocols*, and was immediately surprised by a passage on the first pages:

> For them let that play the principal part which we have persuaded them to accept as the dictates of science (theory). It is with this object in view that we are constantly, by means of our press, arousing a blind confidence in these theories, which our specialists have cunningly pieced together. The intellectuals of the goyim will puff themselves up with their knowledges and without any logical verification of them will put into effect all the information available from science, which our agentur specialists have cunningly pieced together for the purpose of educating their minds in the direction we want. Do not suppose for a moment that these statements are

217

empty words: think carefully of the successes we arranged for Darwinism . . . . (Protocols 2:2-3)

As author of two books exposing Darwinism's myths, I was stunned by this reference. *I* understood Darwinism's relationship to atheism and social destruction, having witnessed it firsthand in the 1960s. But how did the *Czar's police* make that link? And if their goal was to persecute Jews, why bring Charles Darwin into the picture?—he wasn't, to my knowledge, a significant figure in 1900 Russia.

Furthermore, the statement about "arranging the successes of Darwinism" intrigued me, because Darwin lived as a gentleman on a huge estate with up to eight servants. Yet he received no wages from employment, and earned only about 10,000 pounds from his books during his lifetime. Darwin did receive an inheritance from his father, but not enough to maintain such a grand standard of living.

Very few books have discussed Darwin's finances, and only one did in detail: *Darwin Revalued* (1955) by Sir Arthur Keith. This rare book disclosed that Darwin made a fortune through investments. Reviewing Darwin's ledgers, Keith reported:

I note that in some of his earlier dealings there were small losses, but in all his later investments there were only gains, some of them on quite a big scale.[196]

Only gains? Even Warren Buffett will tell you he's occasionally made a bad investment. But not Darwin. To what may we attribute this success? Here's how Keith chose to explain it:

The more we come to know of the man Charles Darwin, the more the wonder grows that he could carry on so many diverse activities. We have been accustomed to think of him as a naturalist brooding over the problem of life in plants, in animals, and in humanity at large, but now we find a man leading a secluded life near a remote village in the country and carrying on a successful business as a financier. No doubt *The Times* helped him; after lunch was the occasion given to it. His biographer tells us: "After his lunch, he read the newspaper, lying on a sofa in the drawing-room. I think the paper was the only unscientific matter which he read to himself."

Thus we may infer that, after assimilating day by day the trend of affairs in the news columns, he did not forget to look at any movements in the stocks which interested him. He had his stock-broker on the Exchange and his lawyer in London to do business for him.[197]

So we're to believe that Darwin, after studying bird eggs all morning, would lie on the sofa, browse the *Times* financial section, and say, "I think I shall invest in *this* one." And somehow he picked only winners. Also, at 22, Darwin's eldest son William was made a partner in the prestigious Southampton and Hampshire Bank, though neither he nor the Darwin family had any background in banking.

Could Darwin's triumphant investing have resulted, not from fortuitous newspaper picks, but careful guidance by financial powers? Might this also explain his son's good fortune in landing a bank partnership? I can't prove it, but as a creationist I don't put much stock in "chance."

But to return to the *Protocols*. I had never read a message so evil. They are often called a "clumsy forgery," but I was personally struck by how they laid out, in sophisticated detail, the very plan for global conquest unfolding today, which *Truth Is a Lonely Warrior* describes, including: world government; banking; the use of socialism, communism, revolution and Masonry; the attempted destruction of Christianity; and establishment of the Antichrist on his throne.

Let's take examples from the *Protocols*. By the way, *selective quotations* can easily distort a book. I want to stress that I haven't strained to find a handful of quotes supporting the thesis that the *Protocols* might be true, while eliminating quotes contradicting that thesis. I encourage you to read the entire *Protocols* for yourself.

Regarding world government they state, for example:

By all these means, we shall so wear down the "goyim" that they will be compelled to offer us international power of a nature that by its position will enable us without any violence gradually to absorb all the state forces of the world and to form a super-government. (Protocol 5:11)

We will not give them peace until they openly acknowledge our international super-government, and with submissiveness. (Protocol 9:4)

Earlier we discussed revolution, and the destruction of kings and nobility, in order to reduce us to an army of pawns.

In the times when the peoples looked upon kings on their thrones as on a pure manifestation of the will of God, they submitted without a murmur to the despotic power of kings: but from the day when we insinuated into their minds the conception of their own rights they began to regard the occupants of thrones as mere ordinary mortals. The holy unction of the Lord's Anointed has fallen from the heads of kings in the eyes of the people, and when we also robbed them of their faith in God the might of power was flung upon the streets . . . . (Protocol 5:3)

In all corners of the earth the words "Liberty, Equality, Fraternity," brought to our ranks, thanks to our blind agents, whole legions who bore our banners with enthusiasm. And all the time these words were canker-worms at work boring into the well-being of the goyim, putting an end everywhere to peace, quiet, solidarity and destroying all the foundations of the goya states. As you will see later, this helped us to our triumph: it gave us the possibility, among other things, of getting into our hands the master card—the destruction of the privileges, or in other words of the very existence of the aristocracy of the goyim, that class which was the only defense peoples and countries had against us. (Protocol 1:26)

Regarding revolution and establishment of the Antichrist:

We appear on the scene as alleged saviors of the worker from this oppression when we propose to him to enter the ranks of our fighting forces—Socialists, Anarchists, Communists. . . . By want and the envy and hatred which it engenders we shall move the mobs and with their hands shall wipe out all those who hinder us on our way. When the hour strikes for our sovereign lord of all the world to be crowned it is these same hands which will sweep away everything that might be a hindrance thereto. (Protocols 3:7-9)

Revolution would destroy the property of wealthy enemies, but never that of the plotters themselves:

These mobs will rush delightedly to shed the blood of those whom, in the simplicity of their ignorance, they have envied from their cradles, and whose property they will then be able to loot. "Ours" they will not touch, because the moment of attack will be known to us and we shall take measures to protect our own. (Protocols 3:11-12)

And again on the coming Antichrist:

We have been leading the peoples from one disenchantment to another, so that in the end they should turn also from us in favor of that king-despot of the blood of Zion, whom we are preparing for the world. (Protocol 3:15)

And yet again, with shades of Orwell's "Big Brother":

Our government will have the appearance of a patriarchal paternal guardianship on the part of our ruler. Our own nation and our subjects will discern in his person a father caring for their every need, their every act, their every interrelation as subjects with one another, as well as their relations to their ruler. They will then be so thoroughly imbued with the thought that it is impossible for them to dispense with this wardship and guidance, if they wish to live in peace and quiet, that they will acknowledge the autocracy of our ruler with a devotion bordering on "apotheosis" [glorification as a god] . . . . (Protocol 15:20)

The *Protocols* discuss the exploitation of "voting, which we have made the instrument which will set us on the throne of the world." (Protocol 10:5). And long before Presidents like Lyndon Johnson and George Bush were sending troops to fight undeclared wars, and "executive orders" began to override the U.S. Constitution, the *Protocols* boasted:

In the near future we shall establish the responsibility of presidents. . . .we shall arrange elections in favor of such presidents as have in their past some dark, undiscovered stain—then they will be trustworthy agents for the accomplishment of our plans . . . . We shall invest the president with the right of declaring a state of war. We shall justify this last right on the ground that the president as chief of the whole army must have it at his disposal . . . . The president will, at our discretion, interpret the sense of such of the existing laws as admit of various interpretation; he will further annul them when we indicate to him the necessity to do so, besides this, he will have the right to propose temporary laws, and even new departures in the government constitutional working, the pretext both for the one and the other being the requirements for the supreme welfare of the State. (Protocols 10:11, 13, 16)

Regarding Christianity's destruction through a "divide and conquer" strategy:

We have long past taken care to discredit the priesthood of the goyim, and thereby to ruin their mission on earth which in these days might still be a great hindrance to us. Day by day its influence on the peoples of the world is falling lower. Freedom of conscience has been declared everywhere, so that now only years divide us from the moment of the complete wrecking of that Christian religion: as to other religions we shall have still less difficulty in dealing with them, but it would be premature to speak of this now. . . . we shall not overtly lay a finger on existing churches, but we shall fight against them by criticism calculated to produce schism. (Protocols 17:2, 5)

Truth Is a Lonely Warrior has discussed pervasive control of the media. The *Protocols* declare:

We must compel the governments of the goyim to take action in the direction favored by our widely conceived plan, already approaching the desired consummation, by what we shall represent as public opinion, secretly promoted by us through the means of that so-called *Great Power*—the press, which, with a few exceptions that may be disregarded, is already entirely in our hands. (Protocol 7:5)

Not a single announcement will reach the public without our control. Even now this is already being attained inasmuch as all news items are received by a few agencies, in whose offices they are focused from all parts of the world. These agencies will then be already entirely ours and will give publicity only to what we dictate to them. (Protocol 12:5)

And if there are any who are desirous of writing against us, they will not find any person eager to print their productions. Before accepting any production for publication in print, the publisher or printer will have to apply to the authorities for permission to do so. Thus we shall know beforehand of all tricks preparing against us and shall nullify them by getting ahead with explanations of the subject treated of. (Protocol 12:7)

There would even be a false opposition press that

will present what looks like the very antipodes to us. Our real opponents at heart will accept this simulated opposition as their own and will show us their cards. All our newspapers will be of all possible complexions—aristocratic, republican, revolutionary, even anarchical . . . .Those fools who think they are repeating the opinion of a newspaper of their own camp will be repeating our opinion. (Protocols 12:11-12)

I suggest that both William F. Buckley's *National Review* (aimed at white-collar conservatives) and Rush Limbaugh (aimed at blue-collar conservatives) fall into this "false opposition" category. Buckley was a member of the Council on Foreign Relations and the super-secretive Skull and Bones, and it has long been rumored that he founded *National Review* with funding from the CIA (for whom he indisputably worked). Like Limbaugh, Buckley ridiculed "conspiracy theories," while giving conservatives the comfortable assurance that they had representation within the media.

Just as in Orwell's *1984*, history would be altered:

We shall erase from the memory of men all facts of previous centuries which are undesirable to us, and leave only those which depict all the errors of the government of the goyim. (Protocol 16:4)

As is common in totalitarian countries, citizens would spy on each other:

One-third of our subjects will keep the rest under observation. . . . It will then be no disgrace to be a spy and informer, but a merit . . . . (Protocol 17:7)

We have discussed the inflationary policies by which the Illuminati control the money supply, destroying our standard of living:

We shall raise the rate of wages which, however, will not bring any advantage to the workers, for, at the same time, we shall produce a rise in prices of the first necessaries of life . . . . (Protocol 6:7)

We have also discussed the strategy of controlling governments through loans:

Loans hang like a sword of Damocles over the heads of rulers, who, instead of taking from their subjects by a temporary tax, come begging with outstretched palms to our bankers. . . . If a loan bears a charge of 5 percent, then in twenty years the State vainly pays away in interest a sum equal to the loan borrowed, in forty years it is paying a double sum, in sixty—treble, and all the while the debt remains an unpaid debt. . . . when we brought up the necessary persons in order to transfer loans into the external sphere, all the wealth of the States flowed into our cash-boxes and all the goyim began to pay us the tribute of subjects. . . ." (Protocols 20:29, 30, 32)

The *Protocols* further state:

In order that the masses may not guess what they are about we further distract them with amusements, games, pastimes, passions, peoples palaces. Soon we shall begin through the press to propose competitions in art, in sport of all kinds. (Protocol 13:3)

The *Protocols* were first published in Russia in 1903. The Olympics had been revived in 1896; meanwhile, spectator sports with professional leagues were born. The first World Series was played in 1903; 1917 marked the National Hockey League's founding and 1922 the National Football League's. Today we have cable TV with 200+ stations; husbands spending an entire day watching football; kids glued to video games. If the *Protocols* are a mere fake, how did the Czar's police foresee a world dominated by amusements?

The Establishment's Explanation

But what about the claim that the *Protocols* were forgeries? After the Czar's fall, all known copies in Russia were destroyed. Owning it there was a capital offense. The *Protocols* first appeared in English in 1920 after Victor Marsden, a British journalist who had suffered imprisonment under the Bolsheviks, returned to

England and translated a copy at the British Museum. He died within a year.

Reaction to the English translation was swift and furious. In 1921, Philip Graves, Constantinople correspondent for the *London Times*, published a series of articles in that paper claiming the *Protocols* were a forgery. He said that, in Constantinople, he had been approached by a mysterious "Mr. X," whom he never identified. According to Graves, Mr. X said he was a Russian émigré and he bore proof that the *Protocols* were a forgery. They had been plagiarized from a satirical novel, *The Dialogue in Hell between Machiavelli and Montesquieu*, published in 1864 by Frenchman Maurice Joly. "Mr. X" supplied Graves with a copy.

In his articles, Graves produced about a dozen quotations from *Dialogue* and contrasted them with similar passages in the *Protocols*. Although the excerpts were not identical, the resemblance was undeniable. Since then, it has been widely proclaimed that Graves refuted the *Protocols* as a hoax.

However, because Joly's book was rare, few people could read it to verify Graves's own allegations. Australian researcher Peter Myers, who has extensively analyzed the two works, reports that only 16.45% of the *Protocols* have correlation with Joly's work—this leaves over 83 percent unaccounted for (see http://mailstar.net/toolkit.html).

The premise of Graves's forgery argument was this: *If two books resemble each other, the second must have been plagiarized from the first.*

However, other explanations exist. For example, both may have relied upon the same sources.

The Bible's three "Synoptic" gospels—Matthew, Mark and Luke—have some passages which are strikingly similar; in cases almost verbatim. Yet I'm aware of no Christians who insist that two of the three were therefore "forgeries." Instead, Biblical scholars believe the authors shared some source(s)—one often proposed is a hypothetical now-lost manuscript called Q.

A similar relationship may explain the resemblance between the *Protocols* and Joly's *Dialogue*. According to William Guy Carr and other analysts, the *Protocols* originated in the 18th century, and were eventually expanded with modifications. A revolutionary, Joly wrote the *Dialogue* as a satire against Napoleon III, whom he hoped would be overthrown. Most French revolutionaries were Freemasons. Was Joly exposed to secret documents at a Grand Orient Freemasonic lodge? If so, he might have incorporated some of what he read into his satire. In that case, one could more accurately say Joly's novel was forged from the *Protocols* (an early version) rather than vice versa.

The *Protocols* cannot be proven authentic; however, they predicted world events with demonstrable accuracy. Who wrote them? Henry Makow (www.henrymakow.com) makes a case for the Rothschilds, especially Lionel Rothschild (1808-1879). The *Protocols* reveal keen understanding of international banking's workings, which should have exceeded the capacities of the Czar's police. And who were the Elders of Zion? Czarist general Count Cherep-Spiridovich believed they were the Committee of 300. The *Protocols* are obviously the work of a small inner circle, and could not possibly be attributed to a broad group, such as the Jewish race.

Considerable debate exists over why the *Protocols* became public. They were originally published by Russian professor Sergei Nilus, who said they were obtained through a cartel member's lover: she'd been shocked to discover them among his effects. But some people doubt that the Illuminati would have been so careless with their documents.

A few believe that, foreseeing exposure, the cartel deliberately let its plans slip—but with a Jewish spin to distract from their true nature. We know the conspiracy is ultimately satanic, not Jewish.

Another theory: they wanted to stir anti-Semitism within Russia to help trigger revolution, as well as drive Khazarian Jews into Palestine; but when the *Protocols* accidentally leaked to England, the document had to be ruthlessly suppressed.

I personally don't even rule out that this was "in your face"—*we're so confident of victory that we can reveal our plan and you won't be able to do a thing about it.* It seems in Satan's prideful nature to boast, so that his evil ingenuity might be admired.

In order to best draw their own conclusions, I suggest that people read the *Protocols*. They may be the closest thing to Satan's plan you can find.

CHAPTER 19
CYBER TYRANNY

We're obviously heading into a cashless society. Electronic transactions increasingly replace money. We swipe cards to pay for gas and groceries.

☺ Hey, Jim, will you catch up with the times? I suppose you want to ban cars too, and go back to horses and buggies! There's nothing "sinister" going on. Electronic transactions are simply the fruit of technological progress. We use them because they're *convenient*. Plus, my credit card gives me cash rebates. It benefits the banks, too: it increases their profits by reducing paperwork—which, by the way, is also great for the environment.

That has truths to it, but I suggest a larger purpose is at hand; the convenience and cash-back rewards are *lures* to help induce the cashless age. Electronic transactions are a bridge toward the point where the Antichrist will control all commerce:

> He also forced everyone, small and great, rich and poor, free and slave, to receive a mark on his right hand or on his forehead, so that no one could buy or sell unless he had the mark. (Revelation 13:16-17)

In 2005, Congress passed the Real ID Act, requiring that states issue drivers' licenses that meet Homeland Security guidelines and that link to a national database. Justifications given: it will "fight terrorism" and "protect against identity theft." Many states oppose the plan, because it is a major step toward a national ID card, which the Establishment has long advocated.

Someday, we will probably all receive a national ID necessary to conduct any business. Most of us, at some time, have known that unpleasant feeling of swiping a credit card that doesn't work. Our national ID card won't work either, once we're classified as politically unacceptable—all transactions will become impossible, and thus the "buy/sell" prophecy about the Antichrist would come true. And with all assets in electronic form, government bureaucrats could wipe out our banks accounts with a few keystrokes.

☹ But the Antichrist is supposed to put a mark on our hands or foreheads.

Be patient. After the national ID card come the implantable chips. The FDA has approved them. *Wired* reported back in 2002:

> The maker of an implantable human ID chip has launched a national campaign to promote the device, offering $50 discounts to the first 100,000 people who register to get embedded with the microchip.
>
> Applied Digital Solutions has coined the tagline "Get Chipped" to market its product, VeriChip.
>
> The rice-sized device costs $200. Those implanted must also pay for the doctor's injection fee and a monthly $10 database maintenance charge, said ADS spokesman Matthew Cossolotto.
>
> The VeriChip emits a 125-kilohertz radio frequency signal that transmits its unique ID number to a scanner. The number then accesses a computer database containing the client's file. Customers fill out a form detailing the information they want linked to their chip when they undergo the procedure, Cossolotto said.[198]

Later, the government could co-opt such devices—to keep its own files on us, monitor our whereabouts, and perhaps even transmit destructive signals *to* us.

☹ You're overlooking the wonderful benefits of these chips. They're already in some pets—if lost, they're easily recovered! Think of the potential for finding kidnapped children! And if someone with Alzheimer's wanders off, the police can scan them to find out who they are! An ER can scan an unconscious accident victim, and know their allergies, medical background, etc. In short, these chips could save lives!

Those are real examples, but such benefits *must* be offered to persuade people to accept the chips, which will ultimately conduct malevolent surveillance and control.

While on the subject of hi-tech, the Internet is worth mentioning. Yes, it's a fantastic place to shop and research, but is probably also the world's greatest spying system.

☺ No one can spy on *my* computer, Jim. It's loaded with security—firewall, anti-spyware, virus protection—you name it!

That's fine against ID thieves and teenage hackers. The Establishment *wants* it to work, so you'll feel secure and use computers without reservations. But the software won't thwart intelligence agencies. The companies that make it depend on the government for licensing and permits. If the authorities say: "For national security, you must allow us to bypass your software, so we can monitor terrorists," the software company won't hinder them.

Neither the government nor software firms would admit this—if they did, public outrage would follow, and monitoring would stop being effective. But if it is happening, the government can know anything about anyone. By reading your email, they'd know what you believe and which of your friends share your political views (very handy for determining who should disappear when the New World Order arrives).

In George Orwell's prophetic novel *1984*, the state was able to bend the hero, Winston, to its will by threatening him with his greatest fear: rats. Could the government know *your* greatest fear? Tabulating your email, as well as those online "opinion surveys," could enable them to form a complete psychological profile. They can also monitor: websites you visit, purchases you make, your electronic bank statements, etc.

☺ Um, news flash, Captain Paranoia. Intelligence agencies don't have enough personnel to monitor every American. Duh!

True, but they have enough to watch *the ones that interest them*. They could care less, of course, about two teenage girls discussing who might invite them to the prom.

Intelligence services' computers are reportedly at least 15 years ahead of our home PCs. I suspect the government can copy every hard drive in America—at least those connected to the Internet. If so, it may be storing that information on super-computers. There it lies until needed by an agent, who can quickly sift the data by "key word" searches.

In *1984*, the government monitored the public through TV sets. I have heard anecdotal evidence that the latest televisions transmit as well as receive. Thus the requirement that everyone "upgrade their TVs to digital." This gives the government an eye and ear in every room in your house equipped with television. As for the latest craze for wide-screen TVs: the bigger the set, the bigger *their* view. The U.S. government is even offering $40 coupons to encourage the public to upgrade to digital TV, as if entertainment were a Constitutional right!

And I hardly need mention that cell phone traffic can be intercepted.

Chapter 3 discussed inflation. Prices are soaring on food, postage stamps, housing, tuition, etc. Have you noticed computers and TVs are exceptions, and actually become *cheaper*? The reason is not just "innovation"; the Establishment wants being spied on to be affordable.

Intelligence gathering has long been the key to winning wars. This will be no less true during the Antichrist's war on the saints.

CHAPTER 20
THE SECRET WAR ON LIFE

Robert McNamara, President of the World Bank:

> We can begin with the most critical problems of population growth. As I have pointed out elsewhere, short of nuclear war itself, it is the gravest issue the world faces in the decades ahead. ... Either the current birthrate must come down more quickly, or the current death rates must go up. There is no other way. There are, of course, many ways in which the death rates can go up. In a thermonuclear age, war can accomplish it very quickly. Famine and disease are nature's ancient checks on population growth, and neither one has disappeared from the scene.[199]

Bertrand Russell, "High Priest of the Committee of 300":

> War has hitherto been disappointing in this respect [population reduction] but perhaps bacteriological war may prove more effective. If a Black Death could spread through the world once in every generation, the survivors could procreate freely, without making the world too full. The State of Affairs might be unpleasant, but what of it? Really high-minded people are indifferent to happiness, especially other people's happiness.[200]

Prince Philip, Chairman of the World Wildlife Fund:

> In the event that I am reincarnated, I would like to return as a deadly virus in order to contribute something to solve overpopulation.[201]

Ted Turner, founder of CNN:

> A total world population of 250-300 million people, a 95 percent decline from present levels, would be ideal.[202]

Ecologist Jacques Cousteau:

> World population must be stabilized and to do that we must eliminate 350,000 people per day.[203]

Paul Watson, President, Sea Shepherd Conservation Club:

> No human community should be larger than 20,000 people . . . .We need to radically and intelligently reduce human populations to fewer than one billion.[204]

There is really only one way, of course, to reduce the world's population from six billion to the one billion Watson desires: kill people.

Zbigniew Brzezinski, advisor and mentor to Barack Obama:

> In earlier times it was easier to control a million people, literally, than physically to kill a million people. Today it is infinitely easier to kill a million people than to control a million people.[205]

The preceding quotes reflect the Establishment's views on population. Some folks ask: if these gentlemen really want to decrease population, why don't they start with themselves?

Though justifications for population reduction are widely publicized, *under*population is what actually threatens the West. For a population to remain steady, fertility rates must be about 2.1 births per woman. Yet the European Union's rate is only 1.5—far below replacement.

Earth looks overpopulated only if you focus on urban areas. If the world's entire population was inside Texas, each person would have over 1,200 square feet of space; a family of four would have 5,000 square feet of land, a typical spread for many American middle-class homes. *I'm definitely not suggesting that all of Texas is habitable, or that this scenario could be implemented in actual practice*; but it gives the numbers some perspective.

It is claimed there isn't enough food for a large global population. But farmers use less than half the world's arable land. And modern agricultural methods have dramatically increased yield per acre. Furthermore, the U.S. government currently pays farmers about $2 billion annually to *not* grow food and keep 40 million farmland acres idle. Why not pay them to *grow* food instead, and give it to the hungry? Hunger's solution is *more food*, not *less people*.

Population reduction also opposes God's command "Be fruitful and multiply."

Why do the Illuminati really want less people?

• When the Antichrist rules, they want a population small enough to control;

• Less people, they believe, means more resources for themselves;

• As Satanists, they share the satanic urge to kill. Jesus told the Pharisees: "You belong to your father, the devil, and you want to carry out your father's desire. He was a murderer from the beginning, not holding to the truth, for there is no truth in him." (John 8:44)

Those are the reasons for population reduction. "Scientific" and "humanitarian" rationales are propaganda.

Abortion, which has slain over 40 million unborn American babies since legalization, was introduced to help achieve this goal. The agitprop "a woman's right to choose" was a facade for population reduction. Eugenics, Planned Parenthood and the birth control push also emerged for this objective.

Conservative Christians oppose abortion. But unknown to most people, another depopulation method is being implemented.

Death in a Disguise

This may seem insultingly obvious, but suppose you were walking along a lake's edge, and saw a little boy drowning, just within arm's reach. What would God expect you to do? Reach in and pull him out, or pray for the child's divine rescue? Obviously,

God would want you to *act*, not just pray. Does it seem probable that He would even answer such a prayer?

Let's vary the situation. Suppose you were watching a little girl in a hospital bed, and an evil-looking person entered the room with a clearly-marked bottle of poison. Let's say you knew this poison would cripple the child for life. Would God expect you to: (A) stop the poison from being given; or (B) let it be given, then pray for healing after it crippled the child? Would God likely honor such a prayer?

I believe the last story illustrates something happening in our culture.

Before making controversial remarks about the medical world, I'll comment that:

• I have been a registered nurse for nearly 40 years, and have worked in major Boston-area hospitals. Though only a tiny part of the "Medical Establishment," I do not speak as a complete layman.

• I have worked with many outstanding doctors and nurses, and have the highest regard for people in these professions.

• Finally, please note: Nothing I say should be construed as personal medical advice. If you are ill, seek care and counsel from a competent, licensed health care professional.

I have a friend whose daughter is mentally and physically incapacitated for life—since the day she received a childhood vaccine at age seven.

One patient I encountered in the hospital was unable to walk; he had become disabled within 24 hours of receiving a flu shot. The doctors did a CT scan and other tests—everything was negative. The man told me: "It had to be the flu shot." I agreed.

☹ Hold it, Jim. Oh boy, I can already see where this is going. I'm surprised at you! As an RN, you of all people should know that every medication has an occasional bad side effect for a few individuals. For vaccines, there's always that one person in 10,000, and you've just selected exceptional cases so you can go on a "vaccines are bad" rant.

It was unfortunate about the people you've mentioned, but those are just the chances we have to take. The benefits of vaccines totally outweigh the risks!

As a more pandemic example, in 1976 President Ford was persuaded to go on television and tell Americans it was urgent they be inoculated against swine flu. Congress appropriated $136 million for the vaccine's manufacturers. The vaccine paralyzed hundreds of people, at least 25 died, and over a billion dollars in lawsuits resulted. The vaccinations were halted—and the swine flu itself turned out to be no threat at all.

For any reader with online access, please go to the following website:

www.vaccinetruth.org/6_out_of_10,000.htm

There you will read innumerable accounts by parents whose children were perfectly normal—until vaccination destroyed their lives. I would love to print some of the stories in this book. But because of their sensitive and personal nature, and because my book makes controversial claims about other subjects, I consider it prudent to direct my readers to the website.

☹ I'm sure there are some gut-wrenching tragedies out there, but again, those are just rare exceptions.

They are not. To start, the incidence of autism, a disease unknown before the 1940s, has been skyrocketing, especially since the 1988 introduction of the MMR vaccine. Thousands of parents have seen their healthy babies descend into autism shortly after receiving the vaccine, including the high-profile case of Doug Flutie, Jr., son of the famed football quarterback.

☹ Parents aren't experts, and can be blinded by personal suffering. Show me one *doctor* who thinks vaccines cause autism.

Bernard Rimland, PhD, founder of the Autism Society of America and the Autism Research Institute:

I was the first to announce the "autism epidemic," in 1995, and I pointed out in that article that excessive vaccines were a plausible cause of the epidemic. As you know, an enormous amount of clinical laboratory research (as opposed to epidemiological research) has been accumulated since that time, supporting my position. . . . The evidence is now overwhelming, despite the misinformation from the Centers for Disease Control and Prevention, the American Academy of Pediatrics and the Institute of Medicine.[206]

Much attention has been focused on the MMR shot itself, whereas in all probability it is a combination of the three factors listed above: the increasing number of vaccines, the large amount of mercury, and the inherent danger of the triple vaccine . . . . The MMR vaccine is also especially suspect because laboratories in England, Ireland, and Japan have found evidence of MMR vaccine viruses in the intestinal tracts of autistic children, but not in control group, non-autistic children.[207]

David Ayoub, MD:

I am no longer "trying to dig up evidence to prove" vaccines cause autism. There is already abundant evidence. . . . This debate is not scientific but is political.[208]

Jaquelyn McCandless, MD:

As a clinician, my current belief which guides my practice with these children is that any child given the HepB vaccination at birth and subsequent boosters along with DPT has received unacceptable levels of neurotoxin in the form of the ethyl mercury in the thimerosal preservative used in the vaccine. In any child with a genetic immune susceptibility (probably about one in six) this sets off a series of events that injure the brain-gut-immune system. By the time they are ready to receive the MMR vaccination, their immune system is so impaired in a great number of these children that the triple vaccine cannot be handled by the now dysfunctional immune system and they begin their obvious descent into the autistic spectrum disorder.[209]

Boyd Haley, PhD, Chairman of Chemistry Department, University of Kentucky:

> I have encouraged parents of autistic children in the USA to get urinary porphyrin profiles done to determine if their child shows signs of mercury toxicity. It is almost 100% that these children, at least those that have reported back to me, are moderate to extremely mercury toxic with regards to this clinical testing procedure. Just where would children less than 7 years of age obtain enough mercury to inhibit their porphyrin pathways? So the IOM [Institute of Medicine] suggests looking everywhere except where the most logical place would be, in the vaccines given to these children that contained thimerosal. The IOM ought to be ashamed of itself, if not for doing something scientifically dishonest, then for being so inept as to think vaccine exclusion from consideration of exclusion for autism causation would be accepted by the American public. Most importantly, while they are looking everywhere else these children lose time before an acceptable treatment for mercury toxicity can be developed—and at least a significant number of autistic children are definitely mercury toxic.[210]

☹ Jim, I've heard it only *looks* like autism is increasing—that the truth is, the rates have always been the same; we're just getting better at recognizing the disease.

If that's true, where are all the 40-year old, 50-year old, and 60-year old autistics? And it's not just autism. Vaccines are linked to Sudden Infant Death Syndrome (SIDS), also known as "crib death" or "cot death." Doctors say no reason is known for this phenomenon, in which babies "just suddenly die." The following testimony—very typical—is from the website www.thinktwice. com/sids.htm.

Our beautiful daughter was born on February 14 and died on April 17. What was unusual was that earlier on the day she died I had taken her to the Military Base hospital for her two month checkup. The doctor told me that she was just perfect. Then the doctor said that she needed four shots. I replied Four!? She assured me that it was completely normal and that it was better to give her all at such an early age (because she wouldn't remember the shots). That evening after feeding [our daughter] we laid her down to sleep and checked on her 45 minutes later and discovered her dead. I told the police, coroner and investigators that I thought it was the shots because she was perfectly fine that day and before the shots. But after 3 weeks we finally got the answer from the autopsy that it was indeed SIDS. To this day I believe that it was the shots and no one can convince me otherwise.

Thomas Levy, MD:

Statistically speaking, the data regarding DPT vaccinated infants is absolutely frightening. The death rate is eight times greater than normal within only three days of receiving a DPT shot. The dreaded Sudden Infant Death Syndrome (SIDS) clusters very strongly around the typical time frame of DPT shot administration.

DPT vaccinations are usually given at ages two months, four months, and six months. SIDS occurs mostly during the same time frame (85% from one to six months), with the largest incidence occurring at two and four months, in a bimodal fashion. This means that most of the SIDS cases actually cluster directly after the injections, and not in smooth fashion over the entire time period. One study showed that of 103 infants who died of SIDS, 70% had received the DPT vaccine within three weeks.[211]

Evidence is growing that vaccines cause many other ill-nesses—for adults as well as children—and prevent none. To again quote Dr. Rimland of the Autism Research Institute:

Autism is not the only severe chronic illness which has reached epidemic proportions as the number of (profitable) vaccines has rapidly increased. Children now receive 33 vaccines before they enter school—a huge increase. The vaccines contain not only live viruses but also very significant amounts of highly toxic substances such as mercury, and formaldehyde. Could this be the reason for the upsurge in autism, ADHD, asthma, arthritis, Crohn's disease, lupus and other chronic disorders?[212]

Robert Mendelsohn, MD:

There is no convincing scientific evidence that mass inoculations can be credited with eliminating any childhood disease. ... The greatest threat of childhood diseases lies in the dangerous and ineffectual efforts made to prevent them through mass immunization.[213]

There are significant risks associated with every immunization and numerous contraindications that may make it dangerous for the shots to be given to your child .... There is growing suspicion that immunization against relatively harmless childhood diseases may be responsible for the dramatic increase in autoimmune diseases since mass inoculations were introduced. These are fearful diseases such as cancer, leukemia, rheumatoid arthritis, multiple sclerosis, Lou Gehrig's disease, lupus erythematosus, and the Guillain-Barré syndrome.[214]

Dr. Viera Scheibner, PhD, developer (with her husband Lief Karlsson) of the Cotwatch Breathing Monitor for infants:

I did not find it difficult to conclude that there is no evidence whatsoever that vaccines of any kind are effective in preventing the infectious diseases they are supposed to prevent. Further, adverse effects are amply documented and are far more significant to public health than any adverse effects of infectious diseases. Immunizations not only did not prevent any infectious diseases, they caused more suffering and more deaths than has any other human activity in the entire history

of medical intervention. It will be decades before the mop-
ping-up after the disasters caused by childhood vaccination
will be completed.[215]

Archie Kalokerinos, MD:

The further I looked the more shocked I became. I found that
the whole vaccine business was indeed a gigantic hoax. Most
doctors are convinced that they are useful, but if you look at
the proper statistics and study the instances of these diseases
you will realize that this is not so.[216]

Philip Incao, MD:

A critical point which is never mentioned by those advocating
mandatory vaccination of children is that children's health
has declined significantly since 1960 when vaccines began to
be widely used. According to the National Health Interview
Survey conducted annually by the National Center for Health
Statistics since 1957, a shocking 31% of U.S. children today
have a chronic health problem, 18% of children require special health care or related services and 6.7% of children have
a significant disability due to a chronic physical or mental
condition. Respiratory allergies, asthma and learning dis-
abilities are the most common of these.[217]

Ted Koren, DC:

Childhood vaccines are giving us a world of chronic illness:
autism, developmental disorders, Asperger's Syndrome, brain
tumors, leukemia, cancers, information processing disorders,
impulsive violence, allergies, asthma, diabetes, Crohn's disease,
intestinal disorders (all conditions rare before mass vaccination) are just some of the vaccine associated disorders.[218]

How about Alzheimer's? Koren states:

According to Hugh Fudenberg, MD, the world's leading
immunogeneticist and 13th most quoted biologist of our times
(nearly 850 papers in peer review journals), if an individual

has had five consecutive flu shots between 1970 and 1980 (the years studied) his/her chances of getting Alzheimer's Disease is ten times higher than if they had one, two or no shots. I asked Dr. Fudenberg why this was so and he said it was due to the mercury and aluminum that is in every flu shot (and most childhood shots). The gradual mercury and aluminum buildup in the brain causes cognitive dysfunction. Is that why Alzheimer's is expected to quadruple?[219]

Dr. Howard B. Urnovitz, Scientific Director, Chronic Illness Foundation:

Had my mother and father known that the poliovirus vaccines of the 1950s were heavily contaminated with more than 26 monkey viruses, including the cancer virus SV40, I can say with certainty that they would not have allowed their children and themselves to take those vaccines. Both of my parents might not have developed cancers suspected of being vaccine-related, and might even be alive today.[220]

Harold Buttram, MD:

Most infants have been receiving up to 15 doses of mercury-containing vaccines by the time they are 6 months old. It is almost inconceivable that these heavy burdens of foreign immunologic materials, introduced into the immature systems of children, could fail to bring about disruptions and adverse reactions in these systems. . . . When arbitrary decisions in the mandating of vaccines are made by government bureaucracies, which frequently work hand-in-glove with the pharmaceutical industry, with no recourse open to parents, we have all the potential ingredients for a tragedy of historic proportions.[221]

Gerhard Buchwald, MD:

Vaccinations are now carried out for purely commercial reasons because they fetch huge profits for the pharmaceutical industry. . . . There is no scientific evidence that vaccinations are of any benefit, but it is clear that they cause a great deal of harm. . . . Today there are 800,000 children and youngsters under the age of 15 years [in Germany] with asthma. 800,000! Neurodermitis, once a rare complaint, has become so common that there are several support networks with many thousands of members. The "Frankenpost" of April 2004 reported an estimated 27 million people now suffer from hay fever, neurodermitis and allergic asthma in Germany.[222]

Eva Snead, MD:

Within a few years of the polio vaccine we started seeing some strange phenomena like the year before the first 300,000 doses were given in the United States childhood leukaemia had never struck in children under the age of two. One year after the first onslaught they had the first cases of children under the age of two that died of leukaemia.[223]

Gordon Stewart, MD, Emeritus Professor of Public Health, University of Glasgow:

My own view, based upon some years of observation and experience, is quite firm. I supported the use of the vaccine in 1951 and subsequently with very little hesitation until about 1972, and gave pertussis vaccine between 1951 and 1956 to each of my four children. I would not dream of doing so again because it has become clear to me not only that the vaccine is incompletely protective, but also that the side-effects which I thought to be temporary are in fact dangerous, unpredictably so. There is no doubt in my mind that in the UK alone some hundreds, if not thousands, of well infants have suffered irreparable brain damage needlessly and that their lives and those of their parents have been wrecked in consequence.[224]

☹ Oh, the various diseases they're talking about were *always* around, just like autism. It's just that it wasn't until the 19th century that doctors become smart enough to diagnose them and think up names for them.

No, they weren't diagnosed and named until the 19th century because that's when they—and compulsory vaccination—began.

☹ So what are you trying to say, chum? That *every* medical problem is from vaccination?

No one would make such a claim; illness has been around since antiquity. It can be caused by nutritional deficiencies, bacterial infections, trauma, and mental (psychosomatic) causes. The Bible also cites spiritual (demonic) causes. And some diseases are congenital—people are born with them. However, even these mutational inherited disorders may be passed to us from ancestors whose genes were deranged by vaccination.

Gerhard Buchwald, MD:

> In 1866, an English physician described a very strange illness. Children looked like Mongols. His name was Down. That's why we call it Down's Syndrome today. . . . I should add that this syndrome is a result of the vaccinations carried throughout England by Jenner in 1796. . . . It (Down's Syndrome) is probably the first congenital disease caused by vaccinations. In Germany, the first child with evidence of Down's Syndrome was reported in 1922. Today, one in every 700 newborns has it.[225]

In addition to physical diseases, let's not forget the emotional and mental problems vaccines have induced. A whole *spectrum* of autism is now acknowledged. How many kids are criticized as "withdrawn," "introverted," "clumsy," "spaced out," or "dorks," when they are 10, 20, 30 percent autistic, completely undiagnosed? How many out-of-control, hyperactive, children are misattributed to bad parenting?

☹ You're wrong! I'm sure these doctors you've been quoting must be *quacks*. I'm also sure the big pharmaceutical companies are *not motivated by profits*, but by the *sheer goodness of their hearts*. Why, I bet they did loads of testing on these vaccines to make certain they were absolutely safe *before* giving them to the public . . . right? . . . I mean, didn't they?

Harold Buttram, MD:

Safety studies on vaccinations are limited to short time periods only: several days to several weeks. There are NO (NONE) long term (months or years) safety studies on any vaccination or immunization. For this reason, there are valid grounds for suspecting that many delayed-type vaccine reactions may be taking place unrecognized as to their true nature.[226]

Tim O'Shea, DC:

The only safety testing that has ever been done on the pertussis vaccine in the past 50 years is an unproven method called the Mouse Weight Gain Test. The "scientists" inject the vaccine to be tested into the stomachs of baby mice. If the mice continue to gain weight and don't die right away, it is assumed the vaccine is safe and effective for humans. That's it! I'm not making this up! ...The only toxicity test required for the initial licensing of the DPT vaccine in the United States was this mouse weight-gain test 60 years ago.[227]

Hugh Fudenberg, MD:

Longest safety trial of the triple vaccine (MMR, all live attenuated viruses) was three weeks.[228]

Bart Classen, MD:

The anthrax vaccine was approved without ever doing a controlled clinical study. There is no long term safety data on the anthrax vaccine. The government admitted this in congressional hearings. It is a distortion of the truth to say there is substantial safety data.[229]

The most logical way to test vaccine safety would be long-term studies comparing vaccinated children to unvaccinated control groups. But that has never been done!

Philip Incao, MD:

The best way to determine the risk-benefit profile of any vaccination is well known and in theory is quite simple: Take
a group of vaccinated children and compare them with a
matched group of unvaccinated children. If the groups are
well-matched and large enough and the length of time the
children are observed following vaccination long enough,
then such a study is deemed the "gold standard" of vaccine
research because its data is as accurate a reflection as medical research is capable of achieving of how vaccinations are
actually affecting our nation's children. Incredible as it sounds,
such a common-sense controlled study comparing vaccinated
to unvaccinated children has never been done in America for
any vaccination. This means that mass vaccination is essentially a large-scale experiment on our nation's children.[230]

Vaccines are virtually *compulsory* throughout the U.S.; most
schools refuse to admit children that aren't "up to date." Thus there
are very few unvaccinated kids to compare with.

☹ But vaccines have wiped diseases off the face of the Earth! It all
started with Jenner defeating smallpox. Polio crippled millions of
children before the Salk and Sabin vaccines eliminated *that* scourge.

The claims for vaccines stamping out diseases are based upon:
• distortions of data;
• diseases naturally declining and running their course, falsely
attributed to vaccines;
• disease reduction from improved hygiene and nutrition,
falsely attributed to vaccines; and
• a final reason we will discuss shortly.

Vernon Coleman, MD:

One of the medical profession's greatest boasts is that it
eradicated smallpox through the use of the smallpox vaccine.
I myself believed this claim for many years. But it simply isn't
true. One of the worst smallpox epidemics of all time took

place in England between 1870 and 1872—nearly two decades after compulsory vaccination was introduced. After this evidence that smallpox vaccination didn't work the people of Leicester in the English midlands refused to have the vaccine any more. When the next smallpox epidemic struck in the early 1890s the people of Leicester relied upon good sanitation and a system of quarantine. There was only one death from smallpox in Leicester during that epidemic. In contrast the citizens of other towns (who had been vaccinated) died in vast numbers. . . . Doctors and drug companies may not like it but the truth is that surveillance, quarantine and better living conditions got rid of smallpox—not the smallpox vaccine. . . . It is worth pointing out that Edward Jenner, widely feted as the inventor of the smallpox vaccine, tried out the first smallpox vaccination on his own 10 month old son. His son remained mentally retarded until his death at the age of 21. Jenner refused to have his second child vaccinated.[231]

Viera Scheibner, PhD:

Polio has not been eradicated by vaccination, it is lurking behind a redefinition and new diagnostic names like viral or aseptic meningitis. . . . According to one of the 1997 issues of the MMWR, there are some 30,000 to 50,000 cases of viral meningitis per year in the United States alone. That's where all those 30,000-50,000 cases of polio disappeared after the introduction of mass vaccination.[232]

William Douglass, MD:

What the vaccinators don't tell you is that communicable diseases have been declining at a steady rate for 150 years and that there is no relationship between the various diseases and the onset of immunization. Without exception, the vaccine program for each of the childhood diseases was inaugurated after that particular disease had begun to disappear. Contrary to what you have been told, this includes polio. What the vaccines have done is cause the various childhood diseases to become adulthood diseases—with far more serious implications, mumps in men and rubella in women for example.

The Salk vaccine failed completely (we'll issue a special report on that at a later date). And the Sabin vaccine was a disaster. It caused many cases of polio and showed no relationship to the disease except for an increase in polio during the early '60s, caused by the vaccine itself. And now we have the sensational findings from the Annals of the New York Academy of Sciences, which strongly indicate that polio did not go away at all, but now manifests itself as chronic fatigue syndrome. . . . When the Coxsackie viruses were first isolated from CFS patients, it wasn't realized that we were simply dealing with a new form of polio. This new polio was caused by the replacement of the polio viruses with their brothers, the Coxsackie viruses. As the researchers didn't get the connection at first, these new polio cases were labeled "post-polio syndrome," "chronic fatigue syndrome," and "myalgic encephalomyelitis."[233]

Gerhard Buchwald, MD:

The "victory over epidemics" was not won by medical science or by doctors—and certainly not by vaccines . . . . the decline . . . has been the result of technical, social and hygienic improvements and especially of improved nutrition. . . . Consider carefully whether you want to let yourself or your children undergo the dangerous, controversial, ineffective and no longer necessary procedure called vaccination, because the claim that vaccinations are the cause for the decline of infectious diseases is utter nonsense.[234]

Guylaine Lanctot, MD:

We are taught by the authorities that vaccines protect us against eventual aggressive viruses and microbes, and, therefore, prevent contagious illnesses and epidemics. This lie has been perpetuated for 150 years despite the INEFFECTIVENESS of vaccines in protecting against illnesses ... the USELESSNESS of certain vaccines, notably, TB & Tetanus ... Diphtheria ... Influenza and hepatitis B.[235]

Peter Morrell, medical historian, Staffordshire University, UK:

In truth, every major infection for which vaccines exist was originally in massive decline before a single vaccine was introduced. This certainly applies to Diphtheria, Tuberculosis, Whooping Cough and Measles.[236]

Dr. J. Anthony Morris, former Chief Vaccine Control Officer at the FDA:

There is no evidence that any influenza vaccine thus far developed is effective in preventing or mitigating any attack of influenza. The producers of these vaccines know that they are worthless, but they go on selling them, anyway.[237]

Russell Blaylock, MD:

They say that if children are not vaccinated against measles millions of children could die during a measles epidemic. They know this is nonsense. What they are using is examples taken from developing countries with poor nutrition and poor immune function in which such epidemic death can occur. In the United States we would not see this because of better nutrition, better health facilities and better sanitation. In fact, most deaths seen when measles outbreaks occur in the United States occur either in children in which vaccination was contraindicated, the vaccine did not work or in children with chronic, immune-suppressing diseases.

In fact, in most studies these children catching the measles or other childhood diseases have been either fully immunized or partially immunized. The big secret among "vaccinologists" is that anywhere from 20 to 50% of children are not resistant to the diseases for which they have been immunized.[238]

☺ OK, so why were old mortality rates so much higher? In 1900, Americans had a life expectancy of only 47 years! Today it's 77! Obviously our health is improving!

But what do the numbers mean? In 1900, people weren't dying from old age at 47. Americans who reached a "ripe old age" then lived as long as old-timers today. Life expectancy simply measures the average life span after birth. It is impacted by anything causing death—including war, disease and hunger. Many of the infectious diseases that increased mortality in 1900 were eliminated or reduced, but not by vaccination.

☹ I don't think you understand how vaccines work. You take a virus, but weaken it. Then you inject it into the child. Because it's weakened, he doesn't get the full-blown disease. However, the immune system creates antibodies to counter the weak virus. Then, later on, when the kid encounters the *real* virus, his immune system's ready to handle it, so he doesn't get sick and die.

Guylaine Lanctot, MD, aptly compares this vaccine methodology to rape:

> Number one, vaccines make people sick. They don't work. They don't protect. The use of vaccines is totally wrong! It's perfect nonsense based on fear. It's fear of the disease. So, in order for you not to get the disease I, as your doctor, am going to give the disease to you right away, but not as strong. This way your body will know about the disease and, if you ever get it in the future, you won't be as sick the second time . . . .What they say is total nonsense. If I came to you and said, "I'm going to perform a little sexual assault on you—a small rape—because, one day you could meet a rapist and you could be raped. But, it won't be as bad the second time as the first time." This is exactly the same thing as giving someone a vaccine, or a little bit of disease. It's nonsense! Immunization is total nonsense! More than that is what's hidden from people about vaccines. They are dangerous. One child out of five has overwhelming disabilities from

vaccines—neurological problems, seizures. I've got a whole list. There are plenty of books on this subject. Doctors don't even read about this.[239]

Vaccination will create some antibodies, but this doesn't mean you can't still get the disease.

Ted Koren, DC:

Whenever we read vaccine papers the MD researchers always assume that if there are high antibody levels after vaccination, then there is immunity (immunogenicity). But are antibody levels and immunity the same? No! Antibody levels are not the same as IMMUNITY. The recent MUMPS vaccine fiasco in Switzerland has re-emphasized this point. Three mumps vaccines—Rubini, Jeryl-Lynn and Urabe (the one withdrawn because it caused encephalitis) all produced excellent antibody levels, but those vaccinated with the Rubini strain had the same attack rate as those not vaccinated at all, there were some who said that it actually caused outbreaks.[240]

In nature, if a person encounters a virus, the body has defense lines, starting with the skin, to keep it out. If inhaled or swallowed, its impact is minimized by more defenses in the gastrointestinal and respiratory tracts. But in vaccination, the body's peripheral defenses are *bypassed* and the virus injected directly under the skin, where it easily accesses the vascular system.

Furthermore, in life we ordinarily encounter one virus at a time. But in today's vaccination protocols, several viruses are injected *simultaneously*. This grotesquely unnatural situation puts incredible strain on a tender infant whose immune system is still under development.

The child's body must also cope with the vaccine's chemicals, such as mercury, aluminum and formaldehyde, as well as monkey protein (which the viruses were cultured in). Most American children receive over thirty vaccinations by the time they enter school. Autoimmune diseases result.

The eminent neurologist Marcel Kinsbourne stated:

The body responds to the vaccine with an immune reaction that attacks its components. Sometimes the immune reaction also attacks a constituent of the body itself, which bears some chemical resemblance to a constituent of the vaccine. Reports of cases in which nerve cells have been attacked have been published for tetanus, influenza and measles vaccines. The "self-attack" is the result of a cascade of biochemical changes which takes at least five days to cause clinically observable disease, and may take at least up to six weeks.[241]

Eva Snead, MD:

Well you can start for instance with monkey protein which, of course, is a contaminant in the vaccine. Monkey protein is extremely similar to human protein. When you become allergic to monkey protein because it was injected into you and you make antibodies, you tend then to attack your own tissues . . . .[242]

Vaccines apparently created the many autoimmune diseases of modern times—lupus, multiple sclerosis, myasthenia gravis, Guillain-Barré syndrome, Crohn's disease, colitis, rheumatoid arthritis, and many others not regularly classed as autoimmune, such as leukemia and Gulf War Syndrome. (Soldiers sent to Iraq have been given innumerable vaccines.) Nearly all chronic diseases have foundations named after them; they collect millions of dollars in donations annually, but none ever find a cure. How can they, when they're looking in the wrong place for the cause?

☹ You're so down on vaccines! What are you trying to say? That doctors and nurses are *deliberately* trying to kill us?

Doctors and nurses, *absolutely not*. They believe they're doing the right thing, based on the information they're given. But at the top of the drug cartel, I believe vaccines are understood as planned genocide.

Guylaine Lanctot, MD:

So, more than that, vaccines are used to test biological weapons. I found that vaccines are used to spread diseases. They are used for targeted genocides.[243]

Archie Kalokerinos, MD:

You cannot immunize sick children, malnourished children, and expect to get away with it. You'll kill far more children than would have died from natural infection. . . . My final conclusion after forty years or more in this business [medicine] is that the unofficial policy of the World Health Organization and the unofficial policy of the "Save the Children's Fund" and [other vaccine-promoting] organizations is one of murder and genocide. They want to make it appear as if they are saving these kids, but in actual fact they don't. I am talking of those at the very top. Beneath that level is another level of doctors and health workers, like myself, who don't really understand what they are doing. But I cannot see any other possible explanation. It is murder and it is genocide.[244]

Today, millions of people, especially in Africa, are dying of AIDS. Why?

Donald W. Scott MA, Msc:

In laboratories throughout the United States and in a certain number in Canada including at the University of Alberta, the US Government provided the leadership for the development of AIDS for the purpose of population control. After the scientists had perfected it, the government sent medical teams from the Centers for Disease Control—under the direction of Dr. Donald A. Henderson, their investigator into the 1957 chronic fatigue epidemic in Punta Gorda—during 1969 to 1971 to Africa and some countries such as India, Nepal and Pakistan where they thought the population was becoming too large. They gave them all a free vaccination against smallpox; but five years after receiving this vaccination, 60%

of those inoculated were suffering from AIDS. They tried to blame it on a monkey, which is nonsense.[245]

The official explanation for AIDS is that a green monkey bit a human being, infecting him with the virus, and then people spread it to each other. However, vaccines are cultured in the kidney cells of *green monkeys*. Clearly, the World Health Organization's mass vaccination program has caused the African AIDS pandemic.

Microsoft founder Bill Gates is on record saying that the world is facing a dire overpopulation crisis. Yet Gates has also donated over $10 billion for vaccine development. Now, if vaccines truly improve health, they would *increase* world population, wouldn't they? Gates is logical enough to understand this contradiction. But if vaccines are intended to kill people, Gates's words and actions become consistent. Check the YouTube video "Bill Gates: Population Reduction Using Vaccinations" (http://www.youtube.com/watch?v=T9vZLlJhI7o), which includes both a news clip on Gates's $10 billion vaccine donation, and a speech he gave decrying overpopulation. In the speech, Gates let it slip that vaccines will *reduce* world population.

☹ Look, if vaccines were designed to kill us, kids should drop dead the moment they're injected.

If that happened, the cause-and-effect would be too obvious for any authority to deny, and no parents would let their children be vaccinated. Therefore, vaccines are designed to work slowly, taking effect after days, weeks—or even years later, when weakness, stress or age may increase one's vulnerability.

Now, as to the final reason infectious diseases declined. I believe some may have been *withdrawn*. Read the works of former MI6 officer John Coleman, and you will learn how deadly viruses are developed in laboratories and intentionally spread. Viruses are generally regarded as non-living. *Wikipedia* states:

It has been argued extensively whether viruses are living organisms. Most virologists consider them non-living, as they

do not meet all the criteria of the generally accepted definition of life.[246]

I suggest:

• that viruses may not be a natural phenomenon of God's
creation, but genocidal agents, possibly manufactured since antiquity;

• that these viruses caused some of the epidemics that were
used to justify vaccination;

• that vaccines became the preferred genocide weapon, because
whereas viruses could go out of control, vaccine distribution is
easily managed, and specific groups precisely targeted;

• that as vaccines were instituted, the dispensing of certain
viruses was halted, creating the illusion that vaccines had eliminated diseases.

For those who consider the *Protocols of the Learned Elders of
Zion* a forgery, Protocol 10:19 says:

> It is indispensable to trouble the peoples relations with gov-
> ernments so as to utterly exhaust humanity with dissension,
> hatred, envy, and even by starvation, want, and *the inoculation
> of diseases.* (emphasis added)

The Protocols were first published over 100 years ago. If, as
claimed, they were a fake orchestrated by the Czar's police, how
did they dream up an idea like "inoculation of diseases"?

☹ Doctors aren't stupid. If vaccines were really harmful, they would
recognize that.

Most doctors rely on journals which (A) are owned by the
Establishment, and (B) depend heavily on drug companies for
advertising revenue. In 1898, leadership of the American Medical
Association was assumed by George Simmons, a journalist and
abortionist with no medical experience, but plenty of political
connections and Establishment backing. Since then, the AMA has
promoted pharmaceutical and surgical treatment of disease while
suppressing alternative, natural healing methods as "quackery."

Doctors who discovered cures for cancer over the past century were ruthlessly suppressed. Among these: Royal Raymond Rife (using specific light frequencies on cancer-causing viruses); Dr. John Beard (using the enzyme trypsin to devour cancer cells); Dr. William F. Koch (cellular oxidation metabolism therapy); Dr. Max Gerson (nutritional healing); and Harry Hoxsey (herbal remedy). All were targeted for ridicule, suppression, and in cases, assassination. A rather long but excellent video that exemplifies the politics of cancer can be found on YouTube under the title "Cancer Cure: Dr. Burzynski Cure for Cancer Documentary" or http://www.youtube.com/watch?v=UvYHdIlqHTA. It deals with attempts to suppress the effective alternative cancer treatments of Dr. Stanislaw Burzynski.

For the pharmaceutical industry, vaccines create a profitable vicious circle of increasing dependence on medication. For example:

- Vaccines create attention deficit disorder in a child;
- He or she is then placed on the medication Ritalin.

Or:

- Vaccines create a certain cancer;
- The victim receives chemotherapy drugs for that cancer;
- But the chemotherapy causes nausea, constipation, and numerous other side effects, so the person receives medications for *those*.

God created us with perfect immune systems. They cannot be improved by shooting viruses and chemicals into them. Man has been tinkering with nature for years—substituting baby formula for breast milk, removing tonsils as "useless appendages," and invariably the original design has proven best.

☹ Oh, yeah? Well, if the immune system is so "perfect," how come people die from infections?

A bullet can pierce your skin and kill you. Your skin is not bullet-proof, but this doesn't mean it's poorly designed. The body is perfect for the world God created. When evil is *added* to the scene, the body can be overwhelmed, whether by manufactured bullets or manufactured viruses.

Postscript: Illness and God's Will

The Bible sometimes attributes illnesses to Satan and his demons. For example, in Luke 3:10-11, we read:

> On a Sabbath Jesus was teaching in one of the synagogues, and a woman was there who had been crippled by a spirit for eighteen years. She was bent over and could not straighten up at all.

After Jesus healed her, the synagogue ruler complained that Jesus had worked on the Sabbath. Jesus replied:

> Doesn't each of you on the Sabbath untie his ox or donkey from the stall and lead it out to give it water? Then should not this woman, a daughter of Abraham, whom Satan has kept bound for eighteen long years, be set free on the Sabbath day from what bound her? (Luke 13:15-16)

In Matthew 17, a man asked Jesus to heal his son, who was suffering from seizures. The Bible records:

> Jesus rebuked the demon, and it came out of the boy, and he was healed from that moment. (Matthew 17:18)

In the book of Job, we read:

> So Satan went out from the presence of the Lord and afflicted Job with painful sores from the soles of his feet to the top of his head. (Job 2:7)

God did *permit* Satan to harm Job (after the evil one disparaged Job's faith), but nonetheless Satan was the perpetrator.

I definitely am not suggesting here that every disease has satanic origins. However, I believe we may sometimes err by attributing to *God* tragedies caused by *Satan*. ("Why did God do this?")

Many Christians have said, when sickness or other misfortunes strike: "This is God's plan. He is in control." If the little girl next door is raped and murdered, they might even say: "It was God's will. He had a purpose to it. He works in mysterious ways." In certain cases, they might be correct.

However, some theologians point out—and I agree—that while God is *omnipotent*, he isn't necessarily *controlling* every situation. In Matthew 12, Jesus rebuked the Pharisees for attributing His miracles to Satan; I believe the Lord is also displeased when we credit Him with Satan's work. God is sovereign; He knows all events that happen; but saying He *caused* them is different.

Let's take an obvious situation. Suppose I'm a corporate CEO, tempted to have an affair with my gorgeous secretary. So I tell myself, "Everything that happens is the Lord's will. Therefore if I commit adultery, it's His will." Then suppose I have this affair, and my wife finds out, so I advise her: "Hey, God's in control—He must have had a purpose in this. Maybe He wants you to learn forgiveness!"

I think we can agree such rationalizations would be absurd. Obviously an affair is not God's will, but a *violation* of His will, of the Seventh Commandment. Likewise, if our neighbor's child is raped and murdered, I believe we shouldn't call that God's will, but its *violation*. And with vaccines increasingly exposed as disease-generating, perhaps we shouldn't automatically call sickness God's will either.

As we previously discussed, while the Bible often speaks of God's sovereignty and power, there are also scriptures such as 1 John 5:19: "The whole world is under the control of the evil one."

In the days of Jesus's ministry on Earth, Satan inflicted disease through demonic attacks. While he still may do so in cases, in modern Western culture demons seem more restrained, perhaps by God's intervention, or possibly because Satan's strategy has been to destroy belief in God through Darwinism and materialism. A materialist would be shocked to see a demon—it would affirm there *is* a spiritual element. After seeing a fallen angel, it's easier to believe in *good* angels, and from this to conclude God is real. Apparently, with demons restrained, the satanic hierarchy has sought to inflict illness and death through alternative means: vaccines, as well as fabricated viruses, drugs, and—some would say— water fluoridation and genetically modified foods. The results of these methodologies can be as cruel as what demons did directly; I almost sense a *creativity* behind it, as though Satan wants to be as inventive in destroying the world as God was in making it.

We often wonder why God does not answer prayers for healing more frequently. Do you recall our examples of one child drowning, and another threatened with poison, and how God would expect us to *act*, not just *pray* in those situations? I must be careful here; it isn't for me to interpret God's will. The Bible warns: "Not many of you should presume to be teachers, because you know that we who teach will be judged more strictly." But I'd like to suggest that *possibly* our prayers go unanswered because God expects us to *act* not *pray*. When we let our children be vaccinated, we are in effect saying, "Lord, we don't trust the way you designed us. We're going to trust pharmaceutical companies to improve it with injections."

For further vaccine information, I recommend the websites www.whale.to, and www.vaccinetruth.org.

Some readers may want to know what can be done to counteract the effects of vaccines. I suggest readers conduct their own research into this, but I will note the following among solutions advocated by vaccine critics:

• Some *homeopathic* practitioners employ their methods to neutralize vaccines.
• Some people use "chelation therapy," which uses substances that bind to poisons, so the body can excrete them.
• Along with exercise, eat a healthy diet—rich in natural organic foods. Because today's American diet is highly processed, vitamin and mineral supplements may be advisable. Some nutri-

tionists say the mineral selenium can bind to mercury and help the body excrete it.

• It has been said water is the drink God gave the world. All animals drink it. I would not neglect drinking water, especially spring or distilled. If you were going to wash something, would you use water or Coke? It may be that you can filter out some of these poisons by increasing your water intake (but never of course, to excess, which can itself be dangerous).

• Some have reported good effects from the use of saunas to "sweat out" toxic substances.

CHAPTER 21
THE WEATHER
FORECAST ISN'T GOOD

God created the heavens and the Earth. And Biblical passages, such as Job 38, address His control of weather:

Have you entered the storehouses of the snow
    or seen the storehouses of the hail,
which I reserve for times of trouble,
    for days of war and battle?
What is the way to the place where the lightning is dispersed,
    or the place where the east winds are scattered over the earth?
Who cuts a channel for the torrents of rain
    and a path for the thunderstorm,
to water a land where no man lives,
    a desert with no one in it,
to satisfy a desolate wasteland
    and make it sprout with grass?
Does the rain have a father?
    Who fathers the drops of dew?
From whose womb comes the ice?
    Who gives birth to the frost from the heavens
when the waters become hard as stone,
    when the surface of the deep is frozen? (Job 38:22-30)

I certainly don't suggest humans control every weather variation; but the elements are manipulated far more than generally realized.

Some Christians may object: "God is sovereign—therefore no one can change the weather." Yet cannot man disrupt and injure the human body, which God sovereignly created? So then can he alter weather. For example, we've been seeding clouds to make it rain since the end of World War II. During the Vietnam War, the U.S. military seeded clouds to extend the monsoon season. With a little research, you'll find far more advanced weather modification is now occurring.

In his 1970 book *Between Two Ages*, Zbigniew Brzezinski quoted geophysicist Gordon J. F. MacDonald:

> Techniques of weather modification could be employed to produce prolonged periods of drought or storms, thereby weakening a nation's capacity and forcing it to accept the demands of the competitor.[247]

In 1972, the United States and Russia signed a weather treaty. It forbade inducing tidal waves, earthquakes and tornadoes, among other phenomena.[248]

William S. Cohen was Bill Clinton's Secretary of Defense. At a 1997 Defense Department briefing he stated:

> Others are engaging even in an eco-type of terrorism whereby they can alter the climate, set off earthquakes, volcanoes remotely through the use of electromagnetic waves. So there are plenty of ingenious minds out there at work finding ways in which they can wreak terror upon other nations. It's real.[249]

Let's underscore Cohen's words *"remotely through the use of electromagnetic waves."*

Nikola Tesla (1856-1943) originated the concept of alternating current, and was the pioneer of electromagnetism. Many say Tesla, not Marconi, was radio's true inventor. He also demonstrated that electromagnetic waves could modify weather, but his work in that area was largely ignored in his day.

The Russians were first to put Tesla's weather technology into practice; the United States has more recently, and lags behind them. Weather can be manipulated through ELF (Extremely Low Frequency) waves, which satellites or ground transmitters aim at a target area. ELF waves are not imaginary; they are just as real as the television and radio signals which, though invisible, carry sights and sounds into our homes.

How do you create a drought in southern California? Figure 19 depicts the jet stream.

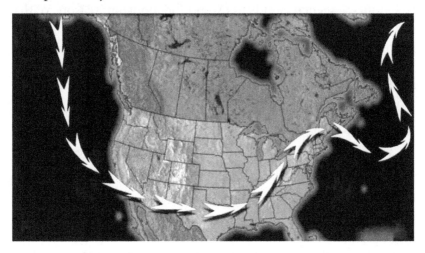

Figure 19

A standing column of ELF waves off the coast (Figure 20) can keep moist fronts out, so the state receives no rain.

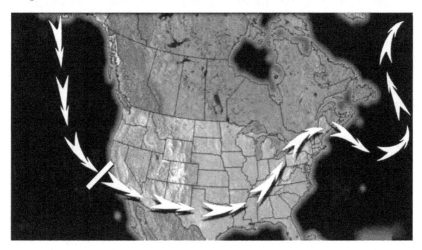

Figure 20

How to cause California *flooding*? Let moist fronts in, but prevent them from leaving with a standing column around the state's eastern border (Figure 21).

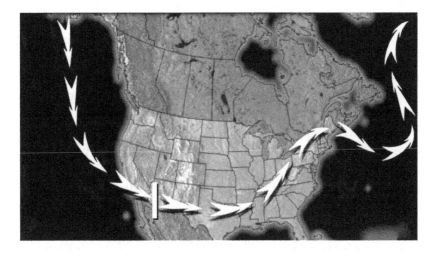

Figure 21

You can divert a jet stream's direction, create high or low pressure areas, change the course of a hurricane or enhance its strength. You can also, through a concentrated blast of electromagnetic energy, trigger an earthquake or tsunami.

Recently, natural disasters have increased exponentially. Is this coincidence, or another weapon in the cartel's arsenal for world population reduction? The 2004 tsunami was the deadliest in history—over 200,000 died. 2005, the year of Katrina, saw the worst U.S. hurricane season ever.

How about tornadoes? In the early 1950s the U.S. was having less than 300 tornadoes per year. But over the past decade it has averaged 1,200 per year, with 2004 experiencing the most in U.S. history—1,819.[250]

☹ There's an easy explanation for that. It's just a coincidence that weather's been getting worse lately. And is it really surprising that when tornadoes increase, hurricanes do too? The whole planet's a single organism, and one weather phenomenon doesn't live in isolation. Plus, there's global warming ...

This book has debunked the "coincidence" explanation for many events. Scientists have often refuted global warming (see for example, www.petitionproject.org and www.junkscience.com).

Global warming claims persist, not because scientifically supported, but because of the Establishment's agenda to regulate the world
based on environmental pretexts. Look for the media to start saying that "the increase in natural disasters is from climate change
due to global warming; therefore we must enact more regulations
and be prepared to sacrifice more freedoms, blah-blah."

The cartel is progressively using weather, along with war,
disease and abortion as part of its genocide campaign. Have you
noticed that weather disasters nearly always destroy "expendable"
people and areas—Midwest farmers (tornadoes), poor urban
blacks (Katrina), island and coastal peoples (tsunami), destitute
Africans (drought-induced famine), and the poorest country in
the Western Hemisphere, Haiti (earthquake).* It's almost never
a city in the northeastern USA, where the U.S. Establishment
mostly resides. Furthermore, rebuilding contracts after these
disasters inevitably go to the same Establishment corporations—
Bechtel, Halliburton—that the Iraq War also benefitted.** They
convert blood and tears into cartel profit. Poor countries pay for
much of the reconstruction through World Bank loans, funded
by American taxpayers.

[*Haiti may have been a rehearsal for a more significant target—Japan, whose prosperity and strong nationalism could make
it difficult to absorb into a world government. **Bechtel swung
an $800 million deal to help rebuild Iraq. Halliburton gave Dick
Cheney a $34 million severance package when he left to become
George Bush's running mate in 2000.]

☹ If Satan really wants genocide, why doesn't he just nuke the whole
planet and be done with it?

Because no one would be left to worship him. He rules through
a hierarchy; to secure its members' cooperation, he must promise
them benefits. He has deceived them into believing they will permanently rule the Earth, while a remnant of the population will
serve as their slaves. Drugs and "vaccine lobotomies" will keep
us docile, like the *Eloi* in H. G. Wells's *The Time Machine*, and
a powerful police force—similar to Orwell's *thought police*—will
ensure against rebellions.

Again, we're not attributing all weather disasters to ELF manipulation; violent storms, of course, existed long before Tesla or any of this technology. But we shouldn't take the other extreme. When calamitous weather strikes, we shouldn't automatically say: "This hurricane was the Lord's will."—as with disease, we could be making God evil's author.

For more information on weather control, search on the Internet for "HAARP" and "woodpecker grid."

It Gets Worse: Chemtrails

People across the United States and the world have increasingly noticed that over the last few years, certain planes have been spewing large trails of chemicals—"chemtrails." Skeptics have tried to explain these away as normal jet exhaust—"contrails." But jet exhaust dissipates rather rapidly—unlike these recent chemtrails, which hang in the air for hours. Examination of the soil in areas heavily dosed with chemtrails suggests that their composition includes aluminum and barium. It doesn't seem likely that the chemtrails are anti-people weapons, because David Rockefeller and the rest of the Illuminati have to breathe the same air as us. But dust from these trails are apparently killing crops, changing the pH of soil, causing bark to fall off trees, and wiping out insects (they may be responsible for the mysterious drop in the population of bees, which we need to pollinate plants). Aluminum is also a fire accelerant, and may explain the upsurge in massive wildfires. Basically, the target of the chemtrails appears to be vegetation. The Illuminati evidently wish to damage the world's food sources—which they can use as justification for further population reduction. They apparently also intend for us to start buying synthetic, genetically modified foods and seeds from corporations like Monsanto. Some also believe the chemtrails are electrifying the atmosphere to make weather weapons more effective.

A very good film on chemtrails is *What in the World Are They Spraying*, co-hosted by G. Edward Griffin. Watch it for free on YouTube.

CHAPTER 22
ARRIVAL OF THE DESPOT

The Bible says of the End Times:

> Because of the signs he [the false prophet] was given power to do on behalf of the first beast, he deceived the inhabitants of the earth. He ordered them to set up an image in honor of the beast who was wounded by the sword and yet lived. He was given power to give breath to the image of the first beast, so that it could speak and cause all who refused to worship the image to be killed. (Revelation 13:14-15)

People have asked: How could they erect an image of the beast (Antichrist) so that everyone on Earth could see it in order to worship it? Some have suggested the image will be on television. But you can turn off a TV—it must be something else.

Serge Monast, a Canadian Christian journalist, conducted research that may explain it. Before dying of an alleged heart attack, he exposed something called Project Blue Beam.

Go to the website http://www.sweetliberty.org/issues/hoax/af.shtml to a picture from a U.S. Air Force web page. It shows a fighter plane and, projecting from it, a *hologram* (three-dimensional image) of itself, *appearing* to be a second fighter plane. The hologram is designed to confuse the enemy, who can't tell which plane is the real one. Hologram technology is very sophisticated—even visitors to Disney World's "haunted house" ride find holograms of ghostly creatures sitting beside them.

I previously mentioned *Report from Iron Mountain*, the summary of a private study done in the 1960s. Again, it asked: in the absence of war, what would be the best way to persuade people to obey government? The report favored environmental threats, and in its wake, numerous eco-scares were publicized. However, the study also explored the possibility of a simulated UFO attack, but did not think it practical given the existing technology at that time:

> Credibility, in fact, lies at the heart of the problem of developing a political substitute for war. . . . The most ambitious and unrealistic space project cannot of itself generate a believable external menace. It has been hotly argued that such a menace would offer the "last, best hope of peace," etc., by uniting mankind against the danger of destruction by "creatures" from other planets or from outer space. Experiments have been proposed to test the credibility of an out-of-our-world invasion threat; it is possible that a few of the more difficult-to-explain "flying saucer" incidents of recent years were in fact early experiments of this kind. If so, they could hardly have been judged encouraging.[251]

But today's technology is far more advanced, and "UFO sightings" more frequent. Incidentally, we can discount the possibility of *real* space aliens visiting us. The closest star to us is Alpha Centauri. Assuming it had a nearby planet with advanced life (unlikely at best), if a spaceship traveled from there to Earth, even at a million miles per hour it would take over 3,000 years to arrive. Would aliens invest that much time, not even knowing if life or anything valuable was here? Could they put a 3,000-year supply of food and fuel on a ship? And after all the generations that would live and die on the voyage, maybe no one would want to complete it. In short, *no* UFOs are coming here from other worlds.

I realize there has been much buzz about Roswell, Area 51, and the "alien autopsy" video. Many say these show the U.S. government is concealing evidence that aliens have landed. I suggest this is *exactly what the government wants us to believe.*

Most UFO "sightings" are probably of *holograms.* If you can put holograms of fighter jets in the sky, you can just as easily project images of spaceships or *any* objects.

Monast says that, in the End Times, the beast's image will be *holograms projected from satellites*. Everyone will see it in the sky; that's why we won't be able to turn it off. In the West, we would mostly view an image of Christ, but other regions would see the chief messiah of their own faiths—Mohammed, Buddha, Krishna, etc.

And this has another dimension. Radio stations, of course, send their signals at various frequencies. It turns out the human nervous system has a specific frequency, on which audible messages can be transmitted via microwaves. Originally, the U.S. military explored this technology's potential for use in combat: making the enemy hear false commands or think he was going mad. Although it could make the deaf hear, the cartel is instead developing it for destructive ends. (Don't overlook this as an explanation for why some "crazy" individuals claim to hear voices.)

People won't just see but *hear* the Antichrist's projected image, because his voice will transmit via this same microwave technology. We won't be able to turn off the voice, which will broadcast in English in England, Japanese in Japan, French in France. The image will proclaim that all the world's religions have gone wrong, that he is God and we must obey him.* As you can imagine, a talking, three-dimensional celestial figure, created by special effects superior to any Hollywood offers, *could be very convincing.*

[*Monast briefly mentioned that "Project Blue Beam" will also include a *false rapture*. This may conceivably help explain the emphasis on a pretribulation rapture in modern Christian theology.]

The Antichrist will probably appear as a "savior" during a crisis. To save us from what? Perhaps war, or artificially created plagues and famines, induced storms and earthquakes, or some combination thereof. He might even rescue us from a fake alien invasion, simulated by holograms of spaceships (accompanied by genuine explosions on the ground). Of course, having contrived these disasters, it will be easy for him to stop them.

The climax of the popular movie *The Incredibles* dramatized this principle. The villain, Buddy/Syndrome, sends his monstrous omnidroid—which he remote-controls—against a city, so he can "save" the people and be hailed as a superhero. In much the same way, Satan plans to rescue us from the very catastrophes he brings us, so we will worship him. But any "saving" will be short-lived because, once enthroned, he will then unleash his greatest cruelties on the world.

Satan may employ supernatural powers in this; but so far, at least, he seems to be building a *high-tech Antichrist.* Is he reluctant to use supernatural powers? If so, why? Could it be that, if he does, God will *intervene* supernaturally?

CHAPTER 23
CONCLUSION

I have seen many cartoons depicting a fool on the street, wearing a sign that says: "The end is near." Nevertheless . . . the end is near!

Some may ask: "Why is God allowing this to happen?" It is not for me to interpret God's will. But according to the Bible, Satan deceived a large number of angels into following him. He has probably boasted, to angels in heaven and to men on Earth, that his rule is superior to God's. Possibly the Lord is letting Satan play out his own hand, so all the world can see what a lie this is. He won't interfere with Satan's free will (any more than he does ours). Otherwise, Satan could say, "You never gave me a chance." But God will limit the time Satan has to rule as an evil despot—apparently, three and a half years, the same time allotted Jesus's ministry of grace.

As the End Times approach, the following suggestions may be considered:

• Above all, put your faith in God, who will send his son, Jesus Christ, to judge the living and the dead. Pray for Him to strengthen you, and to shorten any days of suffering.

• Stay informed. Almost all the facts people need are on the Internet.* It may be a good idea to use it soon—at some point, the Web may become regulated, and all criticism of the cartel outlawed.

[*Bear in mind, of course, that not every conspiracy theory is true; a few wild ones may even be fabricated by the Illuminati in order to discredit *all* theories.]

272

• Weigh alternative views before allowing yourself or your family members to be vaccinated.

• Of course, never let a microchip be implanted under your skin. Such a chip may ultimately constitute the "mark of the beast."

• Do not let your church divide over non-essential issues. "Divide and conquer" is the enemy's universal strategy.

• At the risk of offending some people, I suggest that all believers—Christian, Jewish, and Muslim—stand together against the Antichrist and his New World Order, for his war is on all of us. I am not talking about ecumenically blurring all religions into one—which is something the Antichrist himself will attempt—but a united stand for survival. I hope the distinction is clear. In a battle, when the enemy's artillery is firing, we can't get too fussy about who's sharing the foxhole.

• Although I agree, in principle, with the concept of a "just war," almost all wars today are orchestrated by the Establishment for its purposes: genocide, government borrowing, and nation-destruction to make way for the "new world order." I urge readers not to get caught up in "war fever," or too quickly believe atrocity stories about other nations. I encourage Christians, Muslims, Jews, and people of all faiths, to refrain from violence against each other, and to not harken to voices which promote it. Such voices intend to divide and conquer us all.

• Voting gives the people an illusion that they hold power. The Illuminati introduced voting—whose results they sway through media—to install the politicians and programs they want. And as we have mentioned, some analysts believe the computerized vote-counting systems are being tampered with. Nevertheless, I do not wish to discourage anyone from voting, running for office, organizing referendums, or communicating with their legislators. Some critical issues are decided in Congress by slim margins, and contacting your Senator or congressman may affect their vote.

• Oppose all gun control legislation. The purpose of gun control is to disarm the population in order to facilitate our being enslaved. The prolific recent mass murders, where a "lone" gunman goes on a shooting spree, may have been, in many cases, arranged events designed to soften the public into accepting gun control.

• Investigating the Federal Reserve—an action supported prominently by Texas Congressman Ron Paul—and withdrawing America from the UN are also outstanding legislative goals.

• Become active with groups that oppose the North America Union and seek to uphold U.S. sovereignty and the Constitution, such as the John Birch Society (www.jbs.org).

• As possible, patronize local businesses rather than global corporations.

• Pastors, I encourage you to inform your congregations of the enemy's plan as well as God's.

• Electronic assets will be the easiest for bureaucrats to wipe out. In the End Times, the best assets will be tangible, hard ones—real goods that can be bartered.

• Beware of news headlines that begin "Experts say…" or "Scientists shocked to discover…" The Establishment uses such prefixes to convince the public to trust its agenda.

• In the last days, don't believe every crime the news attributes to Christians, even if "confessed." Today's sophisticated technology can manufacture evidence, and torture can induce confessions.

• Do a little Internet searching, and you will find evidence that FEMA is building concentration camps across America. As I understand it, when the time comes, "undesirable" people will be rounded up swiftly—almost overnight. Evidently these camps will be used not just to *kill*, but to *reeducate*—see the appendix on *1984*. Do not go into these camps expecting that you'll "evangelize the guards." If you try to do so in a camp, you will probably be tasered or drugged or tortured using advanced high-tech weapons unknown to medieval saints.

Now some may ask: Given the Establishment's pervasive control of government, mass media, and banking, is there any use in fighting against this thing?

To answer that, I'm going to paraphrase what a retired U.S. military officer said when asked that very question. Based on combat experience in Vietnam, he replied: "When the going gets tough, and you're surrounded and outnumbered, and it doesn't look good—it's true that if you keep on fighting, you may lose. But you know what? If you give up, you're *guaranteed* to lose. So keep on fighting!"

In the end, God will destroy the satanic cartel. Is it possible for us to defeat it before then? A few people, with determination and initiative, can achieve amazing victories over tyranny.

And let me close with a word of hope. It's true that the Establishment elitists can look in their bank accounts and see billions of dollars. And they may say: "How about you, our enemies? What's in *your* wallet?" Well, we have an asset that the Illuminati *don't*—a commodity called truth. And truth is more powerful than any big lie that the propaganda hacks at CNN can fabricate.

And because we seek to tell the truth, we also have an *ally* the Establishment doesn't have. That ally is God. Jesus Christ said He came to tell the truth; the Ninth Commandment commands us to tell the truth. Therefore it may be said with certainty, the same certainty that God created this remarkable universe: Although a few dark years may lie ahead, in the end the serpent will be crushed, Goliath will fall, and God and the truth, and those of us who seek them, will emerge victorious.

"... the Son of Man will come at an hour when you do not expect him." –Luke 12:40

APPENDIX I
THE MYTHS OF FREE TRADE

Conservatives Got it Wrong.
Protectionism Benefits Us.

This appendix is dedicated to my friend, the late William J. Gill,
an outstanding American patriot who fought tirelessly and selflessly
against NAFTA and GATT until his death.

The United States is so dependent on imports today, it is not easy to find American-made goods. And yet, up until World War II, only two percent of our economy was based on foreign commerce. The transformation did not result from necessity, but from manipulated changes in our trade policy.

The most significant of these changes came in 1994, when Congress approved the GATT Treaty, binding the United States to the World Trade Organization. This sent the nation's economy into a tailspin: a tidal wave of cheap imports, a skyrocketing trade deficit, and massive job losses.

I was covering the GATT for a national magazine, and recorded the Senate Commerce Committee's hearings on the treaty, as well as the very vigorous Congressional debate. In doing so, I witnessed a strange and unique phenomenon:

Normally, on any issue, whether abortion, national defense, or school prayer, conservatives and liberals had clearly defined positions, aligned against each other like cats versus dogs. The GATT Treaty was totally different. A weird mix of liberals and conservatives were on both sides. Illinois Republican Phil Crane, then surveyed as the most conservative congressman in the House of Representatives, strongly favored GATT. But so did well-known liberal Democrats like Al Gore and Ted Kennedy. On the other hand, Jesse Helms, reputed as the Senate's most conservative

Republican, vigorously opposed the treaty. And so did diehard liberals such as Democrat Congresswoman Marcy Kaptur, and consumer advocate Ralph Nader.

One group, however, displayed no divisions on this issue—the Establishment. From David Rockefeller down, they universally favored the treaty. While researching *The Shadows of Power*, I noticed that the Council on Foreign Relations had, throughout its history, unswervingly advocated free trade. This troubled me, because conservatives—of whom I was one—also espoused free trade. Why did we agree with the CFR on this single matter? One of us had to be deceived, and I doubted it was the clever Establishment.

Free trade means nations may trade with each other without restriction—i.e., without *tariffs*, which are charges a country adds to the prices of imports, or *quotas*, which are limits mandated on the number of goods a foreign country can sell. Tariffs and quotas are designed to protect a nation's home industries, and have been labeled "protectionism."

The classic argument for free trade runs something like this. An American manufacturer sells a product at $25 apiece. Then a creative Scotsman devises a more efficient way to make the same item, offering it for sale at $20 each. Fearing his business will collapse, the American manufacturer lobbies his Senator for protection. Congress slaps a $10 tariff on the Scotsman's goods, raising their price to $30 apiece. This is detrimental for several reasons: it punishes the Scotsman's ingenuity, rewards the American producer's inefficiency, and forces consumers to pay higher prices. Conservatives have long castigated protectionism as an *enemy of free enterprise* that brings *big government socialism* into the marketplace. It was with these principles in mind that many sincere conservatives in Congress supported NAFTA and GATT. The treaties largely destroyed our tariffs and quotas; therefore these conservatives deemed the treaties "good."

Adam Smith had articulated the free trade argument in his 1776 book *The Wealth of Nations*. In principle nothing is wrong with it. Free trade is generally healthy—but only between comparable nations whose economies are based on *free enterprise*. Socialism's emergence completely changed the landscape.

The classic free trade argument assumes prices are made low through *efficiency in production*. However, communist countries can make goods inexpensive by manufacturing them in gulags. Slaves-labor products can be sold very cheaply, because wages aren't factored into the price. Most American legislators, Republican and Democrat, agree we should ban slave labor goods. Though such merchandise would be cheap, even free trade advocates usually oppose them on a moral basis. However, although the U.S. supposedly prohibits slave labor goods, huge numbers slip through, because we so poorly monitor the sources of our imports.

Furthermore, when *socialist or semi-socialist* countries swamp us with cheap imports, no opposition is deemed acceptable. Many Americans fail to realize that in nearly all of our trading partners—even Britain—government heavily subsidizes industry.

Foreign governments often do this expressly to undersell American producers. Let us say a U.S. manufacturer retails a stereo component at $100 apiece. A Japanese company wishes to invade the market. To help it, the Japanese government agrees to kick in 25 percent of its costs. The Japanese manufacturer then introduces his comparable product at $75 apiece. Naturally, price-conscious consumers switch to it. The American manufacturer is soon out of business. This is a simple parable of what has become of dead American industries.

If the U.S. manufacturer seeks a protective tariff, conservatives denounce him: "You are seeking to prop up your inefficiency! And even worse, asking for government meddling—that's socialism!" But this situation is very different from that of the ingenious Scotsman. The price differential here did not result from *efficiency*, but from *government subsidies*. While a tariff may appear to taint our marketplace with socialism, far more socialism is introduced by letting subsidized imports destroy an American company that truly operates under free enterprise.

There are, of course, other factors which make domestic goods more expensive than imports. American businesses generally provide better wages and benefits to workers; and they operate under stringent government safety and environmental regulations. Many foreign manufacturers, facing no such standards, can thus sell cheaper wares.

Free trade is splendid only if our trading partners play by the same rules that we do. If they refuse, we may rightly impose tariffs and quotas to keep American industry alive.

Actually, subsidized articles are *also* slave labor products—in this case, the "slave" is the low-wage foreign worker whose highly-taxed salary produced his government's subsidy. This is, of course, more moderate slavery than the gulag, and thus our response should be more moderate: instead of banning them, restraining them via protectionism.

No one criticizes a businessman for protecting his factory from fire with insurance, or from crime with night watchmen. Yet, if he seeks a tariff to protect it from wanton raiding by foreign socialists, "protection" becomes a bad word. In truth, tariffs have long protected something worthwhile—our economic base, which the American way of life depends on.

In his monumental book *Trade Wars against America* (Praeger, 1990), historian William J. Gill resoundingly disproved the notion that protectionism is harmful. George Washington, Thomas Jefferson, James Madison and Alexander Hamilton were all avid protectionists. They helped enact stiff tariffs which not only allowed the fledgling American economy to flourish, but accounted for 90 percent of the U.S. government's revenues during its early decades, eliminating the need to tax our citizens.

Gill documented that over the ensuing two centuries, tariff enactments consistently resulted in American economic upswings, but free trade measures in setbacks. The Smoot-Hawley Tariff Act of 1930 has been widely maligned as the cause of the Great Depression, but as Gill pointed out, the Depression started before Smoot-Hawley, and was subsequently deepened by Franklin D. Roosevelt's free trade measures. (If anyone really believes tariffs are suicidal, they have only to consider Japan. Her markets have always resisted foreign entry, yet she became an economic powerhouse.)

Free-trade advocates claim tariffs are a "tax on consumers." They invariably avoid mentioning that government revenues, lost by destroying tariffs, must be made up for by *increased taxes* (or else by inflation when the Federal Reserve makes money from nothing, as we discussed in Chapter 3).

I have heard this argument: *Even though tariff elimination results in increased taxes, these taxes are offset because American consumers now enjoy lower prices in the form of cheap imports. So it's just a trade-off—we're neither better nor worse for it.* This is false! The import tsunami has thrown millions of Americans out of work. When you have no income, even those cheap imports start to become unaffordable. And when all those unemployed folks go on welfare, government tax receipts fall even further, meaning yet higher taxes for those remaining in the labor force.

The Establishment's real reasons for pushing free trade are as follows:

• A self-sufficient economy is integral to national sovereignty. Making the United States dependent on imports *globalizes* us—an important step toward world government.

• Destroying American industry via imports responded to Étienne Davignon's call to de-industrialize the United States to reduce its power (Chapter 12).

• The wholesale shift of manufacturing overseas to places like China and Mexico enabled multinational corporations to dump their well-paid American workers in exchange for cheap "coolie" labor.

• The international banks have loaned hundreds of billions of dollars to foreign countries. Letting these countries sell vast numbers of exports to America enables them to earn money to repay the loans—thus enriching the banks at the expense of American workers.

• Finally, the flood of unrestricted imports has brought with it a flood of illegal drugs. Drugs usually enter this country through "export companies" serving as fronts. The Illuminati run illegal drugs as well as legal ones.

Appendix II
FOUNDATION FUNDING
OF THE GREEN MOVEMENT

The following numbers were published in *The New American* of April 4, 2005. The figures, which cover the years 2000 to 2003, graphically illustrated that the Green movement is not "grass roots," but is funded by the Establishment.

Alcoa Foundation

National Wildlife Federation, VA	$63,980
Nature Conservancy, VA	$550,000
Resources for the Future, DC	$62,500
World Resources Institute, DC	$898,130
World Wildlife Fund/Conservation Foundation, DC	$850,000

Bank of America Foundation

National Wildlife Federation, VA	$28,400
Nature Conservancy, VA	$320,000
Nature Conservancy, GA	$75,000
Nature Conservancy, AZ	$100,000
Nature Conservancy, OK	$30,000
Nature Conservancy, NV	$10,000
Resources for the Future, DC	$10,000
World Wildlife Fund/Conservation Foundation, DC	$60,000

Carnegie Corporation of New York

Environmental Law Institute, DC	$214,900
Union of Concerned Scientists, MA	$25,000

Citigroup Foundation

Natural Resources Defense Council, NY	$75,000
Nature Conservancy, VA	$50,000
Nature Conservancy, GA	$50,000
Nature Conservancy, NY	$50,000
World Resources Institute, DC	$945,000
World Wildlife Fund/Conservation Foundation, DC	$70,000

DamierChrysler Corporation Fund

Nature Conservancy, VA	$100,000
Resources for the Future, DC	$145,000

Educational Foundation of America

Environmental Defense, NY	$135,000
Environmental Defense, NC	$170,000
Environmental Defense, DC	$175,000
Friends of the Earth, DC	$280,000
International Forum on Globalization, CA	$100,000
National Wildlife Federation, VA	$60,000
National Resources Defense Council, NY	$60,000
Nature Conservancy, NC	$100,000
Rainforest Action Network, CA	$80,000
Union of Concerned Scientists, MA	$200,000
Wilderness Society, CO	$500,000
Wilderness Society, DC	$255,000

Energy Foundation

Center for International Environmental Law, DC	$150,000
Environmental Defense, NY	$2,257, 923
Environmental Defense, DC	$430,000
Environmental Defense, CA	$53,340
Environmental Defense, TX	$140,000
Friends of the Earth, DC	$45,000
National Wildlife Federation, VA	$25,000
Natural Resources Defense Council, NY	$3,442,873
Natural Resources Defense Council, DC	$125,000
Natural Resources Defense Council, CA	$105,000
Resources for the Future, DC	$125,000
Sierra Club Foundation, CA	$1,373,000
Union of Concerned Scientists, MA	$3,749,000
Wilderness Society, DC	$90,000
Wilderness Society, CO	$10,000
World Resources Institute, DC	$955,200
World Wildlife Fund/Conservation Foundation, DC	$570,957

Ford Foundation

Center for International Environmental Law, DC	$1,120,000
Earth Action Network, CT	$50,000
Environmental Defense, NY	$300,000
Environmental Grantmakers Association, NY	$252,000
Environmental Law Institute, DC	$637,000
Friends of the Earth, DC	$350,000
Friends of the Earth International, Netherlands	$155,000

Friends of the Earth Nigeria, Nigeria	$250,000
Institute for Law and Environmental Governance, Kenya	$35,000
National Wildlife Federation, VA	$1,070,000
Nature Conservancy, VA	$409,500
Nature Conservancy, Laikipia, Kenya	$100,000
Natural Resources Defense Council, NY	$150,000
Rainforest Action Network, CA	$290,000
Resources for the Future, DC	$75,000
Union of Concerned Scientists, MA	$860,000
World Resources Institute, DC	$923,000
World Wildlife Fund/Conservation Foundation, DC	$600,000

Hewlitt Foundation, William and Flora

Environmental Defense, NY	$1,200,000
Environmental Defense, TX	$250,000
Environmental Law Institute, DC	$325,000
National Wildlife Federation, DC	$300,000
Natural Resources Defense Council, CA	$1,860,000
Natural Resources Defense Council, NY	$900,000
Nature Conservancy, AK	$750,000
Nature Conservancy, CA	$1,250,000
Resources for the Future, DC	$331,000
Sierra Club, CA	$675,000
Sierra Club of Canada, Canada	$120,000
Union of Concerned Scientists, MA	$1,300,000
Wilderness Society, DC	$1,100,000
Wilderness Society, CO	$172,000
World Resources Institute, DC	$100,000

MacArthur Foundation, John D. and Catherine T.

Center for International Environmental Law, DC	$450,000
Environmental Law Institute, DC	$675,000
Institute of Environmental Law Problems, Russia	$90,000
National Wildlife Federation, VA	$350,000
Natural Resources Defense Council, DC	$300,000
Nature Conservancy, VA	$1,150,000
Nature Conservancy, HI	$470,000
Union of Concerned Scientists, MA	$4,219,000
World Resources Institute, DC	$2,875,000
World Wildlife Fund/Conservation Foundation, DC	$3,135,000

Mott Foundation, Charles Stewart

Center for International Environmental Law, DC	$1,343,000
Environmental Defense, NY	$707,000
Friends of the Earth, DC	$810,000
Friends of the Earth France, France	$420,000
Friends of the Earth International, England	$125,000
Friends of the Earth Netherlands, Netherlands	$472,500
Friends of the Earth Japan, Japan	$565,000
National Wildlife Federation, VA	$2,273,141
National Wildlife Federation, MI	$575,000
Nature Conservancy, VA	$6,542,400
Nature Conservancy of Canada, Canada	$1,000,000
Sierra Club, CA	$520,000

Sierra Club of Canada Foundation, Canada	$66,000
World Resources Institute, DC	$1,550,000
World Wildlife Fund/Conservation Foundation, DC	$291,000

Packard Foundation, David and Lucille

Earth Action Network, CT	$150,000
Environmental Defense, NY	$9,474,343
Environmental Law Institute	$405,000
National Wildlife Federation, VA	$550,000
Natural Resources Defense Council, NY	$725,000
Nature Conservancy, VA	$33,376,441
Nature Conservancy of Canada, Canada	$40,000
Sierra Club Foundation, CA	$250,000
Sierra Club of British Columbia Foundation, Canada	$2,278,000
Union of Concerned Scientists, MA	$397,000
Wilderness Society, DC	$250,000
World Resources Institute, DC	$4,395,957
World Wildlife Fund/Conservation Foundation, DC	$20,709,334

Pew Charitable Trusts

Environmental Defense, NY	$300,000
Friends of the Earth, DC	$300,000
Natural Resources Defense Council, NY	$550,000
Sierra Club, CA	$560,000
Union of Concerned Scientists, MA	$1,000,000
Wilderness Society, DC	$2,145,400
World Resources Institute, DC	$750,000

Rockefeller Brothers Fund

Center for International Environmental Law, DC	$350,000
Friends of the Earth, DC	$50,000
Friends of the Earth International, Netherlands	$70,000
Friends of the Earth Japan, Japan	$400,000
International Forum on Globalization, CA	$300,000
Natural Resources Defense Council, NY	$150,000
Nature Conservancy, VA	$165,000
Rainforest Action Network, CA	$400,000
Sierra Club of British Columbia Foundation, Canada	$180,000
Valhalla Wilderness Society, Canada	$100,000
World Resources Institute, DC	$160,000
World Wildlife Fund/Conservation Foundation, DC	$100,000

Rockefeller Foundation

Center for International Law, DC	$871,487
Environmental Law Institute, DC	$403,933
Nature Conservancy, AR	$50,000
Resources for the Future, DC	$459,594
World Resources Institute, DC	$717,138

Turner Foundation, Inc.

Center for International Environmental Law, DC	$70,000
Environmental Defense, NY	$530,000
Environmental Defense, CO	$28,875
Environmental Defense, DC	$10,000

Environmental Law Institute, DC	$40,000
Friends of the Earth, DC	$200,000
Friends of the Earth Japan, Japan	$30,000
National Wildlife Federation, VA	$1,215,000
National Wildlife Federation, AK	$80,000
National Wildlife Federation, CO	$10,000
National Wildlife Federation, DC	$10,000
National Resource Defense Council, NY	$2,085,000
National Resources Defense Council, CA	$587,500
National Resources Defense Council, DC	$73,875
Nature Conservancy, GA	$539,000
Nature Conservancy, SC	$15,000
Nature Conservancy, ND	$20,000
Nature Conservancy, VA	$200,000
Nature Conservancy of Montana, MT	$15,000
Rainforest Action Network, CA	$130,000
Union of Concerned Scientists, MA	$444,000
Valhalla Wilderness Society, Canada	$110,000
Wilderness Society, DC	$268,000
Wildlands Project, VT	$160,000
Wildlands Project, AZ	$80,000
World Resource Institute, DC	$175,000
World Wildlife Fund/Conservation Foundation, DC	$170,000

Wallace Global Fund

Center for International Environmental Law, DC	$210,000
Environmental Defense, NY	$250,000
Environmental Grantmakers Association, NY	$10,000
Friends of the Earth, DC	$314,000

Friends of the Earth International, England	$214,000
Natural Resources Defense Council, NY	$50,000
Nature Conservancy, PA	$30,000
Rainforest Action Network, CA	$115,000
Sierra Club, CA	$400,000
Sierra Club Foundation, DC	$90,000
Union of Concerned Scientists, MA	$200,000
World Resources Institute, DC	$540,000

APPENDIX III
1984 REVISITED

George Orwell's novel *1984*, published in 1949, portrayed a totalitarian world of the future. According to former MI6 officer John Coleman, Orwell was attached to MI6 and was simply fictionalizing what he knew was to come.

When the actual year 1984 rolled around, the world didn't look just the way Orwell's book envisioned; therefore some criticized the book as a failed prophecy. However, events have increasingly vindicated Orwell and silenced his critics. For those who will complain he missed on the year, we point out that (A) the vigilance of freedom-loving people has forced the Establishment to reset its timetable more than once; and (B) if you read Orwell's novel carefully, it's not even certain that the year *is* 1984—that was simply what the people were told by the government, which controlled all information.

Let's explore ways *1984* has been fulfilled:

• In *1984*, citizens are under constant electronic surveillance by the Thought Police, not only in the city streets, but through their home televisions, which cannot be turned off. To quote the book:

> With the development of television, and the technical advance which made it possible to receive and transmit simultaneously on the same instrument, private life came to an end. Every citizen, or at least every citizen important enough to be worth watching, could be kept for twenty-four hours a day under the eyes of the police . . . .[252]

Today, through computers connected to the Internet, and through cell phone traffic, the government can keep the bulk of

291

the population under surveillance, in the name of "security" under the Patriot Act. This may even be happening through televisions. Years ago, I thought: "Orwell got it wrong. TVs receive, but they don't transmit!" Certainly the TVs of the 1950s didn't transmit, but with the enforced upgrading to digital television, it is increasingly apparent that televisions will probably transmit soon, if they are not doing so already. Google, for example, the article "Is Your TV Spying on You?" at the MIT *Technology Review* (http://www. technologyreview.com/view/427405/is-your-tv-spying-on-you). Orwell was well ahead of the game.

• In *1984*, all people of the world fall under three regional governments—Oceania (where the book's protagonist, Winston Smith, lives), Eurasia and Eastasia. This is reminiscent of the regional approach to world government (European Union, North American Union) now unfolding.

• Just as we have described, power is in a pyramidal structure. At the top of the pyramid is an Antichrist-like figure, Big Brother.

> At the apex of the pyramid is Big Brother. Big Brother is infallible and all-powerful. Every success, every achievement, every victory, every scientific discovery, all knowledge, all wisdom, all happiness, all virtue, are held to issue directly from his leadership and inspiration.[253]

• Winston works in the Ministry of Truth, where newspapers, periodicals, books, and other literature forms are continuously changed according to the government's wishes. For example, if the *Times* reported Big Brother had made a speech predicting something, which later did not happen, the *Times* would be subsequently corrected so that it appeared Big Brother had made the correct prediction.

> Day by day and almost minute by minute the past was brought up to date. In this way every prediction made by the Party could be shown by documentary evidence to have been correct; nor was any item of news, or any expression of opinion,

which conflicted with the needs of the moment, ever allowed to remain on record.[254]

While current society has not advanced to this extreme, history *has* been altered, changing the true nature and records of wars, revolutions, the United Nations, trade treaties, the Federal Reserve, and even the effectiveness of vaccines.

Furthermore, electronic data is increasingly replacing *hard copy* information. In the Internet age, newspapers and magazines are struggling to stay in print. *Newsweek* is no longer published in hard copy. If all information eventually becomes electronic, it will be very easy for bureaucrats to change what back copies of newspapers and magazines say—exactly as in Orwell's novel.

• Although everything in Oceania is in short supply (except that reserved for the elite "Inner Party" members), the government's economics ministry is termed "The Ministry of Plenty." This reminds one of the "Security and Prosperity Partnership" borne out of NAFTA, which claims we are enjoying "prosperity" while millions of jobs are slashed and we drown in inflation. In *1984*, the Ministry of Plenty spews out falsified statistics:

> The fabulous statistics continued to pour out of the telescreen. As compared with last year there was more food, more clothes, more houses, more furniture . . . . [255]

Even today, the U.S. government fudges statistics to make the realities look brighter. For example, the June 23, 2008 *The New American* exposed how the government has continuously altered methods of determining the Consumer Price Index, inflation's main barometer. For example, under Richard Nixon, food and energy costs were simply eliminated from the "core CPI." Later:

> In 1983, the Reagan administration decided that rising real estate costs were causing the CPI to be overstated, so the Bureau of Labor Statistics (BLS) substituted an "Owner Equivalent" measurement, basing housing costs on what homeowners might get if they were renting their houses. Homes were labeled an investment, and the cost of buying

a home (like other investments) was no longer included in the CPI.

The Bush, Sr., Clinton, and Bush, Jr. presidencies each further modified how CPI is determined, each change serving to *lower* it. The end result of all these tweaks is that the U.S. now reports an annual inflation rate of some two percent, whereas true inflation is closer to *ten percent*. This enables the government to cheat senior citizens out of their Social Security, making payment increases based on the *distorted CPI*, rather than the *actual rising costs* the elderly face.

• In the culture of *1984*, the truth is reversed. Two of the government's main slogans are "WAR IS PEACE" and "FREEDOM IS SLAVERY." Today, many of yesterday's truisms have also been reversed. For example, homosexuality, once understood as perverted, is now construed as "normal"; abortion, previously a crime, is today a "right"; advocates of traditional family values, once mainstream, are now "extremists."

• *1984* says:

> It was always at night—the arrests invariably happened at night. The sudden jerk out of sleep, the rough hand shaking your shoulder, the lights glaring in your eyes, the ring of hard faces round the bed. In the vast majority of cases there was no trial, no report of the arrest. People simply disappeared, always during the night. Your name was removed from the registers, every record of everything you had ever done was wiped out, your one-time existence was denied and then forgotten. You were abolished, annihilated: *vaporized* was the usual word.[256]

Many film fans are familiar with the 1995 Sandra Bullock thriller *The Net*, about a woman who no longer "exists" after her identity is destroyed by the cyber-manipulations of the movie's villains. And today, many have been victims of real-world identity theft. Like money and information, the more your identity becomes electronic, the more it becomes erasable. Orwell warns us that someday identity loss may become a *function of government.*

• We have mentioned that the Establishment has *created* much of the "popular" music and literature via the Tavistock Institute. In *1984*, Winston hears a woman singing a song as she hangs clothes on a line:

> The tune had been haunting London for weeks past. It was one of countless songs published for the benefit of the proles [the poor] by a sub-section of the Music Department [at the Ministry of Truth].[257]

• Winston's secret lover, Julia, also works in the Ministry of Truth, where she had

> been picked out to work in Pornosec, the subsection of the Fiction Department which turned out cheap pornography for distribution among the proles. It was nicknamed Muck House by the people who worked in it, she remarked. There she had remained for a year, helping to produce booklets in sealed packets with titles like *Spanking Stories* or *One Night in a Girl's School*, to be bought furtively by proletarian youths who were under the impression that they were buying something illegal.[258]

• Oceania was *continually* at war, the wars never being actually won (sound familiar, Americans?). Bombs would sometimes drop on London (where Winston lived), rousing the people to patriotism. But the bombs "were probably fired by the Government of Oceania itself."[260] Shades of 9-11?

• The war ministry (called the Ministry of Peace) was working on means of "producing artificial earthquakes and tidal waves."[260]

• Oceania had a language called *Newspeak*. It restricted vocabulary to very few words. Each successive *Newspeak* dictionary deleted more words. The eventual result was to eliminate ideas unacceptable to the state, since words for those ideas no longer existed. Orwell pointed out that ultimately an older document, such as the American Declaration of Independence, would become unreadable gibberish. Is this unlike today, when "dumbing down" has left American public school students less and less able to read books of the past?

• In the novel, Winston is exposed as a thought criminal and imprisoned by the Ministry of Love (the secret police). In view of the concentration camps FEMA is now reportedly preparing, certain aspects of Winston's torture are worth mentioning.

The following exchange occurs between Winston and his torturer, O'Brien:

> [O'Brien:] "And why do you imagine that we bring people to this place?"
> "To make them confess."
> "No, that is not the reason. Try again."
> "To punish them."
> "No!" exclaimed O'Brien. His voice had changed extraordinarily, and his face had suddenly become both stern and animated. "No! Not merely to extract your confession, nor to punish you. Shall I tell you why we brought you here? To cure you! To make you sane! Will you understand, Winston, that no one whom we bring to this place ever leaves our hands uncured?"

O'Brien continues:

> "You have read of the religious persecutions of the past. In the Middle ages there was the Inquisition. It was a failure. It set out to eradicate heresy, and ended by perpetuating it. For every heretic it burned at the stake, thousands of others rose up. Why was that? Because the Inquisition killed its enemies in the open, and killed them while they were still unrepentant; in fact it killed them because they were unrepentant. Men were dying because they would not abandon their true beliefs. Naturally all the glory belonged to the victim and all the shame to the Inquisitor who burned him. Later, in the twentieth century, there were the totalitarians, as they were called. There were the German Nazis and the Russian

Communists. The Russians persecuted heresy more cruelly than the Inquisition had done. And they imagined that they had learned from the mistakes of the past; they knew, at any rate, that one must not make martyrs. Before they exposed their victims to public trial, they deliberately set themselves to destroy their dignity. They wore them down by torture and solitude until they were despicable, cringing wretches, confessing whatever was put into their mouths, covering themselves with abuse, accusing and sheltering behind one another, whimpering for mercy. And yet after only a few years the same thing had happened over again. The dead men had become martyrs and their degradation was forgotten. Once again, why was it? In the first place, because the confessions they had made were obviously extorted and untrue. We do not make mistakes of that kind. All the confessions that are uttered here are true. We make them true. And, above all, we do not allow the dead to rise up against us. You must stop imagining that posterity will vindicate you, Winston. Posterity will never hear of you. You will be lifted clean out from the stream of history. We shall turn you into gas and pour you into the stratosphere. Nothing will remain of you: not a name in a register, not a memory in a living brain. You will be annihilated in the past as well as in the future. You will never have existed."

After many tortures, Winston still retains a shred of independent thinking. To finish breaking him, the Thought Police bring him to the place every prisoner dreads—Room 101. Room 101 is different for every person. It contains their greatest horror. In Winston's case, he has a primal fear of *rats*. His head is placed in a two-compartment cage. The furthest compartment is filled with hungry sewer rats. If the connecting door dropped, the rats would devour Winston's face. At this point, Winston completely loses it—he is broken.

How did the Thought Police know Winston's darkest fear was rats? Because they had *monitored his conversations.* Likewise, the government today could know a person's greatest fear, by simply monitoring his emails and phone calls. Compiling a profile of nearly every person would be easy.

At the book's end, the Thought Police have turned Winston free—because he no longer constitutes any threat. He believes every bit of propaganda coming from the telescreen. He gazes at Big Brother's image. And the book closes with these words: "He loved Big Brother." If I may freely translate, he worshiped the Antichrist.

Appendix IV
THE MILLENNIUM

Some years ago I was taking turns hosting a Bible study at a church. We were in the book of Revelation. When we got to Chapter 20, it happened to be my turn to lead. Chapter 20 refers to a 1,000-year reign of Christ, also referred to as "the millennium." Various views of the millennium exist within Christianity. I held no position on it myself at the time, but I researched the different views, and presented them at the Bible study. I was amazed at the wrath that resulted. It seems that the millennium is one of the most debated and emotional "hot spots" of Christian theology.

Scofield

A major impact on views of the millennium was exerted by the *Scofield Reference Bible*. Though it is one of the most influential Bibles ever published, few Christians know the author's background. Cyrus Scofield was involved in numerous confidence games, swindled his mother-in-law out of $1300, and did jail time for forgery.[261] Even after his reported conversion to Christ—and very rapid ordination as a Dallas minister—his wife divorced him for abandonment of her and their two daughters. Scofield traveled to New York, where he was made a member of the exclusive Lotos Club—an unusual affiliation for an evangelical minister. At the Lotos Club he met Samuel Untermeyer, an Establishment insider and one of the country's most powerful Zionists.[262] Untermeyer introduced him in turn to Jacob Schiff, Bernard Baruch, and the bankers at Kuhn, Loeb. They financed his trips to England, where Oxford University Press agreed in advance to publish his proposed reference Bible—even though Scofield had never written a book in his life. He spent months working on the tome in Switzerland—an unlikely place to research a Bible commentary, but long the cartel's center of Masonic, banking and revolutionary activity. (Protecting this center is why Switzerland has always maintained neutrality in wars.) Possibly much of Scofield's book was written, or at least suggested, by others.

The handsomely produced *Scofield Reference Bible* sold millions of copies, and helped advance three controversial concepts in Christian theology:

(1) *The Gap Theory* claimed that, between Genesis 1:1 and Genesis 1:2, there were billions of years not mentioned in Scripture. This "gap" was promoted to accommodate the Bible to atheists and evolutionists, who insisted the heavens and Earth were eons old, contradicting the straightforward Biblical account of a six-day creation.

(2) *Dispensationalism* said, among other less controversial things, that God had a separate plan for the Jews, including the restoration of Israel. Scofield's Bible notes were filled with references espousing Zionism—which is in reality the plot to seize Palestine in order to enthrone the Antichrist in Jerusalem.

(3) *Premillennialism* said that after Jesus returns, he will physically reign on Earth for 1,000 years, prior to the Judgement Day. Millions of Christians today hold this view; it has been the subject of much controversy within the church, with Scriptures extensively quoted both in support and refutation.

The Illuminati spent a fortune to have Scofield, and his predecessor, John Nelson Darby, spread premillennialism among the Christian community. Why? Because when the Antichrist reigns from the rebuilt Jerusalem temple, he will try to persuade Christians that he is the Christ, returned for his 1,000-year reign.*

[*Scofield and Darby also promoted a *pretribulation rapture* (the concept that believers will be taken from this world and united with Christ, before the Antichrist's reign, and thus not suffer under the latter). Some analysts believe the Illuminati publicized this to convince Christians that they need not oppose the rise of the Antichrist, since they won't be around to experience him anyway.]

Some Christian readers will want to know what *scriptures* contradict Scofield's premillennialism.

The Bible and the Millennium

There are, as mentioned, several views of the millennium within Christianity. Very intelligent people are on all sides of the debate. I don't wish to be dogmatic on this subject, and hope my remarks will be understood as *suggestions for consideration*, not assertions.

The verses most frequently cited in favor of a future, coming millennium are Revelation 20:1-6:

> And I saw an angel coming down out of heaven, having the key to the Abyss, and holding in his hand a great chain. He seized the dragon, that ancient serpent, who is the devil, or Satan, and bound him for a thousand years. He threw him into the Abyss, and locked and sealed it over him, to keep him from deceiving the nations anymore until the thousand years were ended. After that, he must be set free for a short time. I saw thrones on which were seated those who had been given authority to judge. And I saw the souls of those who had been beheaded because of their testimony for Jesus and because of the Word of God. They had not worshiped the beast or his image and had not received his mark on their foreheads or their hands. They came to life and reigned with Christ a thousand years. (The rest of the dead did not come to life until the thousand years were ended.) This is the first resurrection. Blessed and holy are those who have part in the first resurrection. The second death has no power over them, but they will be priests of God and of Christ and will reign with him for a thousand years.

No other Bible verses specifically mention a millennium; however, some believe certain Old Testament prophecies refer to it. For example, Isaiah 2:2-4 says:

> In the last days
> the mountain of the LORD's temple will be established

as chief among the mountains;
it will be raised above the hills,
and peoples will stream to it.
Many nations will come and say,
"Come, let us go up to the mountain of the LORD,
to the house of the God of Jacob.
He will teach us his ways,
so that we may walk in his paths."
The law will go out from Zion,
the word of the LORD from Jerusalem.
He will judge between many peoples
and will settle disputes for strong nations far and wide.
They will beat their swords into plowshares
and their spears into pruning hooks.
Nation will not take up sword against nation,
nor will they train for war anymore.

Another support given is the book of Ezekiel, which describes a temple that was never constructed. Some premillennialists believe this temple will therefore be built in the future, and that Jesus will rule from it.

However, Jesus said we were not to look for him in temporal places:

So if anyone tells you, "There he is, out in the desert," do not go out; or, "Here he is, in the inner rooms," do not believe it. For as lightning that comes from east is visible in the west, so will be the coming of the Son of Man. (Matthew 24:26-27)

Scripture indicates that Christ's return is rapid and powerful.

But the day of the Lord will come like a thief. The heavens will disappear with a roar; the elements will be destroyed by fire, and the earth and everything in it will be laid bare. (2 Peter 3:10)

The final judgment appears to occur immediately following Christ's return, not after another 1,000 years:

God is just: He will pay back trouble to those who trouble you and give relief to you who are troubled, and to us as well. This will happen when the Lord Jesus is revealed from heaven in blazing fire with his powerful angels. He will punish those who do not know God and do not obey the gospel of our Lord Jesus. They will be punished with everlasting destruction and shut out from the presence of the Lord and from the majesty of his power on the day he comes to be glorified in his holy people. (2 Thess 1:7-10)

For me, it is hard to see a millennium within that, or in this:

When the Son of Man comes in his glory, and all the angels with him, he will sit on his throne in heavenly glory. All the nations will be gathered before him, and he will separate the people one from another as a shepherd separates sheep from the goats. He will put the sheep on his right and the goats on his left. Then the King will say to those on his right, Come you who are blessed by my Father, take your inheritance, the kingdom, prepared for you since the creation of the world . . . . Then he will say to those on his left, Depart from me, you who are cursed, into the eternal fire prepared for the devil and his angels. (Matthew 25:31-34, 41)

The prophet Daniel also pictured the End Times as immediately followed by resurrection and judgment:

At that time Michael, the great prince who protects your people, will arise. There will be a time of distress such as has not happened from the beginning of nations until then. But at that time your people—everyone whose name is found written in the book—will be delivered. Multitudes who sleep in the dust of the earth will awake: some to everlasting life, others to shame and everlasting contempt. (Daniel 12:1-2)

Regarding the argument that Jesus will rule from the temple Ezekiel described, we need to examine things the prophet said about it:

Also one sheep is to be taken from every flock of two hundred from the well-watered pastures of Israel. These will be used for the grain offerings, burnt offerings and fellowship offerings to make atonement for the people, declares the sovereign Lord. (Ezekiel 45:15)

Jesus will not require us to make such offerings; the Cross eliminated them. And how about:

This is what the Sovereign Lord says: No foreigner uncircumcised in heart and flesh is to enter my sanctuary, not even the foreigners who live among the Israelites. (Ezekiel 44:9)

Will Jesus require physical circumcision and exclude foreigners? The New Testament denies this. Obviously, these verses aren't about Christ's Second Coming.

Who *will* rule from a temple in Jerusalem? The Antichrist. Jesus warned the End Times would occur "when you see the standing in the holy temple the abomination that causes desolation, spoken of through the prophet Daniel." (Matt 24:15). Paul, speaking of the End Times, wrote:

Don't let anyone deceive you in any way, for that day will not come until the rebellion occurs and the man of lawlessness is revealed, the man doomed to destruction. He will oppose and exalt himself over everything that is called God or is worshiped, so that he sets himself up in God's temple, proclaiming himself to be God. (2 Thess 2:3-4)

Revelation 20 discusses Jesus reigning while Satan is bound for a thousand years. Many premillennialists say that, since Satan has not yet been bound, Jesus's thousand-year reign is still to come. Here again are the verses on the binding:

And I saw an angel coming down out of heaven, having the key to the Abyss, and holding in his hand a great chain. He seized the dragon, that ancient serpent, who is the devil, or Satan, and bound him for a thousand years. He threw him into the Abyss, and locked and sealed it over him, to keep him from deceiving the nations anymore until the thousand years were ended. After that, he must be set free for a short time.

Revelation 20:7 elaborates: "When the thousand years are over, Satan will be released from his prison and will go out to deceive the nations in the four corners of the Earth—Gog and Magog—to gather them for battle." I believe this prophecy has already been fulfilled: that Satan *has* been loosed, that his deception of the nations is what this book describes.

But if Satan has been loosed, when was he bound? I believe it was at the time of the Cross. Jesus described Himself as binding Satan:

> But if I drive out demons by the spirit of God, then the kingdom of God has come upon you. Or again, how can anyone enter a strong man's house and carry off his possessions unless he first ties up the strong man? (Matthew 12:28)

Here is the full passage where Paul described the Antichrist:

> Don't let anyone deceive you in any way, for that day will not come until the rebellion occurs and the man of lawlessness is revealed, the man doomed to destruction. He will oppose and exalt himself over everything that is called God or is worshiped, so that he sets himself up in God's temple, proclaiming himself to be God. Don't you remember that when I was with you I used to tell you these things? *And now you know what is holding him back*, so that he may be revealed at the proper time. For the secret power of lawlessness is already at work, but the one who now *holds it back* will continue to do so until he is taken out of the way. And then the lawless one will be revealed, whom the Lord Jesus will overthrow with the breath of his mouth and destroy by the splendor of his coming. (2 Thess 2:3-8) (emphasis added)

Thus, in Paul's day Satan was already being held back (bound).

Some may object that Revelation 20 indicates that, while Satan was bound, believers "came to life and reigned with Christ a thousand years." Since this hasn't happened yet, they say, the millennium clearly lies in the future.

However, the book of Revelation often uses figurative language, and there is scriptural support that "coming to life" and "reigning with Christ" can be contemporary. For example, 1 John 3:14 says "we have passed from death to life," and Revelation 1:6 that Jesus Christ "has made us to be a kingdom and priests to serve his God and Father." Paul wrote:

> God, who is rich in mercy, made us alive with Christ even when we were dead in our transgressions. And God raised us up with Christ and seated us with him in the heavenly realms in Christ Jesus. (Eph 2:5-6)

I suggest the following possibility: that starting with the Cross (or perhaps Pentecost, which occurred shortly after), Satan was bound, and the church grew and thrived for 1,000 years. The first major split (into Catholic Rome and Orthodox Constantinople) occurred in 1054 A.D. Scholars believe the crucifixion occurred about 33 A.D. Was Satan released 1,000 years later? Hassan-I Sabah, the satanic "Old Man of the Mountain"—whose cult of assassins fathered both Freemasonry and the violent Muslim sects—was born in 1033 A.D.

William Guy Carr, perhaps the best analyst of the Illuminati, believed the millennium has passed:

> While we don't wish to labour this matter there is evidence which indicates that with the death and resurrection of Jesus Christ, Satan was cast back into Hell and there bound, as far as his being Prince of this World is concerned, for a thousand years. We believe according to the Apostles' Creed that Christ descended into Hell immediately after the death of his mortal body. Couldn't it have been to see that Satan was secured as well as to release the souls of the Just who had

been detained in that part of Hell called Limbo until Christ had redeemed them?

Then, again, the Luciferian conspiracy seems to have had very poor direction on this earth from the time Christ left us until about A.D. 1000. Christianity had flourished. It was progressing, church and state were trying to get along together. The Church was advising rulers in regard to God's plan for the rule of the universe, and the rulers were seemingly trying to put that plan into effect. Paganism was dying a natural death under the glare of the Light of Holy Scriptures. But as the thousand years ended Satanism broke out again in all its diabolical force and fury, and Satan again became Prince of this World.[263]

If correct, perhaps Satan's current reign will end 1,000 years after it began. We know he sometimes places challenges before God (as in the first chapter of Job). Is it conceivable that, having been bound for 1,000 years, Satan requested—and God granted—equal time: 1,000 years to do his worst?

Will the Antichrist come at the climax of this 1,000 years? The Bible tells us his reign will last 3 and ½ years—like Jesus's earthly ministry. Is God giving Satan the same time measures as his Son? At the risk of facetious comparison, is it like a sports contest, where each side has an equal opportunity to go on offense?

Based on this, Christ's Second Coming—which will mark Satan's end and the Day of Judgement—could happen around 2033 A.D. However, I am mindful that Jesus said "the Son of Man will come at an hour when you do not expect Him," and "No one knows about that day and hour, not even the angels in heaven, nor the Son, but only the Father." (Matt 24:44, 36)

APPENDIX V
A STOLEN LIFE—
MY PERSONAL STORY

A Note of Encouragement (I Hope)
to Those with Asperger's

I suggest that, before reading this section, readers view Chapter 20, the chapter on vaccines.

On reading this appendix, some may say, "Oh, now I see why you're on this big crusade against vaccines. You were affected by vaccines yourself—that's your whole motivation."

Actually, I did not realize that vaccines had impacted me personally until *well after* I discovered the truth about them.

My late mother told me: "When you were a baby you had the most horrible eczema. It was so bad your skin was practically falling off, and you'd cry all night. I went to the doctor, but nothing seemed to work. Finally, he said, 'Mrs. Perloff, it must be that your milk is too rich. Stop breast-feeding him and put him on bottled formula.'"

Of course, that was the worst advice he could have given her. Today, it's widely recognized that formulas are inferior to a mother's milk, which contains an array of nutrients and immune factors that bottled stuff can't compete with. At that time, however, bottled formula was being marketed as supposedly superior.

After my infancy, the eczema vanished. And although I was a quiet child, things went along pretty normally as I adapted to the usual things of life.

I was becoming somewhat athletic. At age seven, I had learned to swim, was perhaps the best four-square player in my second-grade class, and sank the first two hoops I ever fired a basketball at.

After second grade, however, things went downhill for me. Any native athleticism disappeared. I couldn't catch a ball if you threw it at me. I couldn't ride a bike, and was terrified by jungle gyms. I became very shy and withdrawn. I couldn't sleep well and generally became sickly, frequently catching colds. My pediatrician probably doled out some wise-sounding advice to my parents, like, "Don't worry, he's just going through a stage."

The downward spiral continued for me, however. In middle and high school, I was totally withdrawn, sitting clammed up in class, almost never speaking. My lack of athleticism had descended to the point that I was ridiculed as "dork," "geek," "spaz," and much worse words by classmates. I was literally spit on. In gym class, if teams were chosen up, it was guaranteed I'd be picked last.

I didn't know why I was this way—I only knew that I was miserable. I saw the term "introvert" for the first time, and thought, "Wow! That's me! I'm an introvert!" I saw the phrase "inferiority complex" and it rang a bell too. And the problem was—I didn't just have the complex; I really *was* inferior. Tasks that for other people were simple and routine were very difficult for me. While other kids were out having fun, I sat alone at home. Since life was always painful and I had no friends, I fell into a dream-world.

In adulthood, after numerous hard struggles in college and the workplace, I gradually learned to overcome many of my deficits, made some friendships, and by my thirties had developed enough strategies that I generally seemed normal to most people.

A few years ago, well into my fifties, I was having lunch with a friend. He said, "My son has Asperger's." "What's that?" I asked. "It's a mild form of autism," he said.

Curious, when I went home I Googled "Asperger's." As I read about the disease, shock and sorrow came over me. The symptoms were an exact description of my youth—everything from the inability to ride a bike to abnormal fixation on a topic that becomes an area of "expertise." I didn't have *every* symptom—nobody does—but I had enough to strongly overqualify as an "Aspie."

I then examined my old medical records. I found I had received a total of three DPT (Diphtheria-Pertussis-Tetanus) shots during my infancy—the same time frame when I had the so-called "eczema." The "eczema" had curiously gone away after they stopped giving me DPT shots.

Then, in the second grade, I received a DPT booster. My medical record shows this was immediately followed by a fever and "eczema-like" rash. Although the pediatrician was intelligent enough to see that I was reacting to the booster, there is no evidence he connected the dots to what had occurred in my infancy.

Then, at age eleven, I got my final DPT booster. This was followed by a skin rash that lasted for eight months. The doctor (a new one) made no connection to the booster; he sent me to see a skin specialist.

Of course, people can *see* a rash, so they will move to treat it. But something else was happening they could *not* see. *Inside*, my nervous system was being fried. With each shot, I drifted further into withdrawal, clumsiness, and sickliness. Of course, no one connected it to the shots. Somehow, the rather athletic seven-year old had mysteriously become a dork. My life, and its potential, were stolen by injections.

It is obvious today—and recognized even in conventional medicine—that autism exists on a wide spectrum. In full-blown cases, the child is completely unable to function or communicate—he stares off into space in a near-vegetative state, and is recognized as *sick*.

Regrettably, many milder autistics are never recognized as such. Instead, they are called, as I was, "shy," "clumsy," and—in rougher circles—"spaz," "geek," and so forth.

In my experience, I was inevitably blamed for everything that went with my condition. My parents scolded me, my classmates ridiculed me, and my teachers rebuked me. In seventh grade, my social studies teacher bawled me out in front of the class for being so quiet. In retrospect, the words he used to describe me—basically comparing me to slime—could probably have gotten him fired. But I didn't even have the wherewithal to report something like that. And when the guys in my gym class played a particularly cruel prank on me, the gym teacher joined in with their scornful laughter. I guess he figured I deserved to be made fun of. Such things hurt me a lot—but *I* figured I deserved it too.

As a young adult, it was the same. Co-workers and supervisors at jobs blamed me for my inability to work swiftly and competently. Unfortunately, the first Christian church I attended as an adult wasn't much better. I was full of hope after newly coming to Christ, but I was still a quiet person. One day the pastor lit into me in front of the whole congregation. He bawled me out as "aloof" and unfriendly. He made the mistake of confusing *mild autism* with *sin*. I didn't stay at that church much longer.

In this regard, I wish to caution Christians to heed Jesus's words, "Do not judge, or you too will be judged." (Matthew 7:1) Incidentally, I freely admit that I too have passed judgement on others. But in an age of vaccine-induced autism, vaccine-induced ADHD, and a host of other vaccine-induced mental disorders, I believe we need more charity than ever in our views of others.

Now I can hear someone saying this:

*Ah, quit making excuses! Look, I got vaccinated too—it never affected **me** any. Face up to reality, man. The truth is, you really were just a jerk, and all this "vaccines gave me Asperger's" jazz is just an excuse. How do you know you had autism, and how do you know vaccines caused it?*

I understand that viewpoint and respond as follows:

• Nearly all Americans are vaccinated, and most don't get autism. But that doesn't mean they should pooh-pooh others who do. Different people react differently to vaccines, just as some people get an allergic reaction from a medication such as an antibiotic, while others do not. People really are not created equal, especially in their physical state.

Incidentally, contrary to media spin, not all *vaccines* are created equal either. As medical testimony at www.whale.to makes clear, many vaccines were not uniform, but the vials sometimes varied in their potency, purity, and content.

- How do I know I had Asperger's Syndrome? True, diagnosis can be a gray area. However, there is no question that my symptoms more than met the standardized criteria for Asperger's.
- How do I know it was vaccine-induced? Here again, it is logic. After each DPT shot or booster, I had a severe allergic reaction. While this manifested itself *outwardly* as a skin rash, it manifested *inwardly* as further descent into withdrawal, clumsiness, and the various Asperger's symptoms. Furthermore, ample testimony from other victims has clearly linked Asperger's to DPT shots.

Speaking more broadly now, I believe the impact of vaccines has enormous implications for our society. How many "dorks" or "bad kids" are out there who have simply had their brains skewered by vaccines? How many parents have been labeled "lousy parents" when in fact their children were deranged by vaccines? Unfortunately, most parents—like my mother—turn for a solution to the very person who caused the problem in the first place (however unwittingly): the family doctor. He then puts the child on medications which—surprise, surprise—are manufactured by the same Big Pharma cartel that makes the vaccines.

In American culture we have long heard phrases such as:

"You are the result of all the choices you have made in your life."

"If you don't like who you are, you have only yourself to blame."

"You made your bed—now go lie in it."

"We're living in a society of 'victims'—no one's willing to take responsibility for their own actions!"

"Our forefathers were made of sterner stuff."

And in the Christian worldview: "A man's problems are the result of his sin."

Don't get me wrong—all these statements are *true*. However, their truth has been muddled because we live in a culture in which nearly all children are vaccinated, and many have been, to one degree or another, brain-damaged. Their ability to think, respond, and be self-controlled has been *physically* impaired. They don't have the uncontaminated bodies their "hardier" forefathers grew up with. Sure, bad parenting, the removal of prayer and God from public schools, Dr. Spock's "no-spank" teaching, horrible role models, degraded movies-television-music—they've all played their roles in the destruction of American youth. But I'll wager that every one of these things takes a back seat to the invisible destroyer called vaccination.

Vaccines cloud the entire question of individual responsibility. I'm sure my readers would agree that a fully autistic child—one in a vegetative state—should not be slapped, scolded, or told "It's all your fault." But what about the *partial* autistic—one who can still walk around and communicate, is doing their best to cope, but is finding life a horrible struggle? To what degree is *he or she* responsible for their failures? This is a complex, difficult question. I certainly do not deny that sin and bad decisions played a great role in my own miseries. I do not deny that following the precepts and advice laid down in the Bible's book of Proverbs will help any person. But we are living in a culture that has introduced conditions the world never contended with before.

Maybe, like me, you're someone who gave it his or her best, failed, and then … everyone came down on you and said "IT'S ALL YOUR FAULT!"

Well, maybe it's *not* your fault. If it is somebody's fault—try that Big Pharma CEO, who's lying right now on an Aruba beach—countless millions in his bank account, made from vaccines that he *knew* would cripple and kill multitudes of children. Don't get me wrong—I'm all for forgiveness, but my temper runs a little short with people who knowingly injure children for profit.

How did I overcome my Asperger's? To a great degree, I still suffer from it. However, I learned coping mechanisms.

I cannot underestimate the power of change engendered by coming to faith in Christ. My character changed, and while I still suffered from significant deficits, I was much better able to harness them with my feet resting on the stability of the Bible's morals and worldview.

One thing I learned was that I *could* do things—even sports—competently. However, this required lots of practice, much more than the average person needs. I required practice even to learn things that come as second nature to most people.

I also found that I needed to be in jobs and situations that were highly *structured*. In general, Aspies don't do well in environments that require spontaneity and rapid decision-making, unless they have rehearsed each possible situation thoroughly. Since many bosses don't create structure for you, you often have to create it yourself—by sitting down and plotting, on paper or word processor, just how the day might go. You may need to anticipate unlikely situations and rehearse how you would respond to them.

For careers—obvious as it may sound—find out what you do well and pursue it.

As far as friendships go—and I suppose this applies to anyone—seek out people who share your interests. It's amazing how freely words start to flow when you meet someone who's as excited about a subject as you are.

Check also the vaccine-countering suggestions at the end of Chapter 20.

And don't get too down on yourself. It may not be what you've done that's truly caused your failures, but what was done *to* you as a child—shots that you had no control over. An autistic person is not on a level playing field. Seek God, and seek to overcome.

APPENDIX VI
THE UNWRITTEN APPENDIX

Appendix VI could not be written in time for publication. Appendix VI concerns what I consider the most successful lie of the twentieth century. It was the lie that the Illuminati spent more time and money on than any other. For this reason, this lie can only be broken by a comprehensive refutation. Such a refutation could well take up a book in itself. I hope to handle the matter through an appendix added to later editions of *Truth Is a Lonely Warrior*.

NOTES

Where resources cited are on the Internet, the URL is written out. I realize that some web addresses are long, and may be cumbersome to type on a keyboard. In the Kindle version of *Truth Is a Lonely Warrior*, these URLs can be clicked on and instantly accessed. Another option, of course, is to use Internet search engines to locate the material described.

1. "Top Secret Report, Army Pearl Harbor Board," Hearings before the Joint Committee on the Investigation of the Pearl Harbor Attack (Washington, D.C.: United States Government Printing Office), 230. http://www.ibiblio.org/pha/pha/army/tsreport.html.

2. Robert A. Theobald, *The Final Secret of Pearl Harbor: The Washington Contribution* (Old Greenwich, Conn.: The Devin-Adair Company, 1954), 5.

3. Ibid., 43.

4. John Toland, *Infamy: Pearl Harbor and Its Aftermath* (New York: Berkeley Books, 1982), 332-33.

5. Ibid., 272, 350.

6. Martin Dies, "Assassination and Its Aftermath," *American Opinion* (April 1964): 33.

7. Robert B. Stinnett, *Day of Deceit: The Truth About FDR and Pearl Harbor* (New York: Touchstone, 2001), 46.

8. Colin Simpson, *The Lusitania* (Boston: Little Brown, 1972), 147.

9. Ibid., 131.

10. Patrick Beesly, *Room 40: British Naval Intelligence 1914-1918* (New York: Harcourt Brace Jovanich, 1982), 122.

11. Anthony Kubek, *How the Far East Was Lost: American Policy and the Creation of Communist China, 1941-1949* (Chicago: Henry Regnery Co., 1963), 387.

12. Jim and Sybil Stockdale, *In Love & War: The Story of a Family's Ordeal and Sacrifice during the Vietnam Years* (New York: Harper & Row, 1984), 22-23.

13. Ibid., 24-25.

14. Transcript of Powell's UN Presentation, CNN, www.cnn.com./2003/US/02/05/sprj.irq.powell.transcript.

15. "Administration Comments on Saddam Hussein and the Sept. 11 Attacks," *Washington Post*, www.washingtonpost.com/wp-srv/politics/polls/9-11_saddam_quotes.html.

16. "In Quotes: Blair and Iraq Weapons," BBC, http://news.bbc.co.uk/2/hi/uk_news/politics/3054991.stm.

17. Neil Mackay, "Revealed: The Secret Cabal which Spun for Blair," *Sunday Herald*, June 8, 2003, reprinted at http://www.commondreams.org/headlines03/0608-06.htm.

18. http://www.ourrepubliconline.com/OurRepublic/Author/120.

19. "In His Own Words," Theodore Roosevelt Association, http://www.theodoreroosevelt.org/life/quotes.htm.

20. Edith Kermit Roosevelt, "Elite Clique Holds Power in U.S.," *Indianapolis News*, December 23, 1961, 6.

21. "Jimmy Carter," *Wikipedia*, www.en.wikipedia.org/wiki/Jimmy_Carter.

22. Ibid.

23. Gary Allen, *Jimmy Carter, Jimmy Carter* (Seal Beach, Calif.: '76 Press, 1976), 139.

24. Barry Goldwater, *With No Apologies* (New York: William Morrow, 1979), 286.

25. Phyllis Schlafly and Chester Ward, *Kissinger on the Couch* (New Rochelle, N.Y.: Arlington House, 1975), 144-50.

26. *Boston Herald*, "UN Not Immune to Criticism," August 27, 1996.

27. Report, Special House Committee to Investigate Tax-Free Foundations, 1954, 176-77, quoted in John Stormer, *None Dare Call It Treason* (Florissant, Missouri: Liberty Bell Press, 1964), 210.

28. Kenichi Ohmae, "The Rise of the Region State," *Foreign Affairs* (August 1993): 78.

29. Richard N. Gardner, "The Hard Road to World Order," *Foreign Affairs* (April 1974): 558.

30. Philip Kerr, "From Empire to Commonwealth," *Foreign Affairs* (December 1922): 97-98.

31. As quoted in "The New World Order Story," *H du B Reports*, March 1997, 4.

32. Rudolph Rummel, "20th Century Democide," www.hawaii.edu/powerkills/20TH.HTM.

33. Alexander Hamilton, John Jay, James Madison, *The Federalist Papers* (1787-88; reprint, Radford, Virg.: A & D Publishing, 2008), 193.

34. Revelation 13:7, 13:16.

35. Charles Seymour, ed., *The Intimate Papers of Colonel House*, Vol. 1 (Boston: Houghton Mifflin, 1926), 160.

36. Abraham Lincoln, letter to William F. Elkins, November 21, 1864; Archer H. Shaw, ed., *The Lincoln Encyclopedia: The Spoken and Written Words of A. Lincoln* (New York: Macmillan Co., 1950), 40.

37. Frank Vanderlip, "Farmboy to Financier," *Saturday Evening Post* (February 9, 1935): 25, 70.

38. Don Bell, "Who Are Our Rulers?" *American Mercury* (September 1960): 136.

39. *Congressional Record*, December 22, 1913, Vol. 51, 1446-47.

40. Louis T. McFadden, *On the Federal Reserve Corporation*, remarks in Congress, 1934 (Boston: Forum Publication Co., 89), quoted in Gary Allen and Larry Abraham, *None Dare Call It Conspiracy* (Seattle: Double A Publications, 1983), 63.

41. *Congressional Record*, June 10, 1932, 12603.

42. Eustace Mullins, *Secrets of the Federal Reserve* (Staunton, Va.: Bankers Research Institute, 1991), 156.

43. As quoted, Gary Allen and Larry Abraham, *None Dare Call It Conspiracy* (Seattle: Double A Publications, 1983), 62-63.

44. Curtis B. Dall, *FDR: My Exploited Father-In-Law* (Washington, D.C.: Action Associates, 1970), 49.

45. William J. Gill, *Trade Wars against America: A History of United States Trade and Monetary Policy* (New York: Praeger, 1990), 96.

46. As quoted from Marchenches's book *Dans Le Secret des Princes* in *H du B Reports*, April 1987, 4.

47. http://sanders.senate.gov/newsroom/news/?id=9e2a4ea8-6e73-4be2-a753-62060dcbb3c3.

48. http://sanders.senate.gov/imo/media/doc/GAO%20Fed%20Investigation.pdf.

49. Curtis B. Dall, *FDR: My Exploited Father-In-Law* (Washington, D.C.: Action Associates, 1970), 137.

50. Ray Stannard Baker, *Woodrow Wilson and World Settlement*, Vol. I (Garden City, N.Y.: Doubleday, Page & Co., 1923), 214.

51. Charles Seymour, ed., *The Intimate Papers of Colonel House*, Vol. 4 (Boston: Houghton Mifflin, 1926), 38.

52. Advertisement in *Foreign Affairs*, Summer 1986.

53. Hillary Clinton, Address at Council on Foreign Relations, Washington, D.C., July 15, 2009. Full text on State Department website: www.state.gov/ secretary/rm/2009a/july/126071.htm.

54. Laurence H. Shoup and William Minter, *Imperial Brain Trust: The Council on Foreign Relations and U.S. Foreign Policy* (New York: Monthly Review Press, 1977), 169-71.

55. Ibid., 35.

56. Walter Isaacson and Evan Thomas, *The Wise Men* (New York: Simon and Schuster, 1986), 410.

57. "2 International 'Think' Groups Weigh Merger," *H du B Reports*, March 1978, 2-3.

58. "Reference File, For Those Studying the New World Order Europe," *H du B Reports*, November 1993, 4.

59. Joseph Finder, "Ultimate Insider, Ultimate Outsider," *New York Times*, April 12, 1982.

60. *Congressional Record*, December 15, 1987, Vol. 133, S18148.

61. A. K. Chesterton, *The New Unhappy Lords* (London: Candour, 1969), 156.

62. "Drift to Tragedy," *H du B Reports*, October 1977, 1.

63. Hilaire du Berrier, *Background to Betrayal: The Tragedy of Vietnam* (Belmont, Mass.: Western Islands, 1965), viii.

64. Du Berrier's *Background to Betrayal: The Tragedy of Vietnam* extensively documents these facts.

65. Walt Rostow, *The United States in the World Arena* (New York: Harper & Brothers, 1960), 549.

66. James Kunen, *The Strawberry Statement: Notes of a College Revolutionary* (New York: Random House, 1969), 112.

67. William Norman Grigg, "Behind the Environmental Lobby," *The New American* (April 4, 2005): 19.

68. Author's videotape of televised coverage.

69. Henry Kissinger, op-ed, *Los Angeles Times*, July 18, 1993.

70. Andrew Reding, "Trading Away Democracy?" *Ottawa Citizen*, September 10, 1992, A13.

71. Anna Quindlen, "The Terrorists Here at Home," *Newsweek* (December 17, 2001).

72. Robert Pastor, "North America's Second Decade," *Foreign Affairs* (January-February 2004): 125, 133.

73. *Lou Dobbs Tonight*, CNN, June 21, 2006.

74. Dennis Behreandt, "Creating the North American Union," *The New American* (October 2, 2006): 9.

75. Joseph Stalin, *Marxism and the National Question* (New York: International Publishers, 1942).

76. Letter to John Norvell, June 14, 1807, *The Letters of Thomas Jefferson 1743-1826*, http://www.let.rug.nl/usa/presidents/thomas-jefferson/letters-of-thomas-jefferson/jefl179.php.

77. "You've a Right to Know," circular of Congressman John R. Rarick, July 15, 1971.

78. As quoted in "The Masks Are Coming Off," *H du B Reports*, Sept 1991, 1-2. Rockefeller's speech to the 1991 meeting of the Bilderbergers was leaked to the French press; it first appeared in the June 19, 1991 issue of the French weekly *Minute* and the July-August 1991 issue of *Lectures Francaises*.

79. Hans Schmidt, *SS Panzergrenadier* (Pensacola, Fla.: Hans Schmidt Publications, 2001), 241.

80. Barry Domville, *From Admiral to Cabin Boy* (London: Boswell Publishing, 1947), 14.

81. Thomas Jefferson, "A Summary View of the Rights of British America," Philip B. Kurland and Ralph Lerner, ed., *The Founders Constitution* (Chicago: University of Chicago Press, 2000), online edition, http://press-pubs.uchicago.edu/founders/documents/v1ch14s10.html.

82. Anthony Kubek, *How the Far East Was Lost: American Policy and the Creation of Communist China, 1941-1949* (Chicago: Henry Regnery Co., 1963), 272.

83. "How the World Looks as 1997 Approaches," *H du B Reports*, December 1996, 4.

84. Genesis 3:1-5.

85. As quoted in *Don Bell Reports*, February 1, 1980.

86. "As Summer Came in 1988," *H du B Reports*, July-August 1988, 5.

87. "Watergate and the Agency which Could Not Meddle in Chile but which Deposed an Emperor in Vietnam," *H du B Reports*, May 1973, 5.

88. "A Senator Mansfield Primer, for Beginners," *H du B Reports*, July 1971, 5.

89. Romans 9:20-21.

90. John Robison, *Proofs of a Conspiracy against All the Religions and Governments of Europe* (1798, reprint; Belmont, Mass.: Western Islands, 1967), 218.

91. Nesta H. Webster, *Secret Societies & Subversive Movements* (1924, reprint; Brooklyn, N.Y.: A & B Publishers Group, 1998), 241-42.

92. Gary Allen and Larry Abraham, *None Dare Call It Conspiracy* (Seattle: Double A Publications, 1983), 82.

93. William Guy Carr, *Pawns in the Game* (1955, reprint; Boring, Oreg.: CPA Book Publisher, 2005), 92.

94. Eustace Mullins, *Secrets of the Federal Reserve* (Staunton, Va.: Bankers Research Institute, 1991), 85.

95. See, for example, Martin Folly, *The United States and World War II: The Awakening Giant* (Edinburgh: Edinburgh University Press, 2002), 137.

96. James Perloff, *The Shadows of Power: The Council on Foreign Relations and the American Decline* (Belmont, Mass.: Western Islands, 1988), 87-88.

97. *U.S. Naval Institute Proceedings* (August 1983): 73-74, as quoted in Antony Sutton, *The Best Enemy Money Can Buy*, online edition http://www.reformed-theology.org/html/books/best_enemy/chapter_08.htm.

98. Joseph Finder, *Red Carpet* (New York: Holt, Rinehart and Winston, 1983), 177-78.

99. Ibid., 33.

100. Ibid., 237-38.

101. Ibid., 219.

102. Ibid., 156.

103. "Thoughts as Crisis Clouds Hang over the World," *H du B Reports*, July 1983, 3.

104. As quoted in "A Month to Be Remembered," *H du B Reports*, July-August 1989, 5.

105. John Coleman, *The Rothschild Dynasty* (white paper) (Las Vegas: Global Review Publications, 2006), 51.

106. John Coleman, *One World Order: Socialist Dictatorship* (Carson City, Nev.: Bridger House, 1998), 31.

107. Joseph Finder, *Red Carpet* (New York: Holt, Rinehart and Winston, 1983), 262.

108. From transcript at www.supremelaw.org/authors/dodd/interview.htm.

109. Anatoliy Golitsyn, *New Lies for Old* (New York: Dodd, Mead & Company, 1984), 327-28, 338-42, 350.

110. Ibid., 346-47.

111. Quentin Crommelin, Jr. and David S. Sullivan, *Soviet Military Supremacy: The Untold Facts about the New Danger to America* (Los Angeles: Defense and Strategic Studies Program, University of Southern California, 1985), 9-20.

112. Kenneth R. Timmerman, "Inside Russia's Magic Mountain," *WorldNetDaily*, June 6, 2000, www.worldnetdaily.com/news/article.asp?ARTICLE_ID=17518.

113. Barry Goldwater, *With No Apologies* (New York: William Morrow, 1979), 280.

114. Matthew 4:8-10.

115. William Guy Carr, *Pawns in the Game* (1955, reprint; Boring, Oreg.: CPA Book Publisher, 2005), 32-33.

116. John Coleman, *The Committee of 300* (Las Vegas: Global Review Publications, 2006), 45.

117. John Coleman, *The Tavistock Institute of Human Relations* (Carson City, Nev.: Joseph Holding Corporation, 205), 49.

118. Copin Albancelli, *Le Drame Maconnique: Le Pouvoir Occulte contre La France. La Conspiration Juive contre le Monde Chretian*, 43-44, as quoted in Cardinal Caro y Rodriguez, *The Mystery of Freemasonry Unveiled* (1928, reprint; Palmdale, Calif.: Christian Book Club of America, 2006), 33.

119. John Coleman, *Freemasonry from A-Z* (white paper) (Carson City, Nev.: World in Review, 1984), 9.

120. Ibid., 13.

121. Vicomte Léon De Poncins, *Freemasonry and Judaism: Secret Powers behind Revolution* (1929, reprint; Brooklyn, N.Y.: A & B Publishers Group, 1994), 33-34.

122. Nesta H. Webster, *Secret Societies & Subversive Movements* (1924, reprint; Brooklyn, N.Y.: A & B Publishers Group, 1998), 283.

123. Vicomte Léon De Poncins, *Freemasonry and Judaism: Secret Powers behind Revolution* (1929, reprint; Brooklyn, N.Y.: A & B Publishers Group, 1994), 61.

124. H. A. Gwynne, *The Cause of World Unrest* (1920, reprint; Palmdale, Calif.: Christian Book Club of America, 2006), 146.

125. *Acacia* No. 70 (October 1908), as quoted in Gwynne, 144.

126. Arthur Cherep-Spiridovich, *The Secret World Government* (1926; reprint, Hawthorne, Calif.: Christian Book Club of America, 1976), 74.

127. Cardinal Caro y Rodriguez, *The Mystery of Freemasonry Unveiled* (1928, reprint; Palmdale, Calif.: Christian Book Club of America, 2006), 85.

128. Leonard C. Lewin, *Report from Iron Mountain* (1967, reprint; New York: The Free Press, 1996), 60-61.

129. Ibid., 81.

130. John Coleman, *The Committee of 300* (Las Vegas: Global Review Publications, 2006), 159.

131. Ibid., 19.

132. *Great Britain, the Jews and Palestine*, (London: New Zionist Press, 1936), 4-5, as quoted in Robert John, "Behind the Balfour Declaration," Institute for Historical Review online (see footnote 188), http://www.ihr. org/jhr/v06/v06p389_John.html.

133. "Balfour Declaration of 1917," *Wikipedia*, http://en.wikipedia.org/wiki/ Balfour_Declaration_of_1917.

134. "Why Christian Aid Is Speaking Out about Zionism and Islam," *Christian News*, May 5, 2003, 13.

135. Arthur Koestler, *The Thirteenth Tribe* (New York: Random House, 1976), 58-59.

136. Ibid., 69.

137. Ibid., 60, 73.

138. Nicholas Wade, "Geneticists Report Finding Central Asian Link to Levites," *New York Times*, September 27, 2003.

139. Arthur Koestler, *The Thirteenth Tribe* (New York: Random House, 1976), 20.

140. Ibid., 46.

141. Ibid., 81.

142. Josephus, *The Antiquities of the Jews*, Book 1, Chapter 6, Section 1.

143. *New York Times*, April 19, 1972.

144. David Wood, "A Power that Outstrips Even US in Region," *Star-Ledger*, April 9, 2002.

145. *H du B Reports*, August 2001, 2.

146. Www.archives.cnn.com/2002/US/11/08/bush.transcript/ (accessed 2012).

147. "President Bush's Address to the United Nations," CNN online, Sept. 12, 2002, http://articles.cnn.com/2002-09-12/us/bush.transcript_1_generations-of-deceitful-dictators-commitment-peace-and-security/5?_s=PM:US.

148. *Jerusalem Post*, March 6, 1983, as quoted in John Coleman, *How Conspirators Misuse Christian Fundamentalists* (white paper) (Carson City, Nev.: World in Review, 2003), 7.

149. Jack Bernstein, *The Life of an American Jew in Racist Marxist Israel* (1985) (online edition), http://www.biblebelievers.org.au/israel.htm.

150. Sami Hadawi, "Who Are the Palestinians?" *Christian News*, May 5, 2003, 11.

151. John E. Borne, *The USS LIBERTY: Dissenting History vs. Official History* (New York: Reconsideration Press, 1995), 38.

152. Thomas Moorer, "A Fair Probe Would Attack *Liberty* Misinformation," *Stars and Stripes*, January 16, 2004, as quoted at http://www.ussliberty. org/moorer4.htm.

153. Statement of Richard Sturman, www.ussliberty.com/pdf/ sturmanstatememt.pdf.

154. Declaration of Ward Boston, Jr., www.gtr5.com/Witnesses/boston. pdf.

155. Declaration of Steven Forslund, www.gtr5.com/Witnesses/forslund. pdf.

156. Declaration of James Ronald Gotcher, www.gtr5.com/Witnesses/ gotcher.pdf.

157. Statement of Harold Max Cobbs, www.gtr5.com/Witnesses/cobbs. pdf.

158. Victor Ostrovsky, *The Other Side of Deception: A Rogue Agent Exposes the Mossad's Secret Agenda* (New York: HarperPaperbacks, 1994), 143-44.

159. Ibid., 146-48.

160. *Sunday Herald*, Nov. 2, 2003, www.sundayherald.com/37707. (link down at publication time)

161. Patrick J. Buchanan, "Have the Neocons Killed a Presidency?" *WorldNetDaily*, February 16, 2004, www.wnd.com/news/article. asp?ARTICLE_ID=37139.

162. *Rebuilding America's Defenses: Strategy, Forces and Resources for a New Century* (Washington, D.C.: Project for the New American Century, 2000), 51.

163. Ted Gunderson, "The Phoney War on Terrorism," September 4, 2002, www.rense.com/general28/phoney.htm.

164. "Witnesses to the Towers' Explosions," www.911review.com/coverup/ oralhistories.html.

165. Eric Halder, "Twin Towers Engineered to Withstand Jet Collision," *Seattle Times*, February 27, 1993, www.community.seattletimes.nwsource. com/archive/?date=19930227&slug=1687698.

166. The Demartini interview can easily be found on the Web, e.g., www. youtube.com/watch?v=EREolp1G4w.

167. Www.serendipity.li/wot/forbes01.htm.

168. David Harrison, "The Men with Stolen Identities," *Telegraph* (London), September 23, 2001.

169. Www.911research.wtc7.net/disinfo/deceptions/identities.html.

170. Www.archives.cnn.com/2001/US/09/21/inv.id.theft/.

171. As quoted in Albert B. Pastore, *Stranger Than Fiction*, viewable at www. ivanfraser.com/articles/conspiracies/stranger.html.

172. "When Our World Changed Forever," *Guardian*, September 16, 2001, www.guardian.co.uk/world/2001/sep/16/news.september11.

173. "Focus on Florida," CBS News, www.cbsnews.com/stories/2001/09/14/ national/311268.html.

174. Interview, ABC affiliate Channel 4, Venice, Florida, October 21, 2001, www.abc.net.au/4corners/atta/interviews/dekkers.htm.

175. Jim Yardley, "A Trainee Noted for Incompetence," *New York Times*, May 4, 2002, http://www.nytimes.com/2002/05/04/national/04ARIZ.html.

176. Edward Helmore and Ed Vulliamy, "Saudi Hijacker 'Was Key Link to Bin Laden,'" *The Observer*, October 7, 2001, http://www.guardian.co.uk/ world/2001/oct/07/terrorism.afghanistan3.

177. Stan Goff, "The So-Called Evidence is a Farce," www.narconews.com/ goff1.html.

178. "American Airlines Flight 77," *Wikipedia*, accessed 2008.

179. "Former Pentagon Man Has Some Doubts about 9-11," www. patrickcrusade.org/support_alternative_media.htm.

180. "Aviation First for Robotic Spy Plane," BBC News online, April 24, 2001, http://news.bbc.co.uk/2/hi/americas/1294014.stm.

181. Joe Vialls, "Home Run: Electronically Hijacking the World Trade Center Attack Aircraft," October 2001, http://www.serendipity.li/wot/home_ run.htm.

182. Www.hardtruth.navhost.com/brainwashed.html.

183. Victor Ostrovsky with Claire Hoy, *By Way of Deception: The Making of a Mossad Officer* (Scottsdale, Ariz.: Wilshire Press, 1990), 134-36.

184. Jerome Corsi, "Adobe Expert Doubts Obama Birth Certificate," *WorldNetDaily*, June 24, 2011, http://www.wnd.com/2011/06/314717/.

185. William Guy Carr, *The Red Fog over America* (Toronto: National Federation of Christian Laymen, 1957), 225.

186. Cardinal Caro y Rodriguez, *The Mystery of Freemasonry Unveiled* (1928, reprint; Palmdale, Calif.: Christian Book Club of America, 2006), 84-85.

187. John Coleman, *Conspiracy to Create a Holy War: The Temple Mount Conspiracy* (Carson City, Nev.: World in Review, 2005), 14.

188. John Coleman, *The Committee of 300* (Las Vegas: Global Review Publications, 2006), 107.

189. Ed Wallace, "The Importance of Myth," *Star-Telegram*, November 20, 2009, www.star-telegram.com/ed_wallace/story/1779061.html.

190. "One World Is Coming Says Arnold Toynbee," *The Milwaukee Journal*, May 2, 1964, 10.

191. John Foster Dulles, "The Problem of Peace in a Dynamic World," *Religion in Life*, Vol. 6, No. 2 (Spring 1937): 197, as quoted in Alan Stang, *The Actor* (Belmont, Mass.: Western Islands, 1968), 98.

192. "Walter Rauschenbush," *Wikipedia*, http://en.wikipedia.org/wiki/Walter_Rauschenbusch.

193. "Fundamentalist-Modernist Controversy," *Wikipedia*, http://en.wikipedia.org/wiki/Fundamentalist%E2%80%93Modernist_Controversy.

194. "Message from Tony Blair," http://www.tonyblairfaithfoundationus.org/page/message-tony-blair.

195. The grave site can be easily viewed in Google Images by typing "grave" and "Charles Taze Russell."

196. Arthur Keith, *Darwin Revalued* (London: C. A. Watts and Co., 1955), 225.

197. Ibid., 231-2.

198. Julia Scheeres, "Implantable Chip, On Sale Now," *Wired*, October 25, 2002, www.wired.com/politics/security/news/2002/10/55999.

199. Robert McNamara, speech given as President of World Bank, October 2, 1970, quoted in John Coleman, *Diplomacy by Deception*, (Carson City, Nev.: Bridger House, 1993), 117-18.

200. Bertrand Russell, "The Impact of Science Upon Society," 1951, as quoted in John Coleman, *Freemasonry and the One World Conspiracy* (white paper) (Carson City, Nev.: World in Review, 2004), 16.

201. Reported by Deutsche Press Agentur (DPA), August, 1988.

202. From Ted Turner interview in *Audubon* magazine, quoted in Fred Gielow, *You Don't Say* (Freedom Books, 1999), 189, http://www.aim.org/wls/five-percent-of-the-present-population-would-be-ideal/.

203. Bahgat Elnadi and Adel Rifaat, "Interview with Jacques-Yves Cousteau," *The UNESCO Courier*, November 1991, 13, as quoted at www.overpopulation.org/older.html.

204. Paul Watson, "The Beginning of the End for Life as We Know It on Planet Earth?" www.seashepherd.org/news-and-media/editorial-070504-1.html.

205. Zbigniew Brzezinski, "Major Foreign Policy Challenges for the Next U.S. President," address to Royal Institute of International Affairs (the British version of the CFR), November 17, 2008, viewable at www.youtube.com/watch?v=wKzEpQc-yo8&feature=player_embedded.

206. Bernard Rimland, "The (Pretending to) Combat Autism Act," www.whale.to/vaccines/rimland5.html.

207. Bernard Rimland, Autism Research Institute, press release, February 12, 2001, www.whale.to/m/ari.html.

208. David Ayoub, "Discovering the Causes, Treatment of Autism," July 9, 2006, www.whale.to/vaccines/ayoub7.html.

209. Jaquelyn McCandless, "Autism Vaccination Connection?" Letter to *Los Angeles Times*, June 12, 2001, www.whale.to/a/cand.html.

210. Boyd Haley, comments, www.whale.to/v/haley_q.html.

211. Thomas Levy, "Vaccination—the Shot that Keeps on Shooting," www.whale.to/m/levy1.html.

212. Bernard Rimland, Testimony before House Committee on Government Reform, April 6, 2000, www.whale.to/v/rimland.html.

213. Robert S. Mendelsohn, "The Medical Time Bomb of Immunization against Disease," *East West Journal*, November 1984, www.whale.to/vaccines/mendelsohn.html.

214. Ibid.

215. Viera Scheibner, *Vaccination: 100 Years of Orthodox Research* (Co-Creative Designs, 1993), quoted at www.whale.to/m/scheibner9.html.

216. Archie Kalokerinos, Interview, *International Vaccine Newsletter*, June 1995, www.whale.to/v/kalokerinos.html.

217. Phillip Incao, letter of testimony to Representative Dale Van Vyen, Chairman, Health Committee, Ohio House of Representatives, March 1, 1999, www.whale.to/m/incao.html.

218. Ted Koren, July 2001 Newsletter, http://www.whale.to/m/korne7. html.

219. "Recorded from Dr. Fudenberg's speech at the NVIC International Vaccine Conference, Arlington, VA, September 1997. Quoted with permission. Alzheimer's to quadruple statement is from Johns Hopkins Newsletter Nov 1998." http://www.whale.to/a/ted_koren_dc.html.

220. Testimony of Howard B. Urnovitz, Committee on Government Reform and Oversight, House of Representatives, August 3, 1999, http://www.whale. to/vaccines/urnovitz.html.

221. Harold Buttram, "Vaccine Scene 1999: Overview and Update," http:// www.whale.to/vaccines/buttram1.html.

222. Gerhard Buchwald, *The Decline of Tuberculosis Despite "Protective" Vaccination*, trans. Erwin Alber (2004 English edition; originally published as *Der Rückgang der Schwindsucht trotz "Schutz"-Impfung* (Frankfurter, Germany: F. Hirthammer Verlag GmbH, 2002), 130, 132.

223. Radio interview of Eva Snead by Laura Lee, September 19, 1992, http:// www.whale.to/vaccines/snead2.html.

224. Gordon Stewart, "Danger," *Here's Health*, March 1980, http://www. whale.to/vaccines/stewart.html.

225. Gerhard Buchwald, testimony before Quebec College of Physicians Medical Board, http://www.whale.to/vaccines/buchwald9.html.

226. Harold Buttram, "An Open Letter in Support of Parents Wishing to Limit or Avoid Immunization for their Children," http://www.whale.to/a/ buttram.html.

227. Tim O'Shea, *The Sanctity of Human Blood: Vaccination Is Not Immunization* (New West, 2001), 69, http://www.whale.to/vaccines/shea_ q.html.

228. As quoted, http://www.whale.to/vaccines/profits.html.

229. Bert Classen, Congressional testimony, http://www.whale.to/vaccines/ classen3.html.

230. Philip Incao, testimony for Ohio House of Representatives, March 1, 1999, http://www.whale.to/m/incao.html.

231. Vernon Coleman, "Do Vaccines Work and Are They Safe?" www. vernoncoleman.com/vaccines.htm.

232. As quoted, http://www.whale.to/m/scheibner9.html.

233. As quoted, http://www.whale.to/m/douglas9.html.

234. Gerhard Buchwald, *The Vaccination Nonsense: 2004 Lectures* (Norderstedt, Germany: Books on Demand GmbH, 2004), 108, as quoted, http://www.whale.to/m/buchwald9.html.

235. As quoted, http://www.whale.to/a/lanctot_q.html.

236. Peter Morrell, "Vaccination: The Wider Picture," (eLetter, October 13, 2000), as quoted, http://www.whale.to/vaccines/morrell3.html.

237. As quoted, http://www.whale.to/vaccines/morris_h.html.

238. Russell Blaylock, "The Truth Behind the Vaccine Cover-up," 2004, http://www.whale.to/a/blaylock.html.

239. Interview with Guylaine Lanctot by Kenneth & Dee Burke, http://www.whale.to/a/lanctot.html.

240. As quoted, http://www.whale.to/a/ted_koren_dc.html.

241. Marcel Kinsbourne, "Vaccines: Finding a Balance between Public Safety and Personal Choice," presentation to Committee on Government Reform, August 3, 1999, www.whale.to/vaccines/kinsbourne.html.

242. Radio interview of Eva Snead by Laura Lee, September 19, 1992, http://www.whale.to/vaccines/snead2.html.

243. Interview with Guylaine Lanctot by Kenneth & Dee Burke, http://www.whale.to/a/lanctot.html.

244. Archie Kalokerinos, Interview, *International Vaccine Newsletter*, June 1995, http://www.whale.to/v/kalokerinos.html.

245. Donald W. Scott, "Mycoplasma: The Linking Pathogen in Neurosystemic Diseases," *Nexus Magazine*, August 2001, as quoted, http://www.whale.to/m/scott7.html.

246. "Virus," www.en.wikipedia.org/wiki/Virus, accessed 2008.

247. Zbigniew Brzezinski, *Between Two Ages: America's Role in the Technetronic Era* (New York: Viking Press, 1970), 57.

248. John Coleman, *El Nino is Man Made* (white paper) (Carson City, Nev.: World in Review, 2003), 1.

249. William Cohen, Department of Defense Briefing, April 28, 1997, www.en.wikiquote.org/wiki/William_Cohen.

250. See, for example, graph at www.stormhorizon.org/US-tornadoes-1950-to-2008-bar.html.

251. Leonard C. Lewin, *Report from Iron Mountain* (1967, reprint; New York: The Free Press, 1996), 80-81.

252. George Orwell, *1984* (1949; reprint, New York: Harcourt Brace, 1983), 183.

253. Ibid., 185.

254. Ibid., 35.

255. Ibid., 52.

256. Ibid., 17.

257. Ibid., 122.

258. Ibid., 115.

259. Ibid., 136.

260. Ibid., 172.

261. See Joseph M. Canfield, *The Incredible Scofield and His Book* (Vallecito, Calif.: Ross House, 2004).

262. Ibid., 219-20.

263. William Guy Carr, *Satan: Prince of this World*, (Palmdale, Calif.: Omni Publications, 1997), 71-72.

INDEX

Made in the USA
Monee, IL
10 December 2020